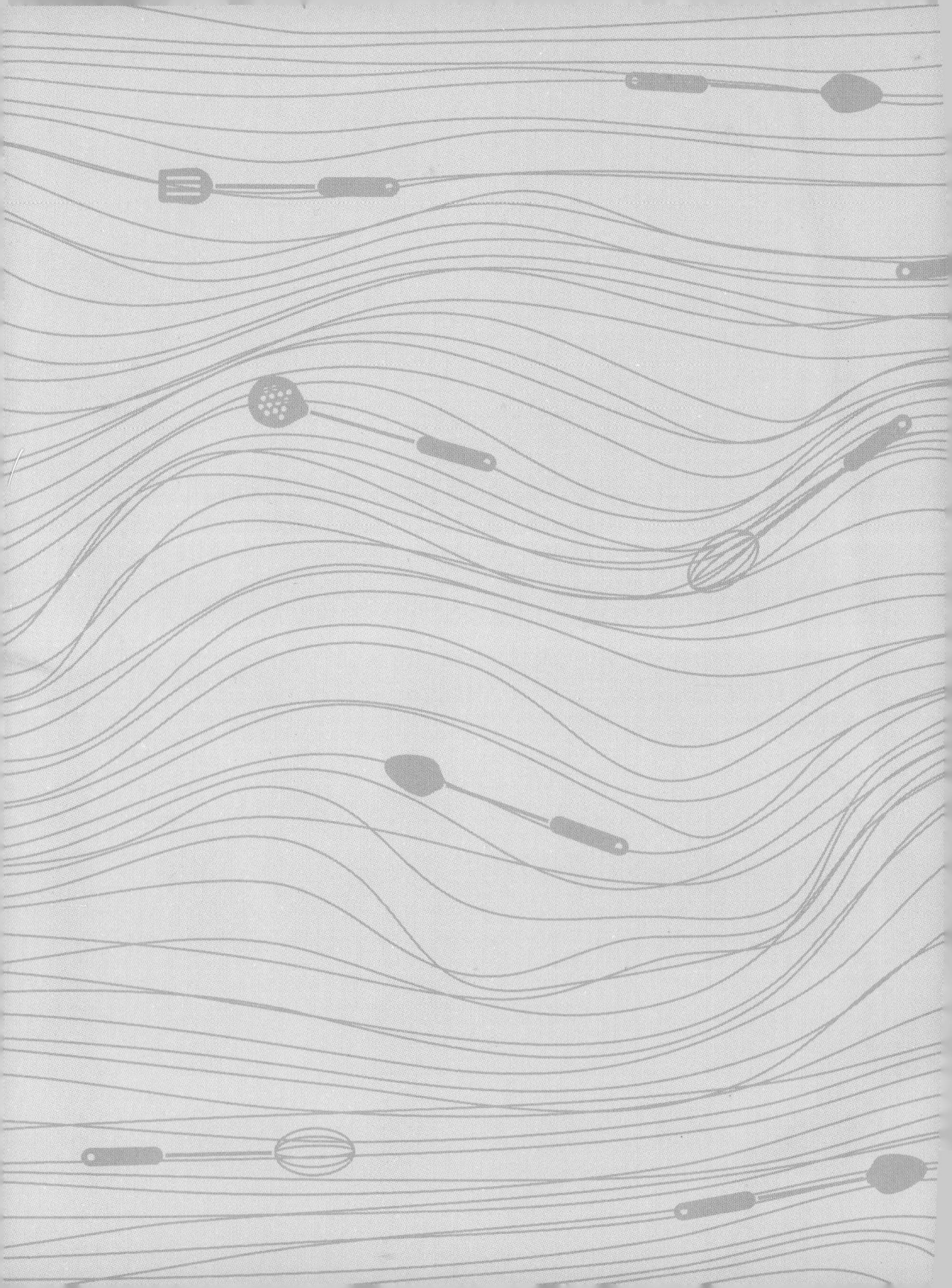

Servings
Simple yet Exotic

Servings
Simple yet Exotic

Roopali Mohanti

Photographs by Roopali Mohanti
Book Design & Illustrations by Nandini Varma

Published by Rupa Publications India Pvt. Ltd 2023
7/16, Ansari Road, Daryaganj
New Delhi 110002

Sales Centres:
Prayagraj Bengaluru Chennai
Hyderabad Jaipur Kolkata Mumbai

© Roopali Mohanti 2023
Book Design & Illustrations by Nandini Varma
Cover & Author Photo by Xoheb Khan Production
Cover Photo Art Direction & Styling by
Shruti Jain, The Leaf bowl

The views and opinions expressed in this book are the author's own and the facts are as reported by her which have been verified to the extent possible, and the publishers are not in any way liable for the same.
All rights reserved.

No part of this publication may be reproduced, transmitted, or stored in a retrieval system, in any form or by any means, electronic, mechanical, photocopying, recording or otherwise, without the prior permission of the publisher.

ISBN: 978-93-5520-523-0
First impression 2023
10 9 8 7 6 5 4 3 2 1
Printed in India
The moral right of the author has been asserted.

This book is sold subject to the condition that it shall not, by way of trade or otherwise, be lent, resold, hired out, or otherwise circulated, without the publisher's prior consent, in any form of binding or cover other than that in which it is published.

To Mama
with Love

Contents

Author's Note | 13
Kitchen Essentials | 15

1 BREKKIE & BRUNCH | 18
- Vegetable Korma
- Mutton Paniyarams
- Vegetable Paniyarams
- Radhaballabi
- Niramish Aloo Dum
- Mangalore Buns
- Mangala Aunty's Onion Sambhar
- Coconut Chutney
- Pratima's Pineapple Sheera
- Kawdhai Pitha
- Ambula Rai
- Kanchaa Dali
- French Toast Casserole
- Strawberry Pistachio Parfait
- Strata
- Green Apple Salad in Vinaigrette
- Summer Fruit Cobbler
- Cinnamon Ice Cream
- Fruity Soda Bread
- Breakfast Tomato Bread Rolls
- Blueberry Muffins with Cinnamon Crumb
- Triple Chocolate Muffins with Salted Caramel Centre
- Jalapeño, Cheese and Onion Muffins
- Chicken Curry Puffs
- Sweet Corn Toasts
- Chocolate Tarts

2 WHETTING YOUR APPETITE | 62
- Makhmali Gulabi Boti
- Hara Bhara Cheesy Kebab
- Prawn Spring Rolls
- Water Chestnut, Corn and Asparagus Spring Rolls
- Fruity Cheese Board
- Beetroot Chop
- Mutton Chop
- Bhai's Asian Red Chilli Prawns
- Salt and Pepper Tofu with a Simple Chinese Dipping Sauce
- Egg Roast
- Chaitra's Goli Bajje
- Paneer Takatak
- Pudina Keema
- Sheermal
- Mansi's Bihari Boti Wings
- Kacche Aam ki Hari Chutney
- Quick Fix Dahi ke Kebab
- Cornmeal Sausage Galette
- Pumpkin Mozzarella Balls
- Yoghurt–Garlic Dip
- Spicy Rasam
- Vada
- Hurida Koli (Pepper and Chilli Fried Chicken)

MAINS

Dilli O Dilli | 100
- Skinny Butter Chicken
- Chicken Tikka
- Baingan in a Baingan
- Mohan's Dal Trimel Tadka
- Stuffed Aloo Kulcha
- Koyla Mirchi Paneer
- Boozy Pantua
- Menu Plan

Timeless Traditions | 114
- Creamy Mustard Chicken with Sun-dried Tomatoes
- Baked Spicy Yoghurt Cauliflower Steaks on a Bed of Roasted Vegetables
- Spinach and Cottage Cheese Casserole
- Keema Scotch Eggs
- Vegetarian Bread Rolls
- Russian Salad
- Mixed Fruit Trifle Cake Layered with Patisserie Crème
- Menu Plan

Mughlai Durbar | 128
- Arshi's Murgh Musallam
- Purani Dilli Yakhni Pulao
- Moradabadi Dahi ki Phulki
- Rawa Laccha Paratha
- Laal Paneer with Moti Hari Mirch
- Pistachio Cake with Rose Muhallabelia Cream
- Menu Plan

Kolkata Chronicles | 140
- Laal Masoor Dal
- Kodhaishutir Chana Bhapa (Steamed Cottage Cheese and Pea Mash in Mustard Paste)
- Sheem, Bodi Diye Jeera Ada Rui Maach (Broad Bean, Dried Lentil Dumplings and Rohu Fish in a Light Ginger–Cumin Gravy)
- Shailashree's Phulkobir Malai Curry (Cauliflower Coconut Cream Curry)
- Lamba Begun Bhaja (Spiced Shallow Fried Brinjal)
- Bhapa Carrot Cake and Doi Medley
- Menu Plan

Odisha | 150
- Rinku's Dahi Bara
- Aloo Dum
- Ghugni
- Peda
- Tankapani Soriso Manso (Mutton Cooked in Mustard Gravy)
- Nayapalli Janhi Chatu Tatitya Basa (One Pot Ridge Gourd and Mushrooms)
- Nadiya Rasa Bhaja Chenna Tarkari (Fresh Cottage Cheese Cubes in Coconut Gravy)
- Abhi Nana's Ou Khatta (Elephant Apple Chutney)
- Nayapalli Posto Bara (Poppy Seed Patty)

- Chitau Pitha (Rice and Coconut Crepes)
- Odisha Rasagola
- Aamba Soriso Chicken (Chicken Cooked with Pickled Mangoes and Mustard)
- Khira Chingudi Saha Tentuli Paga (Milk Prawns with Tamarind Dipping Sauce)
- Poi Putuli and Coconut Black Rice (Malabar Spinach Parcels)
- Chenna Stuffed Pumpkin Flower Fritters
- Kulia Bhai's Junglee Mutton and Coconut Rotis
- Dhingri Chatu – Two Versions (Buttermilk Mushrooms and Mushroom Koftas in Coriander–Coconut Gravy)
- Baked Crabs with Chingudi Sukhua Sambal (Dried Shrimps Sambal)
- Mama's Patrapoda Maacha Bhaata (Steamed Yoghurt Fish with Rice)
- Dalma Bela (Dalma Bowl)
- Traditional Kakara Pitha
- Phulkobi Kakara Pitha and Chicken Kakara Pitha
- Paniya Guda Atta Cake
- Koraput Coffee Flavoured Chenna Burnt Basque and Salted Jaggery Caramel Sauce
- Chatua Peanut Butter Cookies
- Baked Rasabali
- Menu Plan

Darjeeling Diaries | 214
- Clear Soup
- Spicy Chutney
- Thaipo, Momo and Shaphalay Filling
- Thaipo
- Shaphalay (Deep Fried Stuffed Pancake)
- Spinach Momos
- Thukpa
- Plain Momos
- Darjeeling Masala Chai Cake
- Menu Plan

Konkan Express | 228
- Mangala Aunty's Green Mutton Curry
- Mangalorean Gassi with Lobia and Spinach
- Potato Saagu
- Red Chutney
- Chaitra's Alasande Upkari (Yard-Long Beans and Peanut Masala)
- Chaitra's Pan Polo (Rice Pancakes)
- Mango Custard Mini Pies topped with Rasayan
- Menu Plan

Hyderabadi Cuisine | 240
- Ali Family Dalcha
- Murgh Korma
- Baghara Rice
- Mirch Bhindi ka Saalan
- Hyderabadi Lauki Paneer ke Kofte
- Arshi's Gobi Musallam
- Skinny Double ka Meetha
- Menu Plan

Malabar Sadhya | 254
- Mama's Appam
- Anju's Nadan Kozhi Curry
- Mama's Vegetable Stew
- Raju Bhaiya's Red Chilli Chutney
- Anju's Prawn Green Mango Curry
- Mushroom Pepper Fry
- Mama's Avial
- Black Chickpea Tikkis
- Kari Patta Chutney
- Sago Vermicelli Payasam
- Unniyapam with Indian Tres Leches
- Menu Plan

Parsi & Sindhi Flavours | 270
- Hinduja Aunty's Sindhi Kadhi
- Tulu Khudi's Arbi Tuk
- Salli Boti
- Sai Bhaji
- Apple Crème Caramel
- Menu Plan

'Ayo Gorkhali' | 282
- Choila Pork (Spiced Grill Pork)
- Raju's Bhindi ko Bhutuwa (Okra Stir fry)
- Furmeet's Gundruk
- Raju's Golbedha ko Achaar (Tomato Chutney)
- Salina's Karela Sadeko (Bitter Gourd Salad)
- Isskus ko Tarkari (Chayote Squash Curry)
- Sikarni
- Menu Plan

High on Thai | 294
- Thai Green Curry Peanut Butter Tray Bake
- Thai Steamed Fish with Lime and Chilli
- Mama Moon's Som Tam Salad
- Mama Moon's Thai Red Curry
- Basil and Lemongrass Sliced Goat Meat Stir Fried
- Sesame Garlic Bok Choy
- Ginger Nut, Coconut and Lime Cheesecake
- Menu Plan

Moroccan Mazzah | 310
- Shakshouka
- Ulta Tawa Naan
- Yoghurt–Garlic Sauce
- Mint Chicken
- Falafel Pancakes
- Labneh Myriad
- Vegetarian Moussaka Casserole
- Honey Glazed Cumin Carrots
- Saffron Apricot Pilaf
- Almond Crepes with Figs Poached in Orange Syrup
- Menu Plan

Italian Sojourn | 326
- Tagiatelle Aglio Olio
- Shrimp in Garlic and Parsley
- Summer Hues Rocket and Mango Salad
- Tigelle Bread

- Lemon Pound Cake
- Mansi's Cheese Filled Garlic Parsley Braided Wreath Bread
- Creamy Mushrooms and Spinach
- Balsamic Chicken Salad with Yoghurt and Mustard Dressing
- Tiramisu
- Menu Plan

London Diaries | 344
- Mixed Flour Spiced Soda Bread
- Bacon Wrapped Meat Loaf
- Pork Chops in Parsley Demi-Glace
- Cheesy Bubble and Squeak
- Beetroot and Goat Cheese Salad
- Red Pesto, Coriander Garlic Butter Braid
- Chicken Escalope with Creamy Vegetables
- Quattro Formaggi Portobello Mushrooms
- Fresh Cherry Compote Cake with Mascarpone Cheese Frosting
- Irish Cream Cinnamon Crumble Cake
- Menu Plan

CHAI TIME | 364
- Ladi Pav
- Bhaji Puff Patties
- Khari Twist
- Wafer Par Eeda
- Russian Pattice (Gora Chicken Cutlet)
- Jeera Biskut
- 'No Mawa' Cake
- Pradeep's Orange Marmalade
- Orange Almond Cake
- Bacon, Honey, Spiced Buttermilk Scones
- Tartlets
- Chicken Mince Tartlets
- Asparagus Cottage Cheese Tartlets
- Lemon Tarts Topped With Blueberries
- Madras Curry Powder Egg Finger Sandwiches
- Russ
- Nankhatai
- Cantucci (Coffee Almond Biscotti)
- Carrot Cake
- Upside-down Pineapple Yoghurt Cake
- Tutti Frutti Pound Cake
- Sindhi Tuk Chaat with Anardana Chutney and Sai Chutney
- Gurwala Atta Halwa
- Aloo Chop
- Sabudana Vada
- Peanut–Yoghurt Chutney

CRISP, FRESH & TENDER | 412
- Cottage Cheese En Papillote (Cottage Cheese in Parchment with Asian Compound Butter)
- Spiced Hasselback Potatoes with Broccoli in Cheese Chilli Sauce
- Soya Nugget Balls in Barbecue Sauce with Chilli Long Beans and Crisp Fried Lotus Stem
- Akki Roti with Madras Kathal Masala and Tallina's Pineapple Curry
- Arshi's Kabuli Pulao Accompanied with Chukandar ka Saalan
- Nandini's Ratatouille as a Pot Pie with Swati's Rocket and Strawberry Salad
- Chutney Pomfret Stuffed with Caramelized Spicy Prawns
- Sole En Papillote with Compound Basil Butter (Sole in Parchment)
- Chaitan's Beer Batter Fish with Mustard Remoulade Sauce and Bartkartoffein (Potatoes and Bacon)
- Ma Cherry's Ngaa Zabaling Paung and Khayamti Thot (Baked Lemongrass Fish and Tomato Salad)
- Soy Ginger Salmon with Sesame Garlic Kale
- Steamed Asian Chicken with Chilli Oil
- Chicken Baked with Mascarpone and Lime
- Koyla Tawa Murgh
- Slow Cooked Chicken Lollipops with Tangy Dipping Sauce, Sweet potato Fries and Curly Kale Fries

KUNG FU PANDA IN THE HOUSE | 456
- Cream Cheese Pancakes with Chunky Fresh Strawberry Sauce and Home-made Pancake Syrup
- Tom Yum Khao Soi and Sweet Chilli Prawns
- Kung Fu Panda Orange Chicken
- BBQ Chicken Bao
- Bhai's Fried Instant Noodles
- 'Gimbap' Rolls in a Bowl
- Oyakodon (Chicken and Egg Fried Rice)
- 'Chindese' Chopsuey
- Japanese Milk Burger Buns
- Mushroom Burger Patties
- Chicken Burger Patties
- Middle Eastern Plate
- Milk Chocolate Cookies
- Mansi's 'Coco' Cake

...and this is how it all started

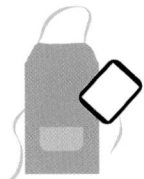

My fascination with laying complete meals and in the right combination on the table somewhere stems from my growing-up years. Introduction to regional food from various parts of India as well as from other countries at an early age was a gift from the partly nomadic life we led with my father being in the Navy. The official mess night menus which I would hear of would fascinate me as there was great emphasis laid on each course and the right combination of dishes. When I finally got down to running my own household and entertaining I decided to keep a notebook with details of what I serve on these occasions and attempt to not repeat dishes with the same guests!

The communities we lived in were a great source of learning about different food habits of people and my mother constantly made an effort to learn from them. I often use her recipe book which has the Remington typewriter script and has yellowed with time. The inspiration of collating recipes is from there. The African philosophy of Ubuntu – 'I am because you are'– literally meaning that a person is a person through other people, holds true in most aspects of my life including this book. All through its pages there is an outpouring of recipes from mothers, aunts, friends, teachers, house staff and sometimes even people I haven't met but whose recipes have been recommended and I have tried. My task with most of their recipes was to quantify the ingredients as most people cook by instinct.

In hotel management school many a session is spent on menu planning. The very basis of what will be on your table during a meal. Balance of colour, flavour, texture, consistency and the process of creating the perfect synergy between dishes depending on the heaviness or lightness of them. More often than not I have come across meals served which are a complete mismatch of regions or flavours, leaving the palette confused. Though my right may not be yours and food is very personal, yet using some basic guidelines can be beneficial.

Travel adds to our gastronomic journey as well – I always come back with vivid memories of what I enjoyed eating on my trips. Sometimes recreating dishes where the recipes were parted with by chefs and locals of the place or using ingredients from the region to recollect the flavours, and in the process create a new dish, is all part of that enriching experience. Some sections in this book are dedicated to those joyful times.

The pages ahead attempt at answering that one question each waking day: 'What should I cook today?' Open a section in this book and the answer lies there. There are menu options created at the end of each main course section where the courses are mentioned with the ideal combinations from different sections of the book. The options are for daily cooking as well as for larger gatherings.

The pandemic and the first lockdown was the beginning of this process. What began as passing on recipes to friends who wanted to try something new became an exchange of ideas. There are some pictures here which were my first ever food shots and many which I retook when I corrected or refined the dish, often making changes to the recipe. It is an iPhone book, the 'Apple of my eye'! Typing the recipes and write-ups on the Notes of my phone since that was the quickest way to WhatsApp the same, and also using the phone to click and save the picture was all a part of this fun activity. However, the improved pictures during the subsequent retest of recipes were on a mini iPad, with photography flat lays, props and a little more thought. It has been a learning experience and the profusion of food photographers, bloggers, stylists and their pictures online is inspirational.

Not a day goes by without my acknowledging the people who helped me learn – my mother for all her strictness and life lessons on running a kitchen and dining area, my father who at a very young age introduced me to the joy of reading and the important aspect of being meticulous, the teachers at my alma mater IHMCTAN (Institute of Hotel Management, Catering Technology and Applied Nutrition) in Kolkata who taught with passion each day, ensuring each of us learnt the techniques and nuances of food production and planning, friends who shared and cared enough to support the process and nudged me to go ahead with the idea, our house staff who like family tolerated and stood by me through all my attempts, sometimes twice and thrice, with a smile, occasionally witnessing my frustration at a high decibel and above all else my husband and son who bravely ate and encouraged me each day!

'Don't die with the music in you' ... a guiding thought for me in the conception and completion of this book, something I had wanted to do for over twenty years. The need to never stop learning no matter your age is a belief that has helped a home cook reach out and be a part of your table.

✱ **Roopali Mohanti,** New Delhi

Kitchen Essentials

Home-made Garam Masala Powder
(Makes 80 gm)

- Cinnamon: 1 inch stick
- Green cardamoms: 5
- Black cardamom: 1
- Black peppercorns: 10
- Coriander seeds: 2½ tsp
- Dried red chillies: 4

1. Put all the ingredients mentioned above in a pan and gently roast on low flame for 5 minutes. Allow all the spices to cool down. Dry grind to a fine powder in a mixer.
2. Store in an airtight jar.

Home-made Chinese Chilli Paste
(Makes 300 gm)

- Dried red chillies: 50 gm
- Refined oil: 200 ml
- Ginger paste: 1 tbsp
- Garlic paste: 1 tbsp
- Kashmiri chilli powder: 1½ tbsp
- Vinegar: 100 ml
- Tomato ketchup: 5 tbsp
- Salt: 1 tbsp

1. Remove seeds from half the quantity of dried red chillies.
2. Soak all the dried chillies overnight in water.
3. Drain out the water and grind dried red chillies to a paste.
4. Heat oil in a pan. Add Kashmiri chilli powder and cook for a minute. Add ginger and garlic paste and sauté till golden.
5. Add dried red chilli paste and cook for 4–5 minutes.
6. Add tomato ketchup followed by vinegar and allow the mixture to simmer for 4–5 minutes. Add salt, mix well and remove from the flame.
7. Allow the paste to cool and then transfer to a clean jar.
8. Store in the refrigerator for up to 2 months.

Cornflour
Refers to cornstarch.

SERVINGS

Butter and cream
Regular salted butter is used in all recipes unless otherwise specified. Cream used is regular double cream unless otherwise specified.

Baking beans
For blind baking, if ceramic baking beans are not available use dried chickpeas or dried kidney beans.

Measuring cup size and spoon measurements
Two sizes of measuring cups have been used, 250 ml and 150 ml. Treat every measurement as a level spoon measurement unless specified as heaped.

Scale
Keep a digital scale handy.

Oven temperature
Every oven has a minor aberration – one has to increase/reduce the temperature or slightly increase/reduce the time taken to bake to get the final result.

Substitutes
While recipes are given to make tart shells, puff pastry, dumpling covers from scratch, to simplify the process, one can use the store-bought options and make the fillings to still get the desired outcome.

BREKKIE & BRUNCH

The Crispy, Crunchy Bomb

The Chettiars were a small community of traders and merchants during the Chola Dynasty's rule in South India. A progressive community, who traded in spices and hence had links with foreign lands. They moved from the Coromandel coast to finally settle in the Karaikudi region of Tamil Nadu.

Their food has locally sourced spices which form the base of all the dishes. Popular spices include star anise, pepper and dried flower pods. The kitchen is a very important area in all Chettiar homes and normally local architecture features prominently, albeit amalgamated with imported artefacts, like mirrors and chandeliers from Belgium and chests and pillars from Burma. The marriage of styles continues on their plates too like in the rice-based accompaniment called idiyappam (string hoppers), the origin of which is actually Burmese. Chettinad restaurants are now popular in many parts of India, as they offer just the right fiery food flavours with a lot of meat, and seafood-based dishes as well.

My love for paniyarams (also called paddu or appadadde and now just 'appe', made in a special mould with small fissures) began at a little coffee stall, simply called 'KBK', in Puducherry, located in one of the by-lanes off the main beach road in White Town. They sell it every morning for breakfast along with amazing filter coffee. It also makes for the perfect brunch dish, when combined with vegetable curry. The mutton keema filling is an attempt to deviate from the normal.

The Japanese also use a similar pan to create a dish called takoyaki, which is an octopus-filled egg and flour batter dish. As they say, same, same – but different!

VEGETABLE KORMA (Serves 4)

(Measuring cup size: 150 ml)

Curry Paste

- Cinnamon: 1–2 inch stick
- Green cardamoms: 5
- Black cardamom: 1
- Fenugreek seeds: 10
- Coriander seeds: 2½ tsp
- Dried red chillies: 4
- Cloves: 3
- Cumin seeds: 1 tsp
- Fennel seeds: 1 tsp
- Black peppercorns: 1 tsp
- Coconut: ½ grated
- Coconut oil: 1 tsp
- Water: as needed

1. Heat coconut oil in a pan.
2. Add all the whole spices including dried red chillies and sauté.
3. Add grated coconut and sauté until light brown.
4. Remove from flame and cool down.
5. Grind to a paste with a few tablespoons of water.

Curry

- Mixed vegetables: 200 gm (carrots, potatoes, beans and peas)
- Onion: 1 large chopped
- Tomatoes: 2 medium chopped
- Garlic paste: 1 tsp
- Ginger paste: ½ tsp
- Turmeric powder: ½ tsp
- Curry leaves: 1 sprig
- Coconut oil: 1 tbsp
- Cashew nuts: 6–8
- Peanuts: 10–12
- Coconut milk: ½ cup
- Salt: 1 tsp
- Water: 1½ cup

1. Dice mixed vegetables and steam until half done.
2. Soak cashew nuts and peanuts in water for 20 minutes, and then grind to a paste.
3. Heat oil in a pan; add curry leaves followed by onions and ½ tsp salt. Allow to sweat and turn translucent.
4. Add ginger and garlic paste and cook well.
5. Add tomatoes and cook covered until they soften.
6. Add turmeric powder, remaining salt and cook further. Now add the curry paste and cook for 5–7 minutes.

7. Add the steamed mixed vegetables.
8. Add ½ cup water and then add the cashew–peanut paste.
9. Simmer for 2–3 minutes and then add 1 cup water followed by coconut milk.
10. Cover and simmer until the vegetables are cooked through.
11. Check seasoning and serve hot.

MUTTON PANIYARAMS
(Measuring cup size: 150 ml)

- Idli batter: 2 cups
- Fruit salt: a pinch
- Mutton mince: 250 gm
- Tomatoes: 100 gm chopped
- Onions: 100 gm chopped
- Green chillies: 2 chopped
- Curry leaves: 10 chopped
- Grated coconut: 3 tbsp
- Ginger paste: 1 tsp
- Garlic paste: 1 tsp
- Coconut oil: 1½ tbsp
- Coriander powder: 1 tsp
- Cumin powder: 1 tsp
- Garam masala powder: 1 tsp
- Black pepper powder: 1 tsp
- Salt: ½ tsp

Filling

1. Heat coconut oil in a pan. Add curry leaves and green chillies.
2. Add chopped onions and cook until pink.
3. Add ginger and garlic paste and sauté further. Add tomatoes followed by all the spice powders and grated coconut.
4. Add mutton mince, salt and cook until it softens completely.
5. Remove from flame and allow it to cool.

Paniyarams

1. Idli batter should be at room temperature. Batter should not be too thin or thick.
2. Add a pinch of fruit salt to it and mix well.
3. Grease the paniyaram pan.
4. Heat the pan over a high flame and then lower the flame.

5. Put 1 tbsp of batter at the bottom of each mould.
6. Place 1½ tsp of the filling on the batter.
7. Cover filling with another tbsp of batter till the moulds are three-fourths full.
8. Allow it to cook for 3–4 minutes on one side over a low flame.
9. Gently turn it over with a skewer or spoon and cook for 3–4 minutes.
10. Turn once or twice to get a uniform colour. Remove and serve.

VEGETABLE PANIYARAMS
(Measuring cup size: 150 ml)

- Idli batter: 2 cups
- Fruit salt: a pinch
- Onion: 1 medium chopped
- Mixed vegetables: ¾ cup (carrot grated and beans finely chopped)
- Green chillies: 2 chopped
- Ginger: ½ inch grated
- Asafoetida powder: a pinch
- Black peppercorns: ½ tsp crushed
- Red chilli powder: ½ tsp
- Curry leaves: 2 tbsp chopped
- Grated coconut: ½ cup
- Salt: ½ tsp
- Refined oil: 1–2 tbsp

Filling

1. Heat oil in a non-stick pan. Add green chillies, curry leaves, ginger and sauté.
2. Add onions and sauté until pink, and then add mixed vegetables. Cook for a few minutes until the vegetables are soft.
3. Add red chilli powder, crushed black peppercorns and asafoetida powder.
4. Add a pinch of salt and remove pan from flame. Let the mixture cool.
5. Now add grated coconut, followed by the idli batter, a pinch of fruit salt and the remaining salt. Mix well and keep aside.

Paniyarams

1. Grease the paniyaram pan.

2. Heat the pan over a high flame and then lower the flame.
3. Fill each mould until three-fourths full with the batter.
4. Cook for 3–4 minutes on one side over a low flame.
5. Gently turn it over with a skewer or spoon.
6. Allow the other side to cook for 3–4 minutes.
7. Turn once or twice to get a uniform colour.
8. Remove and serve.

Janmashtami Special

Radhaballabi may or may not have an association with Radha and Krishna, as the name reflects, but for me it does. Year on year, I have eaten this for Janmashtami at a friend's home in Bhubaneswar. The popular Cuttack Sweet Stall makes a great version too. A halwai was kind enough to explain the process.

Radhaballabi is a deep-fried lentil-stuffed kachori popularly eaten with aloo dum. Since I associate this with Janmashtami, I have made the no onion or garlic version of the aloo dum.

Down this with cups of hot cardamom tea when you aren't aiming to please the gods but only thyself, there is no better way to begin your sunday!

RADHABALLABI (Serves 4)

- White urad dal: 180 gm soaked in water overnight
- Fennel seeds: 4 tsp
- Green chillies: 3–4
- Ginger: 2½ inches
- Salt: ½ tsp
- Water: 55 ml

SERVINGS

1. Strain soaked dal and grind with 55 ml of water until nearly smooth ensuring a slightly grainy texture. Reserve for dough and filling.
2. Grind fennel seeds and reserve for dough and filling.
3. Pound ginger and green chillies in a mortar and pestle, add salt and reserve for dough and filling.

Dough

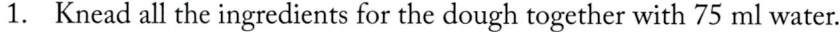

- All-purpose flour: 300 gm
- Dal paste: 130 gm
- Salt: ¾ tsp
- Sugar: 1 tbsp
- Ghee: 1½ tbsp
- Fennel powder: ¾ tsp
- Ginger–chilli paste: 1½ tsp
- Water: 75 ml

1. Knead all the ingredients for the dough together with 75 ml water.
2. Cover and leave dough at room temperature for an hour.

Filling

- Refined oil: 2 tbsp
- Nigella seeds: ¼ tsp
- Asafoetida powder: ½ tsp
- Fennel powder: remaining quantity
- Ginger–chilli paste: remaining quantity
- Salt: 1 tsp
- Sugar: 4 tsp
- Dal paste: remaining quantity

1. Heat oil in a non-stick pan.
2. Add nigella seeds, asafoetida powder, followed by the ginger–chilli paste, and sauté.
3. Sprinkle a little water to prevent it from burning and then add fennel powder, salt and sugar.
4. Cook for 2 minutes until the sugar caramelizes, then reduce the flame and add the remaining dal paste. Let the mixture blend well.
5. Cook for 20–25 minutes until it comes together like a dough. This mixture will be sticky but as you mix further, it will get smoother.
6. Ensure there are no lumps of caramelized sugar in the mix.

Assembling

1. Divide the dough into 12 portions and filling into 12 portions.
2. Press each piece of dough between your palms to make 2½ inch discs. Place the filling in the middle. Bring the sides of the dough together to form a smooth ball. Dip the ball in a little warm oil.
3. Now roll out the ball to a 5½–6 inch disc. Rolling smaller will lead to a thicker edge.
4. Heat oil in a wok/ kadai for frying.
5. Fry the radhaballabi, one at a time over a medium flame, moving the oil with a perforated frying ladle gently pressing down. Fry for 45 seconds or until golden and puffed.
6. Flip and remove to a colander lined with a paper towel. Serve at room temperature.

NIRAMISH ALOO DUM (Serves 6)

- Baby potatoes: 1 kg
- Salt: 3 tsp
- Kashmiri chilli powder: ¼ tsp
- Red chilli powder: ¼ tsp
- Water: 350–400 ml

1. Boil potatoes in water with 2 tsp salt until three-fourths done. Drain and keep aside.
2. When lukewarm peel the potatoes and rub with 1 tsp salt and both chilli powders.
3. Leave for an hour.

Paste

- Roasted cumin powder: 1¼ tsp
- Coriander powder: 2 tsp
- Black salt: ½ tsp
- Ginger paste: 4 tsp
- Water: 2 tbsp

1. Make a paste with all the ingredients and keep aside.

Gravy

- Mustard oil: 50 ml
- Sugar: ½ tsp + ¾ tsp
- Dried red chillies: 2–3
- Bay leaves: 2

- Cloves: 3–4
- Cumin seeds: ¾ tsp
- Asafoetida powder: ¼ tsp
- Turmeric powder: ¾ tsp
- Kashmiri chilli powder: ½ tsp
- Readymade tomato purée: 2 tbsp
- Cashew nuts: 6 soaked and ground to a paste
- Water: 350–400 ml
- Salt: 1 tsp

1. Heat the entire quantity of oil in a non-stick pan and fry potatoes lightly. Remove and keep aside. In the remaining oil, caramelize ½ tsp sugar.
2. Add all the whole spices and let them crackle, add the paste and cook for 3–4 minutes.
3. Add turmeric powder, asafoetida powder and Kashmiri chilli powder.
4. Add tomato purée and cook until the oil separates.
5. Add cashew paste and cook further.
6. Add potatoes, followed by ¾ tsp sugar and salt. Sauté well.
7. Add water gradually, depending on the consistency you prefer, and let the mixture cook for 20 minutes. Serve hot.

Mangalore Tiffin Room

The word tiffin is of Indian English origin, referring to the afternoon tea popular during the British Raj. However, in South India, it refers to the in-between meal in the evening or to brunch during the day. It certainly does not mean that the meal is light! How I love the sound of '*Tiffin saaptacha*', though that's Tamil!

The Mangalore bun is unique. It looks like a poori but has lacy insides like the Western bun. Its origin may have been an attempt to make the actual bun, but the lack of an oven led to an alternative technique. The dough is allowed to ferment and rise, is mildly sweet and goes well with subtly spiced sambhar.

End your meal with the fruity sheera, a recipe given to me by someone I have never met in far-off Atlanta, Georgia! After all, happiness is sharing!

MANGALORE BUNS (Serves 6)

(Measuring cup size: 150 ml)

- All-purpose flour: 4½ cups
- Yoghurt: ¾ cup
- Mashed banana: 1 cup
- Salt: ½ tsp
- Roasted cumin seeds: 1 tsp
- Sugar: 1 cup
- Baking soda: 1 tsp
- Refined oil: 1 tbsp + extra for frying

1. Knead all the ingredients, except the oil, to make a stiff dough.
2. Transfer dough to a greased bowl and pour 1 tbsp oil over it.
3. Leave the dough at room temperature for an hour and then refrigerate overnight.
4. Take the dough out of the refrigerator. Divide into 15–16 equal balls of approximately 55 gm each.
5. Heat oil in a wok/kadai to deep fry.
6. Roll out the balls on a flour-dusted surface into 3–4 inch diameter discs.
7. Fry discs in oil on a medium flame until they are golden and puffed.
8. Serve hot.

MANGALA AUNTY'S ONION SAMBHAR (Serves 4)

Sambhar Masala Paste

- Refined oil: 1½ tbsp
- Coriander seeds: 2 tsp
- Chana dal: 2 tsp
- Cumin seeds: 1 tsp
- Black peppercorns: 7
- Fenugreek seeds: 6
- Mustard seeds: 1 tsp
- Onion: ¼ chopped
- Curry leaves: 6
- Red chillies: 3–4
- Tamarind paste: 2 tbsp
- Asafoetida powder: ½ tsp
- Turmeric powder: ½ tsp
- Water: 2 tbsp

1. Heat oil in a non-stick pan and sauté all the ingredients except the tamarind paste, asafoetida powder and turmeric powder.

2. Add tamarind paste, and cook until the raw smell is no longer there.
3. Remove pan from flame and cool. Grind to a paste with water.
4. Add turmeric powder and asafoetida powder.

Sambhar

- Refined oil: 1 tbsp
- Arhar dal: 85 gm
- Madras onions: 12–14 peeled
- Tomatoes: 2 medium quartered
- Mustard seeds: ½ tsp
- Curry leaves: 1 sprig
- Salt: ¾–1 tsp

1. Soak the dal in water for an hour.
2. Pressure cook the dal with double the quantity of water and a little salt for two whistles. Let it cool, open the cooker and mash dal gently.
3. Boil onions and tomatoes in 250 ml water until partially soft.
4. Heat oil in a non-stick pot, add mustard seeds and curry leaves. Let them crackle.
5. Add sambhar paste and cook. Add boiled onions and tomatoes, dal and remaining salt.
6. Let it boil for a few minutes and serve hot.

COCONUT CHUTNEY

(Measuring cup size: 150 ml)

- Grated coconut: 1 cup
- Yoghurt: 3 tbsp heaped
- Ginger: ¾ inch chopped
- Skinless roasted chana: 3 heaped tbsp
- Green chillies: 2 chopped
- Salt: ⅓ tsp
- Sugar: a pinch

1. Grind all the ingredients except yoghurt in a mixer till semi-smooth. Add yoghurt.

Tempering

- Mustard oil: 1 tsp
- Mustard seeds: ¼ tsp
- Asafoetida powder: a pinch
- Dried red chilli: 1
- Curry leaves: 1 sprig

1. Heat oil in a pan, add curry leaves, dried red chilli and mustard seeds and let them crackle.
2. Add asafoetida powder. Pour tempering over the chutney.

PRATIMA'S PINEAPPLE SHEERA (Serves 4)
(Measuring cup size: 150 ml)

- Ghee: 1 cup
- Semolina: 1 cup
- Sugar: 1–1¼ cups (depending on desired sweetness)
- Chopped pineapple: ¾ cup
- Water: 3 cups
- Green cardamoms: 2 peeled and powdered using a mortar and pestle
- Raisins: 10
- Cashew nuts: 6

1. Heat 2 tbsp of ghee in a wok/kadai and lightly fry raisins and cashew nuts and keep aside.
2. Heat remaining ghee in the same wok/kadai. Reduce flame to medium, add semolina and lightly fry until golden.
3. On another burner, on a medium flame put water and sugar in a wok/kadai and bring it to a boil.
4. Transfer the sugar syrup gradually to the fried semolina, stirring continuously to ensure that no lumps are formed. Be careful during this process as the semolina will bubble.
5. Add pineapple and mix well over a low flame stirring continuously.
6. Cover the pot and let simmer for 2–3 minutes.
7. Open and continue stirring until you get a thick, shiny mass.
8. Add green cardamom powder.
9. Serve hot, garnished with raisins and cashew nuts.

Photo on p. 20: Kuzi paniyaram with Vegetable Korma; Photo on p. 25: Radhaballabi, Niramish aloo dum; Photo on p. 30 (Clockwise): Coconut chutney, Mangalore buns, Pratima's pineapple sheera, Mangala aunty's onion sambhar; Photo on p. 35: Kawdhai pitha with Ambula rai, Kanchaa dali.

SERVINGS

Odiya Steamed Savoury Cake

Brunches in Odisha are part of regular life. My mom always told me stories of eating complete meals before going to school. Meals could be as simple as rice and dal with vegetables or pithas (Rice cakes/pancakes) of various kinds. Unlike the metros, the day starts late in Odisha. I think it's a way of life there. There is no pressure of proving the point of being an early riser. Of course, it might simply be the sheer fact that people are content with a slower pace!

Growing up outside the state, I never had that experience, but marriage gave me an opportunity to live the Odia life. The *nanas* or cooks who knew every part of the cuisine would rustle up various pithas on a regular basis, under the supervision of my mother-in-law. She tried hard to make me enjoy this one early morning activity which was learning the making of unique traditional food like the *phula badi*, the dehydrated flower-shaped wadi or lentil dumpling. However, I was expected to be all dressed up at 7 a.m. in a saree and bindi, only ensuring that I ran away from the task altogether!

Kawdhai pitha is one such wholesome brunch dish, a savoury or sweet rice cake, made in many households. This is the one I learnt at my in-laws', though they do not add vegetables. It is eaten with a boiled dal topped with chopped raw onions and tomatoes and raw mustard oil. Using dehydrated mangoes is also common in Odia cuisine, resulting in really delicious tangy chutneys which are a great accompaniment to any pitha.

KAWDHAI PITHA (Serves 4)
(Measuring cup size: 250 ml)

Kawdhai Pitha Batter

- Raw rice: 1 cup
- Urad dal: ¼ cup
- Flattened rice (poha)(optional): ¼ cup
- Water: 1½ cups approximately
- Salt: 1 tsp

1. Soak rice and urad dal separately in water for 6–8 hours.
2. Soak flattened rice in water for 5 minutes, if using.

3. Strain and grind dal until smooth.
4. Add strained flattened rice if using and grind further.
5. Add strained rice and continue to grind, adding water along the way.
6. Once the batter is smooth, leave it at room temperature overnight.
7. Add salt before using.

Pitha

- Batter: 400 gm
- Peas: 75 gm shelled
- Beans: 100 gm chopped
- Carrots: 100 gm chopped
- Cauliflower: 100 gm chopped
- Onion: 1 large sliced
- Green chillies: 2 chopped fine
- Mustard seeds: 1 tsp
- Curry leaves: 1 sprig
- Coconut: 2 tbsp finely chopped
- Sugar: 1–1½ tsp
- Ghee: 2–3 tbsp
- Fruit salt: ¾ tsp or baking powder: ¾ tsp
- Salt: 1 tsp

1. Heat 1 tbsp ghee in a pan. Add sugar and let it dissolve.
2. Add mustard seeds and let them crackle.
3. Add curry leaves.
4. Add sliced onions and green chillies with ½ tsp salt.
5. Cook until onions are translucent and pink.
6. Add all the vegetables and coconut pieces and stir fry.
7. Ensure that vegetables and coconut pieces are cooked through but crunchy.
8. Add the vegetable mixture to the batter and mix well.
9. Add fruit salt/baking powder, ½ tsp salt and aerate with a ladle.
10. Heat a thick-bottomed wok/kadai well greased with ghee.
11. Add the vegetable batter in it and pour a few drops of ghee along the sides.
12. Cover wok/kadai tightly with a lid and cook over a low flame for 20 minutes.
13. Remove from the flame. Gently loosen the pitha from the sides using a spatula.
14. Turn the wok/kadai over to transfer the pitha to a hot tawa to cook the other side.
15. Remove from tawa, cut into slices and serve.

SERVINGS

AMBULA RAI (Serves 4)

- Yellow mustard seeds: 1 tbsp
- Black mustard seeds: 1 tbsp
- Garlic: 2 cloves
- Ginger: ½ inch
- Green chillies: 2
- Coconut: 150 gm grated
- Yoghurt: 125 ml
- Dried mango kernels: 3 cut and soaked in water
- Jaggery: 1 tbsp
- Salt: to taste

1. Soak yellow and black mustard seeds, garlic, ginger with green chillies in water for 30 minutes. Strain and grind to a paste with a little water in a mixer.
2. Strain the paste again. Strain dried mango kernels and keep aside.
3. Mix grated coconut, yoghurt, dried mango kernels and jaggery.
4. Add salt and mustard paste and mix well.

Tempering

- Ghee: 1 tsp
- Black mustard seeds: ½ tsp
- Curry Leaves: a few

1. Heat 1 tsp ghee in a pan.
2. Add ½ tsp black mustard seeds and a few curry leaves. Let them crackle.
3. Pour tempering over the mango kernel mix.

KANCHAA DALI (Serves 4)

- Arhar dal: 275 gm
- Water: 600 ml
- Salt: 1–1½ tsp
- Turmeric powder: ½ tsp
- Tomatoes: 2 finely chopped
- Onion: 1 large finely chopped
- Green chillies: 1–2 finely chopped
- Coriander leaves: 1 tbsp finely chopped
- Mustard oil: 2 tbsp

SERVINGS

1. Soak dal for an hour in 600 ml of water.
2. Heat a pressure cooker.
3. Add dal and water with turmeric powder and salt.
4. Pressure cook for one whistle. Open the cooker once it cools down.
5. To serve dal, top with a mixture of onions, tomatoes, coriander leaves and green chillies.
6. Pour mustard oil on top.

Petit Déjeuner

The French toast was probably my first introduction to anything firang on my breakfast plate. Every Indian home makes this version of eggs and bread either sweet or savoury, fried in Amul butter and served with tomato ketchup.

This dish dates back to the Roman era, when stale bread was softened in a slurry of eggs and cream, with an added sweetener, and then fried. This was followed by the British who coined their own versions and then by the Americans. The French version is called *pain perdu*, literally meaning stale bread.

The word 'pain' means bread in French, it always brings back memories of a senior in college telling me, a fresher then, that during meal service if I saw *petit pain* on the menu card, it didn't actually mean 'little pain', but bread rolls. This version of French toast is a casserole and can be made into an overnight version, a lot like a bread and butter pudding, a Sunday brunch treat.

FRENCH TOAST CASSEROLE (Serves 6)
(Measuring cup size: 250 ml)

- White bread: 8 slices
- Eggs: 8
- Peanut butter: ½ cup + 2 tsp melted for topping
- Milk: ⅔ cup
- Bananas: 2 + 1 to garnish
- Honey: 2½ tbsp + 1 tbsp to drizzle while serving

- Salt: ½–¾ tsp
- Cinnamon powder: 1 tsp
- Vanilla essence: 1 tsp
- Icing sugar: 2 tsp

1. Take a 10 x 8 inch baking dish.
2. Divide each slice into 6 pieces. Place in the dish.
3. Slice 2 bananas and place evenly in the dish.
4. For the overnight version, add bananas in the morning.
5. Beat eggs with honey, peanut butter, milk, cinnamon powder, vanilla essence and salt.
6. Pour egg mixture over bread pieces and press down gently with your fingers.
7. Melt 1 tsp peanut butter and drizzle all over.
8. Cover with cling film tightly and leave for 2 hours. Refrigerate if making the overnight version. Then take out and let it stand for 15 minutes to reach room temperature.
9. Remove cling film. Replace with a foil and bake at 170°C for 30 minutes.
10. Remove foil and bake for another 10 minutes till it is firm in the middle.
11. Serve hot, topped with remaining bananas sliced and a drizzle of 1 tbsp warm honey and 1 tsp peanut butter mixed together and dust with icing sugar.

STRAWBERRY PISTACHIO PARFAIT (Serves 4)

- Strawberries: 300 gm hulled and quartered
- Greek yoghurt: 500 gm hung
- Honey: 3–4 tbsp
- Pistachios: 100 gm shelled and sliced
- Muesli: 4 tsp

1. Whisk honey and hung yoghurt together.
2. Layer fruit at the bottom of a mason jar, top with a few spoons of hung curd mixture and then add a layer of pistachios.
3. Repeat layers till the jar is full.
4. Top with muesli for crunch.

All American Diner

Everything American is what this meal is about. Strata or Stratta is a layered casserole and popular in America. It's basically a savoury bread pudding with sausages, eggs and milk. I love this dish for its simplicity. It's a saviour for a brunch table as it can be put together the previous night and baked in the morning and it looks and sounds more exotic than the usual bread, eggs and meat on the table. A variant can be made with mushrooms for the vegetarian or rather 'eggetarian' on the table. It's a put-anything-together dish. Adding an Indian tamatar–pyaz masala element enhances the flavour. Served alongside a fruit and leaf salad, it's a complete meal.

Top this with another favourite: a summer fruit cobbler. This is an American variant of the crumble, and the appearance of the dish is where the name is derived from. Essentially, it is a simple mixture of stewed fruit topped with a stiff batter of flour, butter, eggs and sugar.

I have one person to thank for the cinnamon ice cream trick. While he was at the Chambers in Taj Bengal, I have been fed and spoilt by Chef Basu on many an occasion when the going got tough. He served the ice cream with his legendary apple pie, a version I so regret not learning from him, but back then, working in the hotel kitchen was so not my thing!

STRATA – LAYERS OF GOODNESS (Serves 4)

(Measuring cup size: 250 ml)

- White bread: 9 slices (preferably a day old)
- Refined oil: 1 tbsp
- Chicken sausages: 350 gm
- Tomatoes: 1½ large sliced
- Onions: 1½ large sliced
- Tomato ketchup: 2 tsp
- Coriander leaves: 5 tbsp chopped
- Green chillies: 2–3 chopped fine
- Chicken masala/Curry powder: ¾ tsp
- Nutmeg powder: a pinch
- Cream: ½ cup
- Milk: 1½ cups
- Eggs: 5
- Salt: 1½ tsp
- Black pepper powder: ½ tsp

- Butter: to grease dish
- Cheese: ½–¾ cup grated (combine whatever cheese is available)

1. Slice sausages to ½ cm thick pieces.
2. Whisk together eggs, cream, milk, nutmeg powder, 1 tsp salt and black pepper powder.
3. Heat oil in a pan, add onions and stir fry with ½ tsp salt until translucent.
4. Add green chillies, 2 tbsp coriander leaves and tomatoes and let soften.
5. Add chicken masala/curry powder, tomato ketchup and sliced sausages.
6. Mix well. Check seasoning.
7. Take a 10 x 8 inch baking dish and grease with butter.
8. Cut each bread slice in 6 pieces. Layer half the quantity in the dish.
9. Pour ⅓ of the milk and egg mix.
10. Top with half the quantity of sausage mix and ⅓ the quantity of cheese and some coriander leaves.
11. Place another layer of bread, top with ⅓ of the egg–milk mix, the remaining sausage mixture and ⅓ of the cheese mix. Top with the remaining egg–milk mix and cheese.
12. Top with coriander leaves and press the bread pieces down with your palms.
13. Cover dish with a cling film and let it rest at room temperature for 2 hours. The dish can be refrigerated overnight and taken out an hour prior to baking.
14. Preheat oven to 170°C for 10 minutes. Remove cling film and bake covered with a foil for 30 minutes.
15. Increase oven temperature to 180°C, remove foil and bake for 15–20 minutes for a golden colour. Check if cooked in the centre with a toothpick. Serve hot.
16. Be careful while using a salty cheese. Reduce the salt in the egg–milk mix accordingly.
17. Baking time will decrease if the dish is larger as the ingredients will be layered thinner.

GREEN APPLE SALAD IN VINAIGRETTE (Serves 2)

- Green apple: 1 medium sliced and placed in ice cold water
- Fresh pomegranate seeds: 3 tbsp
- Balsamic vinegar: 15 ml
- Cheddar cheese: 60 gm cubed
- Extra virgin olive oil: 45 ml
- Cherry tomatoes: 6 halved
- Cottage cheese: 75 gm cubed

- Salt: ½ tsp
- Black pepper powder: ½ tsp
- Powdered sugar: ½ tsp
- Lettuce: 2–3 leaves shredded and placed in ice cold water

1. Mix balsamic vinegar, olive oil, salt, black pepper powder and powdered sugar together in a bowl. Strain apples and lettuce.
2. Add apples, lettuce, cottage cheese, Cheddar cheese, cherry tomatoes, pomegranate seeds to the bowl and toss. Serve cold.

Cobble to My Gobble

SUMMER FRUIT COBBLER (Serves 6)

Fruit Layer

- Peaches: 2 deseeded and chopped
- Plums: 2 deseeded and chopped
- Raspberries: 25 gm
- Blueberries: 25 gm
- Lemon zest: ½ tbsp
- Cornflour: 1 tbsp
- Honey: 40 ml
- Brown sugar: 2 tbsp
- Mint leaves: a few shredded

1. Mix all the ingredients in a bowl, except blueberries, raspberries and mint leaves.
2. Keep aside for a few minutes.

Cobble Batter

- All-purpose flour: 125 gm
- Baking powder: ½ tsp
- Butter: 100 gm
- Brown sugar: 100 gm
- Eggs: 2
- Vanilla/Lemon essence: ½ tsp

1. Ensure eggs and butter are at room temperature.
2. Sieve flour and baking powder.
3. Cream butter and sugar in a mixer. Add eggs, one at a time.
4. Add essence and the sieved flour. Fold the batter.

Assembling the Cobbler

1. Preheat oven to 170 °C and grease a 5 x 4 inch pie dish with butter.
2. Layer the fruit mix at the bottom and place the mint leaves in the gaps under it.
3. Using a scoop, put the cobbler batter, into the pie dish leaving a little space between each scoop. Place raspberries and blueberries in the gaps.
4. Bake in the oven for 30–35 minutes. Insert a toothpick in the centre, it should come out clean.
5. Remove from the oven and let it cool.
6. Serve at room temperature with cinnamon ice cream.

CINNAMON ICE CREAM (Serves 4)

- Vanilla ice cream: 500 ml
- Cinnamon powder: 2 tsp heaped

1. Soften ice cream with a whisk. Add cinnamon powder and mix well.
2. Reset in a bowl and place in the freezer for 6 hours before serving.

Spotted Dog – Fruity Brekkie

Soda bread is popular in Ireland though the early American Indians were the first to use soda to leaven bread. The method for making this bread is easy and requires just basic flour and makes for a nice simple breakfast. Commonly made with herbs and nuts, the raisin variety is called 'Spotted Dog' for its Dalmatian-like appearance. Another story tells of marking a cross on the round bread to ward off evil and protect the household. And if you forget to do that, do not fret because bingeing on yummy carbs can only bring joy.

This is a very child-friendly treat and is meant to awaken the child in the adult too. Home-made white butter is a welcome addition. Hallelujah!

FRUITY SODA BREAD (Serves 4)

- All-purpose flour: 250 gm
- Salt: ¼ tsp
- Baking soda: ½ tsp
- Trail mix berries: 50 gm
- Cranberries: 50 gm
- Raisins: 50 gm
- Orange zest: 1½ tbsp
- Sugar: 1 tbsp
- Butter: 25 gm
- Whole milk: 200 ml
- Lemon juice: 1 tbsp

1. Roughly chop cranberries, raisins and trail mix berries.
2. Sieve flour with baking soda.
3. Cream butter and sugar.
4. Mix milk with lemon juice in a bowl and leave it for 10 minutes.
5. Put the flour in a bowl and make a well in the centre. Into this well, pour the lemon and milk mix. Add creamed butter.
6. Now add orange zest, raisins, cranberries and trail mix berries. Using a whisk or a stand mixer with a hook mix together to form a soft dough.
7. Apply butter on your palms and make the dough into a ball.
8. Ensure the dough ball is not too high to get an even rise.
9. Make a deep cross on top of the dough.
10. Place on a parchment-lined baking tray.
11. Preheat the oven to 220 °C for 10 minutes.
12. Bake for 25–30 minutes. Apply melted butter on top to brown the crust at the 20-minute mark. Insert a toothpick in the centre to check if done.
13. Serve warm or toasted with butter.

Cut slices and bake again for 10 minutes in the oven at 200 °C fan and the end result is a fruity biscotti!

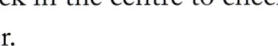

El Desayuno – Pan Con Tomate

Popular in the Catalan region, tomato bread is basically bread rubbed with olive oil, garlic and tomato paste. But one does find versions of this all over Europe, the popular bruschetta being one such version.

In India, many of us were introduced to the Tomatina festival held in Bunol through a popular Hindi movie and the equally popular song that goes, '*Oo, aa, take the world and paint it red!*' The song celebrates the sheer magic of tomatoes, rolling in them, jumping in their slurry, all to a catchy song-and-dance routine. I must admit, though, that if I were to get another chance, I would visit Barcelona again, with its grid of perfect perpendicular streets and amazing architecture. As a vegetarian, the food doesn't delight you, but yes, breakfast was my main meal, while I sat on the sidewalks, watching people go by.

This version of bread uses the star of the show and the accompanying sidekicks in a braided version. Tomatoes would have been used to soften dry bread and that's why this bread also requires no fat in it to yield a soft product. Now, all you have to do is toast it and dip it in herb olive oil or get creative and fill it with whatever you can find. I am a sandwich buff, be it breakfast, brunch, lunch or dinner. I love the ease of making and eating them. Tomato bread is a great base to build your own sandwich.

BREAKFAST TOMATO BREAD ROLLS (Serves 4)

- All-purpose flour: 250 gm
- Active dry yeast: 5 gm
- Tomatoes: 2 blanched and peeled
- Sugar: 1 tbsp
- Salt: ½ tsp
- Mixed herbs: ¼ tsp
- Garlic powder: ¼ tsp
- Onion powder: ¼ tsp
- Eggs: 2
- Egg yolks: 2

1. Put tomatoes and eggs in a blender and give them a quick mix.
2. Mix all dry ingredients together with yeast.
3. Make a dough by gradually adding the tomato–egg mix into the dry ingredients.
4. Proof the dough in a warm place for 1 hour covered with a moist cloth.
5. Knock back the dough, give it a quick stretch and fold. Divide into 12 equal balls.
6. Lengthen balls into cylinders of 4 inches each.
7. Place one cylinder across the other to form a cross. Braid 2 lengths with each other.
8. Bring the other 2 lengths down and continue braiding.
9. Place rolls on a parchment-lined baking tray and proof for 30 minutes.

10. Brush rolls with egg yolk. Preheat oven to 200 °C for 5 minutes.
11. Bake for 18–20 minutes. Let the rolls cool on a rack.
12. Store in an airtight container.

Cottage Cheese and Arrabiata Vegetable Filling (Makes 1 sandwich)

- Cottage cheese: 75gm
- Milk: 1–2 tbsp
- Mixed herbs: ¼ tsp
- Chilli flakes: ¼ tsp
- Salt: ½ tsp
- Sun-dried tomato: 1 tbsp
- Long aubergine slices: 4
- Mushroom: 1 sliced thick
- Refined oil: 2 tbsp
- Rice flour: 1 tbsp
- Red chilli powder: ¼ tsp
- Water: 1 tbsp
- Lettuce: 1 leaf
- Marinara sauce: 2 tbsp kept warm with ¼–½ tsp paprika to make the arrabiata sauce

1. Mash cottage cheese and soften with milk.
2. Add chilli flakes, sun-dried tomato, mixed herbs and ¼ tsp salt.
3. Mix rice flour with red chilli powder and ¼ tsp salt and a little water to make a paste.
4. Heat oil in a non-stick pan
5. Dip mushroom and aubergine in the rice flour paste.
6. Place in the pan and fry until crisp.

Assembling the Sandwich

1. Lightly toast bread roll in a pan and slice through the centre. Apply a little butter.
2. Apply a thick layer of cottage cheese.
3. Top with arrabiata sauce and then place aubergine and mushroom.
4. Drizzle some arrabiata sauce.
5. Top with crisp lettuce.
6. Serve.

Simple Chicken Filling

1. Apply a layer of mayonnaise on to the sliced roll.
2. Sauté onions and bell peppers in paprika, mustard, salt and pepper. Add shredded boiled chicken. Place on the roll.
3. Then layer with slices of boiled egg and season.
4. Top with some more onions, mayonnaise, mustard and crisp lettuce. Serve.

Wake Up Treat - Muffins

Muffins are a great breakfast offering and also work well in lunch boxes. As we see them today, muffins are an American creation and each family has their own recipe. In recipe books, the appearance of muffins coincides, interestingly, with the discovery of potash or potassium carbonate, which provides an alternative to yeast to make the dough rise. The earlier version of muffins were less sweet, with lower fat content, because the combination of fat with potash led to a soapy taste.

However, the discovery of baking soda changed all that. This is when experiments with different grains, flavours and fruits began. Baked initially in 'gem irons' or lozenge-shaped pans, muffins moved to circular pans for convenience. Muffin liners further eased the process involved in making them. Muffins were a hot breakfast dish to begin with, and today they exist on the menu of every coffee shop.

BLUEBERRY MUFFINS WITH CINNAMON CRUMB
(Serves 6)

Cinnamon Crumb Topping

- All-purpose flour: 35 gm
- Granulated sugar: 45 gm
- Butter: 45 gm
- Cinnamon powder: ½ tsp

1. Mix all the ingredients to make a crumble, and refrigerate.

Muffins

- Sugar: 90 gm
- Egg: 1
- Sour cream: 20 gm
- Cream cheese: 20 gm
- Refined oil: 75 ml
- Milk: 50 ml
- Vanilla essence: ¾ tsp
- All-purpose flour: 120 gm
- Baking powder: ¾ tsp
- Salt: ¼ tsp
- Blueberries: 75 gm fresh or frozen

1. Grease the muffin pan and place liners in it. You can make parchment liners by cutting 6 inch squares. Place each square over the base of a soft drink can and press the parchment down along the sides. This will make a pleated muffin cup.
2. Preheat the oven to 190 °C for 10 minutes.
3. If using fresh blueberries, clean, wash and dry them. If they are large, halve them. Toss in a spoon of flour such that they are coated, and keep aside.
4. Sieve together flour, baking powder and salt.
5. In a bowl, combine sugar, egg, sour cream, cream cheese, oil, milk and vanilla essence. whisk until well combined.
6. Add the sieved flour and whisk until just combined and fold in the blueberries.
7. Evenly distribute the batter between the prepared muffin liners, filling them almost to the top.
8. Take out the cinnamon crumb from the refrigerator and put a generous tablespoon of crumb topping.
9. Bake muffins for 40–45 minutes or until a toothpick inserted into the centre of the muffins comes out clean.
10. Remove the muffin pan from the oven and cool before taking out the muffins.

40 gm of thick yoghurt can be used instead of sour cream and cream cheese.

Photo on p. 38: Peanut butter french toast casserole with a strawberry pistachio yoghurt parfait; Photo on p. 41 (Clockwise): Strata, Cinnamon ice cream, Summer fruit cobbler and Granny smith apple salad in a vinaigrette; Photo on p. 44: 'Spotted Dog' – Fruity soda bread with white butter; Photo on p. 47: El desayuno pan con tomate – Breakfast tomato bread; Photo on p. 50: Blueberry muffins with cinnamon crumb.

TRIPLE CHOCOLATE MUFFINS WITH SALTED CARAMEL CENTRE (Serves 6)

Salted Caramel

- Sugar: 200 gm
- Butter: 90 gm
- Salt: 1 tsp
- Cream: 125 ml

1. In a heavy-bottom saucepan, melt sugar and butter, whisking continuously.
2. Once the mixture comes together and softens, remove from flame and continue whisking. Add salt.
3. Gradually add in the cream and continue whisking.
4. Place back on the flame and whisk. Boil for a minute.
5. Remove from the flame and cool.
6. This can be bottled and refrigerated for a month.
7. Reheat when you want to use it.

Muffins

- Milk chocolate: 50 gm
- Chocolate chips: 75 gm
- Cocoa powder: 15 gm
- All-purpose flour: 50 gm
- Baking soda: ¼ tsp
- Vanilla essence: ½ tsp
- Sugar: 75 gm
- Butter: 50 gm
- Yoghurt: 40 gm
- Eggs: 1½
- Salted caramel: 6–8 tsp heaped

1. Melt milk chocolate for 10 seconds in the microwave or in a double boiler.
2. Sieve flour with cocoa powder and baking soda. Preheat oven to 220 °C for 8 minutes.
3. Whisk together butter, sugar, yoghurt, vanilla essence, melted milk chocolate and eggs.
4. Fold in the dry ingredients well and then fold in chocolate chips.
5. Grease the muffin pan and place liners in it. You can make parchment liners by cutting 6 inch squares. Place each square over the base of a soft drink can and press parchment down along the sides. This will make a pleated muffin cup.
6. Fill the muffin liners halfway with batter, then put a heaped teaspoon of salted caramel sauce and then top with some more batter.

7. Tap the pan on the counter to remove air pockets and bake in the oven at 220 °C for 5 minutes.
8. Reduce temperature to 165 °C and bake further for 13–15 minutes.
9. Insert a toothpick to check if done – the caramel centre will be moist.
10. Remove from the pan and cool in the liners on a rack.

JALAPEÑO, CHEESE AND ONION MUFFINS
(Makes 6 small)

- All-purpose flour: 50 gm
- Whole wheat flour: 30 gm
- Egg: 1
- Milk: 35 ml
- Refined oil: 35 ml
- Baking soda: ¼ tsp
- Baking powder: ½ tsp
- Onion: 30 gm
- Butter: ½ tsp
- Jalapeño: 20 gm + 5 gm sliced for topping
- Cream cheese: 30 gm
- Sun-dried tomato: 10 gm
- Garlic powder: ¼ tsp
- Onion powder: ½ tsp
- Chilli flakes: ½ tsp
- Salt: ½ tsp
- Cheddar cheese: grated, for topping

1. Preheat oven to 200 °C for 8–10 minutes.
2. Grease the muffin pan and place liners in it. Alternatively, you can make parchment liners by cutting 5 inch squares. Place each square over the base of a soft drink can and press parchment down along the sides. This will make a pleated muffin cup.
3. Sieve both flours along with baking soda and baking powder.
4. Chop sun-dried tomato, 20 gm jalapeño and onion.
5. In a non-stick pan sauté onions in ½ tsp butter.
6. Whisk cream cheese and eggs.
7. Add oil followed by flour mix, chilli flakes, garlic powder, onion powder and salt. Fold sautéed onions, jalapeño, sun-dried tomato and milk into the batter.
8. Divide batter equally between muffin liners.
9. Top with jalapeño slices and grated Cheddar cheese.

10. Bake for 20 minutes at 200 °C, reduce temperature to 180 °C and bake further for 5–6 minutes.
11. Insert a toothpick and check if it comes out clean.
12. Remove from oven and serve warm.

Legendary Flury's

Built by a Swiss couple Mr and Mrs J. Flury this iconic tea room and bakery located on Park Street in Kolkata dates back to 1927. I have distinct memories of walking into Flury's at 11 a.m. and being served by bearers dressed in starched white – many of them had spent 40-odd years working there! To my mind, there's no better way to begin a lazy day than to eat up the savoury, gulp down the cold coffee and indulge in the best chocolate boats.

Today, of course, the interiors of Flury's do not look like what they did in the 1990s. A renovation had to be done in 2010 after a blazing fire ravaged the building. Reminiscing those flavours while recreating them was fulfilling!

CHICKEN CURRY PUFFS (Makes 8)

- Puff pastry squares: 8 (4x4 inch)
- Chicken mince: 250 gm
- Onion: 1 medium chopped
- Garlic–ginger paste: 1 tsp
- Coriander leaves: 2 tbsp chopped
- Red chilli powder: 1 tsp
- Madras curry powder: 2 tsp
- Refined oil: 1 tbsp
- Salt: ¾ tsp

1. Heat oil in a non-stick pan.
2. Add onion and stir fry with salt until it is translucent and pink.
3. Add ginger–garlic paste and sauté. Add chicken mince.

4. Cook the mince for 4–5 minutes and add curry powder, coriander leaves and red chilli powder. Continue cooking till the mince softens.
5. Remove from flame and cool.
6. Blitz half the chicken mix in a blender for a few seconds.
7. Add it to the rest of the chicken mix. Soften the mix with your fingers to make a smoother mash and divide it into 8 equal portions.
8. To assemble the puff, place a portion of the chicken mix in the centre of the puff pastry square. Apply water along the edges and fold the square to make a triangle.
9. Lightly press the edges with a fork.
10. Place on a parchment-lined baking tray.
11. Brush with melted butter or egg wash.
12. Preheat oven to 200 °C for 10–12 minutes.
13. Bake puffs for 20–22 minutes.
14. Broil on upper rack for 2 minutes or until golden.
15. Remove and cool on a wire rack.
16. Serve warm or store in an airtight container.

SWEET CORN TOASTS (Serves 2)
(Measuring cup size: 150 ml)

- Cream of sweet corn: 1 cup
- Corn kernels: 1 cup boiled
- Butter: 1 tbsp
- Onion: 1 small chopped
- Garlic: 2 cloves minced
- Milk: ½ cup
- Grated Cheddar cheese: 1 cup
- Salt: ½ tsp
- Black pepper powder: ½ tsp
- Parsley leaves: 1 tbsp chopped

1. Preheat oven to 180 °C for 10–12 minutes.
2. Heat butter in a non-stick pan.
3. Sauté onions with salt until they turn pink, then add garlic and continue to sauté.
4. Add cream of sweet corn, followed by boiled corn kernels and sauté until soft.
5. Add black pepper powder and parsley leaves.

SERVINGS

6. Add milk and mix well along with half the quantity of cheese. Remove from flame and divide into 3 equal portions.
7. On a heated flat pan, place 3 slices of white bread.
8. Crisp on one side for 3 minutes and remove from flame.
9. On the soft side of the bread, spread the corn mixture.
10. Top each slice with the remaining cheese and parsley.
11. Preheat 170 °C for 8 minutes. Place slices on a wire rack and bake for 13–15 minutes or until crisp. Serve hot.

CHOCOLATE TARTS (Serves 8)

(Measuring cup size: 250 ml)

Tart Shells

- All-purpose flour: 100 gm
- Butter: 50 gm
- Egg: ½ beaten
- Icing sugar: ½ tbsp

1. Using your fingers mix flour and butter until crumbly.
2. Add egg and knead to a dough.
3. Wrap in cling film and let it rest in the refrigerator for 30 minutes.
4. Take out of the refrigerator and place dough between two layers of cling film and roll out to ½ cm thickness.
5. Remove upper layer of cling film and cut dough into 6 cm discs.
6. Transfer discs carefully into 5 cm tart tins.
7. Press the edges with your fingers. Prick the base with a fork.
8. Preheat oven to 180 °C for 8 minutes.
9. Place baking beans on the tart dough and blind bake for 15 minutes.
10. Remove baking beans and bake further at 170 °C for 6–8 minutes.
11. Remove from the oven. Allow shells to cool.

Chocolate Ganache

- Dark chocolate covertures: ¾ cup
- Milk chocolate covertures: ¼ cup
- Vanilla essence: 1 tsp

SERVINGS

- Honey: 4 tsp
- Pink salt: ¼ tsp
- Cream: 1 cup

1. In a heat-proof bowl, place both chocolate covertures, vanilla essence, honey and pink salt.
2. Heat cream in a heavy-bottomed saucepan and let it boil.
3. Pour the hot cream over the chocolate mix and cover the bowl.
4. Leave the bowl at room temperature for 25–30 minutes.
5. After that mix the chocolate and cream together to get a shiny ganache.
6. Fill each tart shell with the ganache and allow it to set in the refrigerator for at least 30 minutes.
7. Top with halved strawberries or any other topping of choice.
8. Serve cold.

Photo on p. 53: Triple chocolate muffins with salted caramel centres; Photo on p. 54: Jalapeño, cheese and onion muffins; Photo on p. 59 (Clockwise): Sweet corn toast, Chocolate tarts and Chicken curry puffs.

WHETTING YOUR APPETITE

Start Up

Starters or appetizers are small portions or bite-sized delicacies – the precursor to a meal. They set both the palate and tone of what to expect from the main course. Appetizers were served as a buffet, as early as the third century. But they weren't very popular, because the meal had no main course – and people went away hungry! Fruit, wine, olives and cheese were the main focus here, quite like the grazing tables we see today. Creative appetizers are an integral part of any meal. They not only add to the quality of the time spent together, but also to the conversations around the table, stretching out the mealtime too. While planning a menu, it's always a good idea to try and ensure that the starters are similar to the cuisine you are serving in the main course. Diverse flavours may adversely impact the culinary experience.

The recipes have been created as sets with a vegetarian and a non-vegetarian option.

MAKHMALI GULABI BOTI (Serves 4)

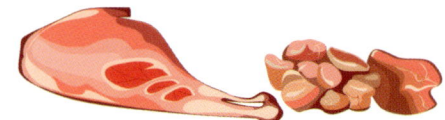

- Boneless mutton: 500 gm

1. Cut mutton into cubes around 1½ inches in size.

Marinade

- Raw papaya paste: 50 gm
- Onion: 50 gm
- Fried onion: 50 gm
- Yoghurt: 50 ml
- Home-made garam masala powder: ½ tsp
- Yellow chilli powder: 1 tsp
- Coriander powder: ¾ tsp
- Meat masala: 1 tsp

SERVINGS

- Ginger paste: 1½ tsp
- Salt: 1 tsp

1. Boil onion and grind to a paste.
2. Grind fried onions with yoghurt to a paste.
3. Marinate mutton with all the ingredients for 8 hours or overnight.

- Ghee: 3 tbsp
- Cloves: 2
- Green cardamoms: 2
- Cashew nuts: 5–6
- Almonds: 5–6
- Roasted coconut powder: 1 tbsp
- Roasted gram flour: 1 tbsp
- Saffron: 6–7 strands
- Dried rose petals: 10–12
- Home-made garam masala powder or rose petal garam masala powder: ¼ tsp
- Milk: 20 ml
- Salt: ¼ tsp

1. Soak cashew nuts and almonds in warm water for 30 minutes. Strain, peel almonds and grind both to a paste.
2. Soak rose petals and saffron in warm milk.
3. Heat 2 tbsp of ghee in a non-stick pan.
4. Add cloves and cardamoms and let them crackle.
5. Add marinated mutton and roasted gram flour.
6. Sauté for a few minutes until the mutton changes colour and then cover with a lid and cook for 20 minutes on a low flame. Check seasoning and add salt.
7. Remove the lid and add cashew–almond paste and remaining ghee.
8. Add coconut powder and home-made garam masala or rose petal garam masala.
9. Add saffron and dried rose petals soaked in milk.
10. Cook until the mutton is completely soft. This will take another 15–20 minutes at least. Remove from flame and serve.

HARA BHARA CHEESY KEBAB (Serves 4)

- Baby spinach: 115 gm
- Green peas: 125 gm
- Potatoes: 120 gm
- Green chillies: 2 finely chopped
- Ginger: 1 inch
- Refined oil: 1 tsp + 1½ tbsp for frying
- Chaat masala powder: ½ tsp
- Dried mango powder: ½ tsp
- Salt: ¾ tsp
- Mozzarella cheese: 40 gm
- Breadcrumbs: 2½–3½ tbsp

1. Blanch spinach leaves in boiling water for 1–2 minutes.
2. Strain and place in cold water for 5 minutes. Drain, squeeze dry and chop.
3. Boil potatoes in salt water, drain, cool, peel and mash.
4. Cut mozzarella cheese into 8 cubes.
5. Heat oil in a non-stick pan and lightly sauté ginger and green chillies.
6. Add peas and toss until soft. Remove, cool and mash.
7. Add spinach to the same pan and gently stir fry until well done.
8. Remove from flame and mix spinach with the peas, boiled potatoes, spices and salt.
9. Mix well and mash together. Add breadcrumbs and mix further.
10. Divide into 8 portions, approximately 35 gm each.
11. Shape into balls and flatten. Place a piece of mozzarella cheese in the centre.
12. Reshape into a ball and flatten.
13. Heat 1½ tbsp of oil in a non-stick pan and gently fry the kebabs, 2–3 minutes on each side. Serve hot with ketchup.

Photo on p. 65: Makhmali gulabi boti, Hara bhara cheesy kababs.

PRAWN SPRING ROLLS (Serves 4)

Filling

- Roasted sesame oil: 1 tbsp
- Onion: 1 small chopped
- Prawns: 300 gm chopped
- Cornflour: 2½ tsp

- Powdered sugar: 1½ tsp
- Salt: ¼ tsp
- Ginger: 1 tsp minced
- Black pepper powder: ¼ tsp
- Oyster sauce: 1½ tbsp

1. Heat oil in a non-stick pan and sauté onions.
2. Add ginger and sauté lightly.
3. Add chopped prawns and stir fry.
4. Add all the other ingredients and sauté gently till the ingredients blend well.
5. Remove from flame.
6. Transfer mixture to a bowl and let it rest for 10 minutes.
7. Divide the mixture into 10 equal portions of approximately 15 gm each.
8. To make spring rolls refer to the picture on p. 67 and process on p. 69.

WATER CHESTNUT, CORN AND ASPARAGUS SPRING ROLLS (Serves 4)

Filling

- Onion: 1 small chopped
- Ginger: 1 tsp minced
- Water chestnut: 70 gm
- Asparagus: 50 gm
- Fresh corn: 30 gm

- Hoisin sauce: 2 tbsp
- Black pepper powder: ½ tsp
- Salt: ¼ tsp
- Powdered sugar: ½ tsp
- Roasted sesame oil: 1 tbsp
- Cornflour: 1 tsp

Photo on p. 67: The process of making Prawn spring rolls, Water chestnut, Corn and Asparagus spring rolls.

1. Peel and chop water chestnuts, asparagus finely and mix with corn.
2. Remove excess water with a salad spinner or by squeezing gently.
3. Heat oil in a non-stick pan and sauté onions. Add ginger and stir fry.
4. Add all other ingredients and stir fry gently till everything blends well. Remove from flame. Place in a bowl and let it rest for 10 minutes.
5. Divide the mixture into 10 equal portions of approximately 15 gm each. To make the springrolls refer to pictures below and process on p. 69.

Assembling the Spring Rolls

- Spring roll sheets: 20
- All-purpose flour: 2 tsp
- Whisked egg/Water: 3–4 tsp
- Refined oil: to deep fry

1. Mix flour and egg or flour and water to make a sticky paste and keep it aside.
2. Keep the spring roll sheets wrapped in a moist cloth to avoid drying out.
3. Place a spring roll sheet on a clean board such that it resembles a diamond shape.
4. Place a portion of the filling about 1½ cm from the corner.
5. Fold the edge over the filling and then roll once more to ensure the roll is tight.
6. Fold the left and right corners inwards to form an envelope.
7. Keep rolling till it takes the shape of a cylinder.
8. Secure the edge with the flour paste.
9. Place the spring rolls on a flat plate.
10. Heat oil in a wok on a medium flame to deep fry the spring rolls.
11. Gently drop a few pieces at a time into the oil and fry till golden.
12. Remove from the oil and place in a colander lined with a paper towel.
13. Serve hot with sweet chilli sauce and chilli oil mixed with soy.

FRUITY CHEESE BOARD

WASABI AND CHEESE–FILLED LITCHIS

- Deseeded canned litchis: 24 drained
- Blanc cheese: 75–100 gm
- Wasabi paste: ¾ –1 tsp (depending on the pungency of the wasabi)

1. Smoothen blanc cheese and add wasabi paste to it, check taste for sharpness.
2. The quantity of cheese required will vary depending on the size of the litchis.
3. Fill the wasabi–cheese mixture into a piping bag.
4. Pipe the wasabi–cheese mixture into the litchis. Chill before serving.

SERVINGS

CHEESY DATES

- Dates: 12 deseeded
- Ricotta cheese: 115 gm
- Basil leaves: 8–10 chopped
- Garlic cloves: 2 large minced
- Pistachios: 10–12 chopped

1. Soften ricotta cheese.
2. Add chopped basil leaves, minced garlic and chopped pistachios. Mix well.
3. Stuff dates with the cheese mixture and serve at room temperature.

Building a Cheese Board

1. Place the containers for the ingredients on a board. The containers can be used for jams, dips or filled fruit. These can be metal or glass bowls, jars or glasses.
2. Place different varieties of cheese you want to serve. Three is a good number to start with, and you can go up to five.
- Familiar cheese – like Cheddar or gouda
- Aged cheese – for depth in flavour like a blue cheese
- Exciting cheese – something that catches the eye like a spiced cheese
- Soft cheese – like Brie
- Milk cheese – like goat or cow
3. The cheese can be cut or served whole for guests to cut.
4. Place bunches of fruit like grapes, sweet tomatoes, apricots or sticks of vegetables like carrots and cucumbers around the cheese.
5. Add meats like sliced salami or prosciutto folded into either a half circle or triangle.
6. Place just a few crackers on the outside edge of the board. Serve the extra crackers in a container or glasses off the board.
7. Fill gaps with nuts like pistachios, almonds and olives.
8. Create a visual of different heights for better impact.

Photo on p. 68: Prawn spring rolls and Water chestnut, Corn and Asparagus spring rolls;
Photo on p. 71: Fruity cheese board.

CHOP CHOP

Chop is a concept of small deep fried croquettes popular in east India, be it Bengal or Odisha. It is not a cutlet and nor is it a Western chop. The origin could be Anglo-Indian and as it is a combination of the kebab with the hammered and crumb fried rib bone meat.

The chop is sold at tea stalls, which is the place for *khatti*, small groups of people sitting together and chatting or rather gossiping while drinking lots of tea.

Chop Masala (Makes 1 portion)

- Bay leaf: 1
- Dried red chilli: 1
- Cloves: 3
- Cinnamon: 1½ inch stick
- Cumin seeds: ½ tsp
- Fennel seeds: 1 tsp

1. Dry roast all the ingredients in a pan, cool grind in a mixer and keep aside.

BEETROOT CHOP (Serves 4)

- Beetroot: 200 gm diced
- Beans: 50 gm diced
- Carrots: 50 gm diced
- Peanuts: 1½ tbsp
- Potatoes: 200 gm boiled, peeled and mashed
- Black salt: 1¼ tsp
- Refined oil: 1 tbsp
- Ginger: 1½ tbsp chopped
- Green chillies: 1–2 chopped
- Ghee: ½ tbsp
- Sugar: ¾ tsp
- Chop masala: 1 portion (recipe above)
- Cornflour: 2 tbsp heaped
- Flour: 2 tbsp heaped
- Water: 150 ml
- Breadcrumbs: as required

1. Pound green chillies and ginger in a mortar and pestle.
2. Heat oil in a non-stick pan. Add the peanuts. Gently fry, remove from oil and keep aside. Now add pounded green chilli–ginger mixture and sauté.
3. Add beetroot, carrot and beans. Let them soften. This will take 8–10 minutes on a medium flame.
4. Add chop masala, black salt and sauté.
5. Add sugar and ghee and mix well.
6. Add mashed potatoes and mix. Do not mash the vegetables.
7. Turn off the flame. Add the peanuts and let the mixture cool.
8. Shape into 8 oblong croquettes, approximately 40 gm each.
9. Make a slurry of cornflour and flour with 150 ml water.
10. Spread breadcrumbs on a flat pan.
11. Dip chops in slurry and then coat with breadcrumbs.
12. Repeat the process of dipping and coating and then freeze on a tray for 3 hours.
13. Deep fry and serve with ketchup or chilli sauce.

MUTTON CHOP (Serves 4)

- Mutton mince: 250 gm
- Potatoes: 100 gm boiled, peeled and mashed
- Refined oil: 1 tbsp + for deep frying
- Eggs: 2 whisked
- Ginger paste: ½ tbsp
- Garlic paste: 1 tbsp
- Onion: 1 medium chopped
- Coriander leaves: 1 tbsp chopped
- Sugar: ¾ tsp
- Ghee: ½ tbsp
- Tomato ketchup: ¾ tbsp
- Chop masala: 1 portion (recipe on p. 72)
- Salt: 1 tsp
- Green chillies: 1–2 chopped
- Cornflour: 2 tbsp
- Flour: 2 tbsp
- Water: 150 ml
- Breadcrumbs: as required

1. Heat oil in a non-stick pan. Add sugar and caramelize.
2. Add the onions and ½ tsp salt, sauté until pink.
3. Add chopped green chillies, ginger and garlic paste, and sauté. Add the mince and cook for a few minutes.
4. Add chop masala and coriander leaves, followed by ghee, remaining salt and tomato ketchup. Cook covered for 8–10 minutes until mince softens.
5. Add potatoes and mash. Remove from flame cool and blitz in a chopper for 30 seconds.
6. Divide into 8 portions, approximately 35 gm each.
7. Make a slurry of cornflour and flour with 150 ml water.
8. Whisk eggs in a bowl and season.
9. Spread breadcrumbs in a flat pan.
10. Dip chops in slurry, then in the eggs and then coat with breadcrumbs.
11. Repeat the process of dipping and coating and then freeze on a tray for 3 hours.
12. Deep fry and serve with ketchup or chilli sauce.

BHAI'S ASIAN DRY RED CHILLI PRAWNS (Serves 4)

- Prawns: 6–8 with head approximately 600 gm
- Garlic: 60 gm chopped
- Onion: 1 medium chopped
- Dried red chillies: 10 flat large
- Ginger: ½ inch chopped
- Salt: 1 tsp
- Sugar: ¾ tsp
- Fish sauce: 1 tbsp
- Dark soy sauce: 1 tbsp
- Refined oil: for deep frying

1. Remove the head and legs of the prawns. Keeping the shell intact.
2. Lay prawns on their back on a chopping board, make a slit through the stomach and devein.
3. Deseed half the quantity of dried red chillies and chop along with the remaining lot.
4. Heat oil in a wok. Deep fry garlic until it is light golden and keep aside on a paper towel to drain the excess oil.

5. Strain remaining oil. Take 2 tbsp of the oil again in the wok and heat it.
6. Fry prawns in the oil, a minute on each side. Do not overcook.
7. Remove prawns and keep aside
8. In the same wok, add another 2 tbsp of oil and stir fry chopped ginger and chopped onions until brown.
9. Add dried red chillies and stir fry.
10. Add prawns, salt and sugar.
11. Add soy sauce, fish sauce and stir.
12. Add fried garlic and toss well for 2 minutes.
13. Serve hot.

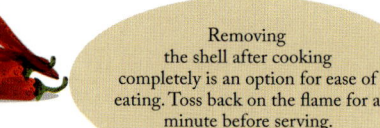

Removing the shell after cooking completely is an option for ease of eating. Toss back on the flame for a minute before serving.

SALT AND PEPPER TOFU WITH SIMPLE CHINESE DIPPING SAUCE (Serves 4)

Tofu

- Packaged extra firm tofu: 350 gm
- Salt: ¾ tsp
- White pepper powder: 1 tsp
- Castor sugar: 1 tsp
- Chinese five spice: ¼ tsp
- Cornstarch: 2–3 tsp
- Refined oil: 3 tbsp
- Spring onions: 2 heads chopped and greens sliced
- Garlic: 2 heaped tsp chopped
- Thai chillies: 2 chopped
- Light soy sauce: 1 tbsp
- Sesame oil: ½ tsp

1. Cut tofu into cubes.
2. Place on a paper towel and allow it to dehydrate for an hour.
3. Pat dry tofu, sprinkle salt, castor sugar, Chinese five spice and white pepper powder.
4. Spread cornstarch on a plate and coat each piece of tofu on all sides.
5. Brush a non-stick flat pan with 2 tbsp refined oil and place the tofu in it.
6. Cook the tofu on both side for 2 minutes each. Also brown the sides of the tofu cubes by making them stand vertical in the pan.

7. Place on a rack once done.
8. Heat 1 tbsp refined oil and sesame oil in the same pan on a medium flame.
9. Lightly sauté spring onions heads, garlic and chillies. Add soy sauce.
10. Add prepared tofu and toss lightly.
11. Top with spring onion greens.

Simple Chinese Dipping Sauce

- Mint leaves: 1 tbsp chopped
- Coriander leaves: 1½ tbsp chopped
- Ginger: 1 tsp chopped
- Garlic: 1 tsp chopped
- Salt: ¼ tsp
- Black pepper powder: ¼ tsp
- Tomato ketchup: 3 tbsp
- White vinegar: 2 tbsp
- Chinese chilli paste: 1 tsp
- Castor sugar: ½ tsp

1. Mix all the ingredients to make a dipping sauce.

EGG ROAST (Serves 4)

- Eggs: 5 boiled, peeled and halved
- Refined oil: 1 tbsp
- Ghee: 1 tbsp
- Curry leaves: 2 sprigs
- Whole bydagi chillies: 2
- Garlic: 8 cloves chopped
- Kashmiri/Bydagi chilli powder: ¼ tsp
- Turmeric powder: ¼ tsp
- Coriander powder: ½ tsp
- Mustard seeds: ¾ tsp
- Cumin seeds: ½ tsp
- Salt: ¾ tsp

1. In a non-stick pan, heat ghee and oil on a medium flame.
2. Add cumin seeds, mustard seeds, whole bydagi chillies, curry leaves and let them crackle.
3. Add chopped garlic and sauté lightly. Do not let it brown.
4. Lower flame and add Kashmiri/bydagi chilli powder, turmeric powder and coriander powder. Mix well and add salt.

5. Keep the flame low, otherwise the spices will burn and will taste bitter.
6. Add the boiled eggs.
7. Coat eggs with the masala.
8. Cook till the eggs are golden.

CHAITRA'S GOLI BAJJE (Serves 4)

- All-purpose flour: 80 gm
- Gram flour: 40 gm
- Baking powder: ½ tbsp
- Thick yoghurt: 50 ml
- Fresh coconut: 3 tbsp diced
- Ginger: 2 tsp chopped
- Green chillies: 2 chopped
- Curry leaves: 2 sprigs chopped
- Water: 75–80 ml
- Salt: ¾ tsp
- Refined oil: to deep fry

1. Sieve flour, gram flour and baking powder together.
2. Add yoghurt and whisk together.
3. Add fresh coconut, ginger, green chillies and curry leaves. Gradually add water and whisk to aerate batter.
4. Add salt. Check seasoning and let the batter rest at room temperature for an hour.
5. Heat oil in a wok/ kadai for deep frying.
6. Shape batter into balls with your fingers, and drop into hot oil.
7. Deep fry 5–6 balls at a time until golden in colour. This will take 3–4 minutes.
8. Remove and drain excess oil on a paper towel.
9. Serve immediately with a coconut chutney of your choice.

Photo on p. 74: Beetroot chop and Mutton chop; Photo on p. 77: Bhai's asian dry red chilli prawns; Photo on p. 78: Salt and pepper tofu with Simple Thai chi sauce; Photo on p. 80: Egg roast and Chaitra's goli bajje.

SERVINGS

PANEER TAKATAK (Serves 6)

- Paneer (cottage cheese): 850 gm
- Onions: 3 chopped
- Garlic paste: 1 tbsp
- Tomatoes: 4 chopped
- Coriander powder: 1 tbsp
- Red chilli powder: ¾ tsp
- Kashmiri chilli powder: 1 tsp
- Roasted cumin powder: 1½ tsp
- Turmeric powder: 1 tsp
- Green chillies: 2 slit
- Cream: 60 ml
- Ghee: 2–3 tbsp
- Refined oil: 1½ tbsp
- Salt: 1¼ tsp

1. Cut paneer into cubes. Heat ghee and oil in a pan.
2. Add onions with a little salt and cook until translucent.
3. Add garlic paste and cook for 1–2 minutes.
4. Add tomatoes and cook, add coriander powder, both chilli powders, roasted cumin powder and turmeric powder.
5. Cover and cook until the tomatoes soften and the oil separates.
6. Add paneer, remaining salt and let the mixture blend well.
7. Cover and cook for 10 minutes.
8. Add green chillies and cook, gently mashing the paneer cubes.
9. Finish with cream, and mix.
10. Serve with sheermal.

Photo on p. 83: Paneer takatak, Pudina kheema, Sheermal.

PUDINA KEEMA (Serves 6)
(Measuring cup size: 250 ml)

- Mutton mince: 1 kg
- Onion: 4 largish sliced
- Ghee: 75 ml
- Refined oil: 50 ml
- Garlic paste: 1 tbsp
- Ginger paste: 1 tbsp
- Red chilli powder: ¾–1 tbsp
- Coriander powder: 2 tbsp
- Meat masala: 1 tsp level
- Garam masala: 1 tsp
- Yoghurt: 150 ml
- Green chillies: 1–2 slit
- Mint leaves: 1 cup chopped
- Salt: 2–2½ tsp
- Water: ½–¾ cup

1. Heat half the quantity of both oil and ghee in a heavy-bottomed pan.
2. Add mutton mince and let it cook till the water evaporates. Remove from flame.
3. In the same pan, add remaining ghee and oil. Add ginger and garlic paste and cook.
4. Add onions with a little salt and fry until golden brown.
5. Add mince back into the pan followed by spice powders and cook until brown on a low flame.
6. Add a little boiling water and soften the mixture, mashing the mince to a soft consistency. Add slit green chillies.
7. Add beaten yoghurt and cook. Add remaining salt.
8. Cover for 15 minutes and let the mixture soften.
9. Add chopped mint, mix and cover again for 25 minutes, adding hot water to keep softening the keema. Serve hot with sheermal.

SHEERMAL (Serves 6)
(Measuring cup size: 250 ml)

- All-purpose flour: 1 cup
- Semolina: ¼ cup
- Egg: 1
- Ghee: 2 tbsp
- Salt: ½ tsp
- Powdered sugar: ¼ cup
- Milk: 75 ml

1. Mix all of the above ingredients except milk.
2. Add milk gradually and knead to a dough.
3. Let the dough rest for 3 hours.
4. Divide into 12–14 equal balls. Roll out into 5 inch discs.
5. Heat ½ tsp ghee on a non-stick flat pan.
6. Cook sheermals on each side for 3–4 minutes until light golden and crisp.

Sheermal can be made in advance, half-cooked and frozen.

MANSI'S BIHARI BOTI WINGS (Serves 6)
(Measuring cup size: 250 ml)

- Chicken wings: 750 gm
- Lemon juice: 2 tbsp
- Salt: 1 tsp
- Kashmiri chilli powder: 1 tbsp
- Nutmeg powder: 1 tsp
- Mace: 1 piece
- Mustard oil: ¼ tsp
- Kachri powder: 1 tbsp
- Poppy seeds: ¾ tbsp
- Roasted chana: 2 tbsp
- Coriander seeds: 1 tbsp
- Yoghurt: 1 cup
- Fried onions: 1 cup
- Ginger paste: 1 tbsp
- Garlic paste: 1 tbsp
- Refined oil: 2–3 tbsp

1. Grind poppy seeds, roasted chana and coriander seeds in a mixer and add to the chicken wings.
2. Mix yoghurt, fried onions, ginger paste, garlic paste together and add to the chicken wings.
3. Add lemon juice, salt, Kashmiri chilli powder, nutmeg powder, mace, mustard oil and kachri powder to the chicken wings.
4. Marinate overnight in the refrigerator.
5. Take out the marinated chicken from the refrigerator and leave it outside for an hour.
6. Heat oil in a large non-stick pan. Spread chicken wings and cook on a medium flame.
7. Allow one side to darken for 4 minutes. Flip and cook the other side.
8. Continue flipping till the chicken wings are cooked through.
9. Serve hot.

KACCHE AAM KI HARI CHUTNEY

- Raw mango: 100 gm chopped
- Mint leaves: 10 gm
- Coriander leaves: 25 gm
- Ginger: ½ inch
- Salt: 1 tsp
- Green chillies: 3–4
- Yoghurt: 3 heaped tbsp

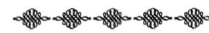

1. Grind raw mango, coriander leaves, ginger, mint leaves and green chillies together in a mixer. Add salt, yoghurt and mix well.

QUICK FIX DAHI KE KEBAB (Serves 6)
(Measuring cup size: 250 ml)

- Yoghurt: 400 ml
- Chenna: ½ cup
- Onion: 1 medium finely chopped
- Green chillies: 2 finely chopped
- Pink salt: 1¼ tsp
- Roasted cumin powder: 1 tsp
- Ginger: ½ tsp grated
- Coriander leaves: 2 tbsp finely chopped
- Garam masala powder: ½ tsp
- Roasted gram flour: 1 tbsp
- White bread: 10–12 slices
- Refined oil: to deep fry

1. Hang yoghurt in a muslin cloth for 8 hours.
2. Hang chenna and compress with a heavy object for 1½ hours.
3. Mix yoghurt and chenna well, add onions, green chillies, gram flour, coriander leaves, pink salt, garam masala powder, roasted cumin powder and ginger. Mix well with a whisk.
4. The mixture should be firm enough to not fall when a spoon of it is overturned.
5. If the mixture is not firm enough, add a little more roasted gram flour.
6. Divide the mixture into 10–12 portions.
7. Place slices of white bread on a board and cut into 3 inch discs. Grind the remaining portions into breadcrumbs in a mixer.
8. Dip a disc of bread in a bowl of water for a few seconds.

9. Take out and compress lightly between your palms to remove excess water. Place back on the board.
10. Place the yoghurt mix on each disc and shape into kebabs. Repeat the process for all.
11. Toss a small quantity of the ground breadcrumbs on it.
12. Place on a plate and put them in the freezer for 10–15 minutes.
13. Take out and deep fry in hot oil on a medium flame.
14. Place on a kitchen towel to remove excess oil if any. Serve hot with mint chutney.

CORNMEAL SAUSAGE GALETTE (Serves 4)

Galette

- All-purpose flour: 60 gm
- Fine cornmeal: 50 gm
- Butter: 50 gm
- Chilled water: 2 tbsp

1. Sieve both flours together. Add melted butter. Rub with your fingers to make a crumble.
2. Add chilled water gradually and knead to make a dough.
3. Wrap in cling film and refrigerate the dough ball for 30 minutes.
4. Between two cling film sheets roll the pastry into a 5 mm thick disc 9–9½ inches in diameter.
5. Remove cling film and transfer to a parchment-lined baking tray and keep refrigerated.

Filling

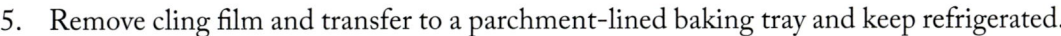

- Olive oil: 1 tbsp
- Sugar: ½ tsp
- Garlic: 2 big cloves sliced
- Onion: 1 small sliced thin
- Chicken/Pork sausage: 75 gm sliced
- Cherry tomatoes: 8–10 halved
- Paprika powder: ½ tsp
- Mixed herbs: ½ tsp
- Basil leaves: 4 leaves chopped
- Salt: ½ tsp
- Cream cheese: 2 tbsp softened
- Chilli flakes: ½ tsp

Photo on p. 85: Mansi's Bihari boti wings, Kachche aam ki hari chutney; Photo on p. 88: Quick fix dahi ke kabab.

1. Heat olive oil in a non-stick pan on a medium flame.
2. Add sugar and let it caramelize.
3. Add onion and sauté until pink. Add garlic and cook until golden.
4. Add paprika powder, salt and mixed herbs.
5. Add sausages and stir fry for 2–3 minutes.
6. Add cherry tomatoes and let them cook till soft.

Assembling the Galette

1. Preheat oven to 200 °C for 8 minutes. Take out the refrigerated galette, spread cream cheese on the base of the rolled-out pastry disc leaving a border of 2 inches.
2. Spread the sausage mixture on the cheese.
3. Fold the edges of the galette inwards. The dough will be brittle, and may crack a little. Fix the cracks with your fingers.
4. Reduce oven teperature to 190 °C and bake for about 20–25 minutes.
5. Top with basil leaves and chilli flakes before serving.

PUMPKIN MOZZARELLA BALLS (Serves 6)
(Measuring cup size: 250 ml)

- Olive oil: 2 tbsp + 1 tbsp
- Onion: 1 large chopped
- Ripe pumpkin: 1 cup grated
- Sugar: ½ tsp
- Mozzarella: 1 cup grated
- Parsley leaves: 2 tbsp
- Salt: ¾–1 tsp
- Black pepper powder: ½ tsp
- Cornflour: 4 tbsp heaped
- Water: 100 ml
- Panko bread crumbs: 1 cup
- Refined oil: to deep fry

1. Heat 2 tbsp olive oil in a pan.
2. Add onions, salt, sugar and cook until caramelized.
3. Remove from flame and keep aside.

4. Heat 1 tbsp olive oil in the pan. Add grated pumpkin and cover. Cook for 4–5 minutes, until soft and mushy.
5. To the pumpkin add onion mixture, black pepper powder and mix well. Let it cool in the refrigerator for 30 minutes.
6. Add parsley leaves, grated mozzarella and divide into 10–12 portions. Shape into balls.
7. Mix cornflour with water and make a slurry in a bowl. Spread panko on a plate.
8. Dip each ball in the slurry and then coat with panko bread crumbs. Repeat the process again for a double coating. Place on a flat plate and freeze for 2 hours uncovered.
9. After this, either store for later use frozen or on a medium flame, deep fry in hot oil a few pieces at a time.
10. Serve hot with the yoghurt–garlic dip.

YOGHURT– GARLIC DIP

- Yoghurt: 3 tbsp heaped
- Garlic: 1 tbsp finely chopped
- Parsley leaves: 1 tbsp finely chopped
- Olive oil: 1 tsp
- Shallot: 1 finely chopped
- Black pepper powder: a pinch
- Pink salt: ½ tsp

1. Hang the yoghurt in a muslin cloth for 30 minutes.
2. Mix all the other ingredients with the hung yoghurt and serve.

Photo on p. 91: Cornmeal sausage galette; Photo on p. 92: Pumpkin mozzarella balls, Yoghurt–garlic dip.

SERVINGS

Kabini Life

As I have written earlier, I am a huge fan of South Indian food. This could be because I grew up largely in the south, or maybe that's a sign of my past life!

A trip to Kabini was an opportune time to just gorge on food, begin one's day with filter coffee, and eat all the vadas and dosas available along with delectable curries and sheera. Yum is the word! Food more than made up for not sighting a tiger, a leopard or a panther, the only sighting being a nilgai!

While the forest was gorgeous, the chef at the resort agreeing to part with a recipe or two was the real highlight. This time I got lucky and was actually able to cook while he instructed me, so it was a real-time experience. These recipes are versions of the same.

SPICY RASAM (Serves 4)

Green Paste

- Onion: ½ large
- Green chillies: 2
- Black peppercorns: ½ tbsp
- Cumin seeds: ½ tbsp
- Curry leaves: ½ sprig

1. Grind all the ingredients together in a mixer to a coarse paste.

Dal Paste

- Arhar dal: 4 tbsp
- Water: 8 tbsp
- Salt: ¼ tsp
- Turmeric powder: ¼ tsp

1. Pressure cook dal with water, salt and turmeric powder for 4–5 whistles.
2. Release pressure and let the dal cool.
3. Open pressure cooker and mash the dal.

SERVINGS

Rasam

- Refined oil: 2 tbsp
- Fenugreek seeds: 1 tsp
- Byadgi chillies: 2–3 chopped thick
- Onion: 2 tbsp chopped
- Tomato: 2 tbsp heaped, chopped
- Green paste: 2½ tbsp heaped
- Water: 250 ml + 150 ml
- Turmeric powder: ¾ tsp
- Kashmiri chilli powder: ¾ tsp
- Tamarind paste: 1 tbsp
- Dal paste: 2 tbsp heaped
- Salt: 1 tsp
- Coriander leaves: 2 tbsp chopped

1. Heat oil in a non-stick pan.
2. Add fenugreek seeds, chopped bydagi chillies and let them crackle.
3. Add onion, cook until pink and then add tomato with ½ tsp salt.
4. Sauté for 4–5 minutes. Add the green paste.
5. Add 250 ml water and let it boil for 3–4 minutes.
6. Add turmeric powder, followed by Kashmiri chilli powder and tamarind paste. Boil for 5 minutes. Add dal paste, mix and add 150 ml water.
7. Add ½ tsp salt. Garnish with coriander leaves and serve hot.

VADA (Serves 4)

(Measuring cup size: 250 ml)

- Urad dal: 1½ cups
- Ginger: 1 tbsp chopped/grated
- Green chillies: 1 tbsp chopped
- Curry leaves: 1 tbsp chopped
- Coconut pieces: 1½ tbsp chopped
- Asafoetida powder: ⅙ tsp
- Salt: 1 tsp
- Water: 150 ml

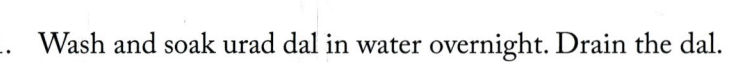

1. Wash and soak urad dal in water overnight. Drain the dal.
2. Place dal in the grinder and add water gradually, 2 tbsp to begin with, and continue grinding to make a smooth batter.
3. Add all remaining ingredients to the batter.
4. Use your hands like a whisk, adding a few drops of lukewarm water to help make the batter lighter. Mix well for 4–5 minutes. Let the batter rest for 45 minutes to rise.

5. Add salt and give it a good mix again for 4–5 minutes to aerate the batter.
6. Heat oil on a medium flame in a wok/kadai for deep frying.
7. Moisten fingers and take a small portion of the batter and make a ball.
8. Flatten to make into a disc. Make a hole in the centre with the index finger.
9. Gently drop the discs into the oil, two to three at a time.
10. Gently move the oil around and fry vadas till golden.
11. Line a colander with a paper towel.
12. Remove vadas from the oil and place in the colander.
13. Serve vadas with rasam and chutney of choice.

> Do not add salt to the batter, in case refrigerating, add just before making the vadas.

HURIDA KOLI (Pepper and Chilli Fried Chicken) (Serves 4)

- Oil: 2 tbsp
- Onion: 2 heaped tbsp chopped
- Curry leaves: 1 sprig
- Green chillies: 2–3 chopped
- Ginger–garlic paste: 1½ tbsp
- Water: 75 ml + 75 ml
- Turmeric powder: 1 tsp
- Byadgi chilli powder: 1 tbsp
- Coriander powder: 1 tbsp
- Boneless chicken breast: 2–3 cubed
- Black pepper powder: 1 tsp
- Salt: ¾ tsp

1. Heat oil in a non-stick pan, add onion and ½ tsp salt. Sauté until light pink.
2. Add curry leaves, chopped green chillies, ginger–garlic paste and sauté.
3. Add 75 ml water and cook well.
4. Add turmeric powder, byadgi chilli powder and coriander powder.
5. Add the chicken pieces and ¼ tsp salt.
6. Cook on a low flame and add another 75 ml of water gradually. Check seasoning.
7. Once the chicken is well cooked, add black pepper powder to finish.
8. Serve hot.

Photo on p. 95: Spicy rasam and vadas; Photo on p. 97: Hurida koli.

DILLI O DILLI

Cauldron of Flavours

Delhi is the culinary capital of the nation for a reason!

The city I live in is the ultimate food haven and because of its cosmopolitan population, it has adopted cuisines from far and wide. The cuisine is primarily Indo-Persian, brought in by the Mughals, but with influences from Europe as well as the refugees who made the city their home after the Partition. Today, you can see the city thriving on kebabs and chaats in Old Delhi or kathi rolls and fish cutlets in Chittaranjan Park or momos and thukpa in Majnu ka Tilla.

The cuisine we know today is 'Dehlvi', of which the literal translation from Urdu is 'from Delhi'. Refinement to the cuisine came from the Mughals who amalgamated Persian techniques with Indian tastes. They say that Emperor Akbar had 400 cooks from Persia and India in his kitchen – quite a retinue! I can only imagine that the clanking of pots and pans would have been a great sound-and-light show!

As the capital of several kingdoms in the past, the adoption of flavours has been a part of the journey. As William Dalrymple aptly describes Delhi, 'A portrait of a city disjointed in time, a city whose different ages lay suspended side by side as in aspic, a city of djinns.' The taste of the food found here leaves you possessed and spellbound.

With the Partition of India in 1947, the refugee population from Punjab increased by leaps and bounds. Their hearty food was adopted by most residents of Delhi. Butter chicken or murgh makhni is their addition to the food scene which has now been adopted in every part of India. In fact, it is probably the one dish that is recognized worldwide. The credit goes to an experiment of mixing leftover chicken with tomato and butter at the Mukhe da Dhaba renamed Moti Mahal in Peshawar, Pakistan which then crossed borders to its current location at Daryaganj in Delhi. Every household makes their version. This is ours with no cream and less butter but I think it works. The coal-infused method of cooking gives the dish the desired smokiness when a tandoor is not used. The dhaba-style dal with anda and baingan bharta is comfort food.

SKINNY BUTTER CHICKEN (Serves 4)

- Chicken tikka: 400 gm (recipe on p. 102)
- Butter: 60 gm
- Tomatoes: 1 kg
- Onion: 1 large
- Sugar: 1 tsp
- Salt: 1 tsp
- Kashmiri chilli powder: 1 tsp
- Ginger paste: 1 tsp
- Garlic paste: 2 tsp
- Kasuri methi: 1 tbsp
- Melon seeds: 1 tsp
- Cashew nuts: 6
- Milk: 60 ml
- Water: 200–220 ml
- Coal: 1 piece
- Ghee: 2 tbsp
- Refined oil: 2 tbsp

1. Heat water in a pot. Mark the skin of the tomatoes with a cross on the bottom with a knife. Peel onion. Add both to the water.
2. Boil for about 8 minutes until the tomatoes soften.
3. Take the tomatoes and onions out of the pot and let them cool. Remove the peel of the tomatoes and mash while passing through a strainer, so that the seeds separate from the pulp. Similarly mash the boiled onion as well.
4. Heat oil in a non-stick thick-bottom pan. Add ginger and garlic paste and sauté for a few minutes.
5. Add the tomato and onion paste to this with sugar and allow it to cook over a low flame for 30 minutes. Add salt and Kashmiri chilli powder.
6. Add butter and let it melt. Allow the mixture to simmer.
7. Soak melon seeds and cashew nuts in water for 20 minutes, then strain and grind in a mixer to a smooth paste.
8. Add the melon and cashew nut paste to the gravy and cook for another 20 minutes over a low flame until the oil separates.
9. Add the cooked chicken tikka to the gravy. Blend it well and let it simmer for 5–7 minutes. Add milk, water and let it simmer for 3–4 minutes.
10. Add kasuri methi. Put ghee in a small steel bowl.
11. Heat the coal piece over an open flame until it glows red. Then add it to the warm ghee. Place the bowl of ghee with the coal in the pan with chicken and cover.
12. After 5 minutes, remove the bowl of ghee, add 1 tsp of the charcoal-infused ghee to the gravy. Mix and serve hot.

SERVINGS

CHICKEN TIKKA   (Serves 4)

- Boneless Chicken thighs: 500 gm cut into chunks
- Ginger paste: 1 tsp
- Garlic paste: 1 tsp
- Thick yoghurt: 200 gm
- Cream: 100 gm
- Garam masala: 1 tsp
- Chicken tikka masala: 2 tsp
- Kasuri methi: 1 tsp
- Red chilli powder: 1 tsp
- Refined oil: 1 tbsp
- Salt: to taste

1. Mix all the ingredients except chicken to make a marinade. Season with salt if needed.
2. Add chicken chunks, coat well and let them marinate for 3–4 hours at room temperature.
3. Line a baking tray with foil and place marinated chicken.
4. Preheat the oven to 210 °C for 10 minutes.
5. Grill for 20–25 minutes until the chicken is cooked.

Skewer tikkas before grilling to serve as an appetizer.

BAINGAN IN A BAINGAN   (Serves 4)

Brinjal Shell

- Brinjal: 1 large
- Salt: ½ tsp
- Red chilli powder: ½ tsp
- Refined oil: 2 tsp

1. Cut the brinjal into two vertically.
2. Remove the insides keeping the skin intact. Prick with a fork on the inside of the shell.
3. Rub the brinjal with oil, salt and red chilli powder.
4. Preheat the oven to 200 °C for 5 minutes.
5. Place the brinjal shell and bake for 20 minutes. Remove and keep aside.

Bharta Filling

- Large brinjal: 600–700 gm
- Salt: 1 tsp
- Onions: 1½ large chopped thick
- Tomatoes: 2 chopped thick
- Cumin seeds: 1 tsp
- Ghee: 1 tsp

* 102

- Refined oil: 1½ tbsp
- Garlic: 1 tbsp sliced
- Ginger: 1 inch, cut into juliennes
- Coriander powder: ½ tsp
- Cumin powder: ½ tsp
- Red chilli powder: ¾ tsp
- Turmeric powder: ¼ tsp
- Home-made garam masala powder: ½ tsp
- Green chilli: 1 chopped
- Coriander leaves: 1 tbsp chopped
- Mozzarella cheese: for garnish

1. Prick the skin of the brinjal and rub 1 tsp oil on it and place directly on the burner over a medium flame until the outer skin is charred.
2. Remove from flame and cool. Then peel, remove head and roughly mash with a fork.
3. Heat remaining oil and ghee in a non-stick pan. Add cumin seeds and let them crackle.
4. Add onion with ½ tsp salt and let it cook until pink and translucent.
5. Add garlic and ginger and stir fry. Add tomatoes, green chillies followed by coriander powder, cumin powder, red chilli powder, turmeric powder, remaining salt and home-made garam masala. Cover and cook until the tomatoes soften.
6. Add the mashed brinjal and stir fry. Add chopped coriander leaves and mix well.
7. Cover and let the mixture remain moist and soft.
8. Check seasoning.
9. Stuff the brinjal mixture into the baked brinjal shell.
10. Grate a little mozzarella cheese over it.
11. Place in a preheated oven on grill mode at 180 °C for about 10 minutes until the cheese melts and the top is golden. Serve hot.

MOHAN'S DAL TRIMEL TADKA (Serves 4)

- Urad dal: 125 gm
- Arhar dal: 125 gm
- Chana dal: 125 gm
- Turmeric powder: ½ tsp
- Salt: 1½ tsp

- Refined oil: 2 tbsp
- Green chillies: 2 slit
- Ginger: 1 tbsp julienned
- Garlic: 1 tbsp sliced
- Onions: 1½ large sliced
- Tomatoes: 2 sliced
- Bay leaf: 1
- Kasuri methi: 1 tbsp
- Butter: 50 gm
- Kashmiri chilli powder: 1 tsp
- Eggs: 2 (optional)
- Water: 750 ml

1. Soak all the dals together in water for 1 hour.
2. Pressure cook dals in 750 ml water with ½ tsp salt and turmeric powder for 4 whistles.
3. Heat oil in a pan and add bay leaf.
4. Add onions, ¼ tsp salt and stir fry until translucent, then add ginger and garlic.
5. Cook for 3–4 minutes. Add green chillies, tomatoes and cook until soft.
6. Add Kashmiri chilli powder and kasuri methi.
7. Add butter, whisked eggs if using. Cook for 4–5 minutes, then add the boiled dals.
8. Add remaining salt. Boil for 8–10 minutes and serve hot.

STUFFED ALOO KULCHA (Serves 4)

(Measuring cup size: 250 ml)

Dough

- All-purpose flour: 2 cups
- Sugar: 1 tsp
- Salt: 1 tsp
- Baking powder: 1 tsp
- Yoghurt: ¼ cup
- Refined oil: 2 tsp
- Lukewarm water: to knead

1. Sieve flour and baking powder together.
2. Knead with all the remaining ingredients, adding lukewarm water as required, to make a soft dough.
3. Cover with a moist cloth and allow it to rest for 2 hours at room temperature.

Aloo Stuffing

- Potatoes: 2 large boiled and mashed
- Green chilli: 1 finely chopped
- Kashmiri chilli powder: ½ tsp
- Carom seeds: ½ tsp
- Dried mango powder: ½ tsp
- Coriander leaves: 2 tbsp chopped
- Ginger: 1 inch grated
- Salt: ½ tsp

1. Mix all the ingredients in a bowl. Divide into 8 portions and keep aside.

Kulcha

- Nigella seeds: 2 tsp
- Butter: 2 tbsp
- Coriander leaves: 3 tbsp chopped

1. Stretch and fold the dough and divide into 8 portions.
2. Make a ball and roll it into a 5 inch disc.
3. Place a ball of stuffing in the middle.
4. Pleat the outer dough towards the centre such that it completely encases the stuffing.
5. Pat and twist at the centre. Place some nigella seeds and chopped coriander leaves on it and gently roll to an oval shape.
6. With a brush apply water and place kulcha face down on a hot tawa for 1 minute to make the kulcha stick.
7. Immediately invert the tawa on the open flame and let the kulcha cook until it is golden brown. Apply butter and serve hot.

KOYLA MIRCHI PANEER (Serves 4)

- Paneer (cottage cheese): 300 gm cut into 1½ inch cubes

Tomato Masala

- Tomatoes: 400 gm
- Green chillies: 3
- Dry red chilli: 1
- Cashew nuts: 5–6
- Cumin seeds: ½ tsp
- Ginger: 1 inch
- Green cardamoms: 1–2
- Cloves: 2
- Black peppercorns: 4
- Cinnamon: 1 inch stick
- Refined oil: 1 tbsp

1. Heat oil in a pan and add whole spices and dry red chilli. Let them crackle.
2. Add ginger, followed by tomatoes, cashew nuts and green chillies.
3. Let the tomatoes soften.
4. Remove from flame, cool and grind to a paste.

Gravy

- Refined oil: 1 tsp
- Cumin seeds: 1 tsp
- Kasuri methi: ½ tbsp
- Coriander powder: ½ tbsp
- Kashmiri chilli powder: ½ tsp
- Turmeric powder: ½ tsp
- Coriander leaves: 1 tbsp chopped
- Tomato masala: entire quantity cooked earlier
- Capsicum: ½, cut into large squares
- Water: 100–125 ml
- Coal: 1 small piece
- Ghee: 2 tsp
- Asafoetida powder: a pinch
- Salt: ¾–1 tsp

1. Heat oil in a pan. Add cumin seeds and let them crackle.
2. Add turmeric powder, Kashmiri chilli powder, asafoetida powder and coriander powder.
3. Add tomato masala. Add chopped coriander leaves and crushed kasuri methi.
4. Add paneer, capsicum and salt. Cook until the oil separates.
5. Add water and allow the gravy to simmer for 5–7 minutes. Check seasoning.
6. In the meantime take a small steel bowl. Burn a piece of coal until it glows red and place it in the steel bowl.
7. Place the bowl with the burning coal in the gravy pan and add ghee over it.
8. Cover the pan tightly and simmer for 8–10 minutes.
9. Remove the coal-filled steel bowl add ghee from it to the gravy and serve hot.

Punjabi Bagh Meets CR Park

The gulab jamun, is a dark wonder – a melt-in-your-mouth delight, rose scented and jamun fruit-like in appearance. Folklore credits its origins to a mistake in Shah Jahan's royal kitchen when a Persian delight was being replicated.

The 'pantua' is the gulab jamun's Bengali brother, but made with chenna and flour, instead of only khoya and flour. He can be a *golap jaam* if golden or its darker brother *kalo jaam*. If a thinner sister is made, she is called *ledikeni*, in honour of Lady Canning or Lady Kenny, the wife of the first Viceroy of India under the British Raj. Ledikeni was made by Bhim Chandra Nag, a confectioner in Kolkata. That's quite the bonded family – though I finally bonded with 'pantua' only on my third attempt! In my state of exhilaration at finally getting the jaam right, I decided to get the golden sibling drunk, so I dunked him in a little rum, something I had read about in the past. You can choose to keep him sober, though.

BOOZY PANTUA (Serves 8)

Sugar Syrup

- Sugar: 375 gm
- Water: 500 ml
- Green cardamoms: 3
- Rose water: 1½ tsp
- Saffron: a few strands
- Green cardamom powder: ¼ tsp
- Lemon juice: a few drops

1. In a wide pan with a flat bottom, heat water with sugar, cardamom powder and whole cardamoms.
2. Bring the sugar syrup to a boil and add lemon juice.
3. Add rose water and saffron strands.
4. Lower the heat and let the syrup simmer for 8–10 minutes. It should be sticky between your fingers.
5. Remove from flame and keep aside, ensuring it stays warm.

SERVINGS

Gulab Jamun

- Chenna: 200 gm (recipe on p. 166)
- Mawa: 40 gm
- All-purpose flour: 30 gm
- Fine semolina: 1 tsp (optional for binding)
- Baking soda: ⅙ tsp
- Green cardamom powder: ½–¾ tsp
- Refined oil: to deep fry

Quick Fix Mawa Substitute (in case mawa is not available)

- Milk powder: 50 ml (use a measuring cup)
- Milk: 20 ml
- Butter: ½ tsp

1. Heat butter and milk powder in a non-stick pan.
2. Add milk and cook until it solidifies.
3. Let it cool. This will give you 40 gm of mawa.

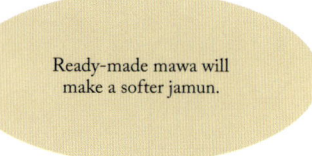

Ready-made mawa will make a softer jamun.

Making the Jamuns

1. Knead the chenna for 7–8 minutes until smooth.
2. Add grated mawa and knead for 2 minutes. Add flour mixed with baking soda.
3. Knead for 4–5 minutes to make a smooth dough.
4. In case dough is too soft, add fine semolina, green cardamom powder and knead.
5. Divide dough into 16 equal portions of approximately 18 gm each, keeping a little for test frying.
6. Apply oil on your palms.
7. Shape dough into balls without applying pressure.
8. Ensure there are no cracks in the balls.
9. Cover the balls with a moist cloth.
10. Heat oil in a wok/kadai over a high flame for 2–3 minutes. After which lower the flame.

11. Fry the test ball to check for colour and to see if it cracks.
12. The test ball should sink and then rise up to the surface of the oil. This indicates that the oil is at the right temperature for frying.
13. Fry the balls in batches until they turn dark golden brown and are completely cooked through.
14. Move the balls in the wok/kadai while frying.
15. Remove the balls and keep aside for 7–8 minutes to cool.
16. Add the balls to the warm syrup.
17. If the balls float in the syrup, the jamuns have been made correctly.
18. Leave the jamuns in the syrup for at least 4 hours. Overnight is best.
19. Top with pistachios and serve, or for a boozy version, heat 3 tbsp of syrup in a pan, add 1 tbsp of rum and give it a quick boil. Add 2 jamuns.
20. Toss the jamuns, cover for a few seconds, serve hot.

Note

1. Chenna should be soft.
2. The dough should not be too dry or moist.
3. If the dough is right, you will not need to grease your palms.
4. If the test ball breaks, then add 1 tsp of semolina.
5. Ensure the balls are fried over a low flame.
6. Ensure there is enough oil in the pan so that the balls can move around.
7. Fry a few balls at a time.
8. Ensure that the sugar syrup is sticky, not ektaar or single-string syrup.
9. The sugar syrup should be warm, not too hot or too cold.
10. Always use a flat-bottomed pan to make the syrup.

Photo on p. 104 (Clockwise): Mohan's dal trimel, Baingan in a baingan, Skinny butter chicken, Stuffed aloo kulcha, Koyla mirchi paneer;
Photo on p. 109: Boozy Pantua.

For the Love of Food
(Suggested Menu Plan)

LET'S PARTY

Starters

Sabudana Vada with Peanut–Yoghurt Chutney	pp. 407, 408
Sindhi Tuk Chaat	p. 401
Chutney Pomfret	p. 430
Chicken Tikka	p. 102

Mains

Murgh Korma	p. 242
Kulia Bhai's Junglee Mutton	p. 182
Koyla Mirchi Paneer	p. 106
Arshi's Gobi Musallam	p. 247
Stuffed Aloo Kulcha/Ulta Tawa Naan	pp. 105/312
Baghara Rice	p. 242

Dessert

Boozy Pantua with Vanilla Ice Cream	p. 108

FAMILY TIME

Koyla Tawa Murgh	p. 448
Baingan in a Baingan	p. 102
Paneer Takatak	p. 82
Sheermal	p. 84

Dessert

Gurwala Atta Halwa	p. 405

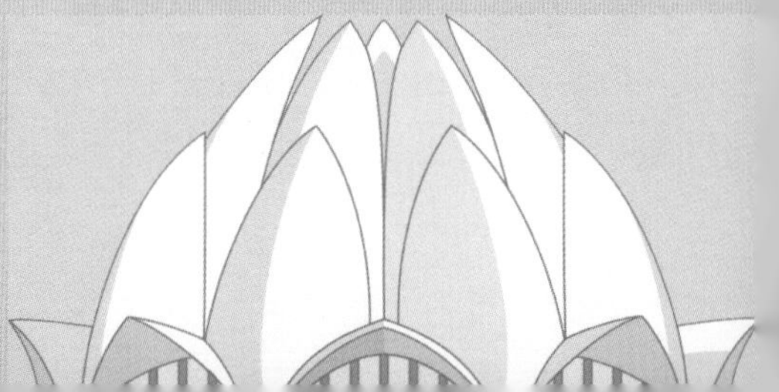

TIMELESS TRADITIONS

Boarding School Dining Rooms

Boys and girls in British boarding schools are usually served old-fashioned 'English' meals. My father went to one of them – the erstwhile Prince of Wales Royal Indian Military College in Dehradun, now the Rashtriya Indian Military College. 'Rimcollians' are what its students call themselves. Each student will tell you stories of Scotch eggs, trifle pudding or 'tipsy pudding' (sans the alcohol!). Dinners there are all about baked dishes and bread rolls. Since I never experienced the boarding school life, this kind of food is a reminder of Enid Blyton's Malory Towers or the St Clare's series or even Harry Potter's Hogwarts.

The recipe for the Spinach and Cottage Cheese Casserole evolved over the years. I would often make spinach in white sauce with a layer of mashed potatoes on top for my evening meal after work. That became a layer of mashed potatoes baked crisp and then topped with spinach in white sauce. Much later, yet another version took shape – cottage cheese mixed in a spinach masala on a potato base.

Going beyond béchamel sauce, a spicy yoghurt sauce and a mustard cream sauce just add more variety to the base sauces which can be made with other meats and vegetables as well.

'Scotties' were what Scotch eggs were called in the good old days. These were usually eggs wrapped in fish paste, which originated in Whitby, Yorkshire. Now, fish paste has been replaced by sausage meat for better shelf life. In India, Scotch eggs are made with spiced minced mutton or keema and also have evolved to become 'Deemer Devil', which is a Bengali version of boiled eggs wrapped in mashed potatoes and deep fried. There is everything Russian about the evergreen Russian salad, also called the Olivier salad. This was created in the mid-1800s by Chef Lucien Olivier at the Hermitage Restaurant in Moscow. The original recipe still remains a secret, but it had a special kind of mayonnaise with crayfish, capers, veal tongue and potatoes. Olivier's sous chef sold him out to publishers at some point, but even that version, they say, has something missing. We are always happy to put bright vegetables in fresh mayonnaise though, adding fruit when we feel like it – and if you have ever been a member of SODA (Serving Officers' Daughters Association), then you will know that every officers' mess or club has this on its menu.

CREAMY MUSTARD CHICKEN WITH SUN-DRIED TOMATOES (Serves 4)

- Boneless chicken thighs: 4 (cut into 8 pieces)
- Olive oil: 1 tbsp
- Salt: 1 tsp
- Black pepper powder: 1 tsp
- Onion: 1 big chopped
- Garlic: 4 cloves chopped
- Rosemary: a few sprigs
- Chicken stock: 250 ml
- Dijon mustard: 2–2½ tbsp
- Cream: 150 ml
- Milk: 125 ml
- Brown sugar: 1 tsp
- Sun-dried tomatoes: 4–5 chopped

1. Toss chicken with ½ tsp salt and ½ tsp black pepper powder and leave aside for 30 minutes.
2. Heat olive oil in a heavy-bottom pan.
3. Add chicken and stir fry until three-fourths done.
4. Transfer chicken with its juices to a bowl.
5. In the same pan, sauté onions with ½ tsp salt until translucent. Add garlic followed by chicken stock.
6. Add rosemary sprigs.
7. Add Dijon mustard and stir.
8. Reduce flame or take the pan off the flame and add cream.
9. Let the sauce cook until it thickens.
10. Add milk and continue to stir. Adjust seasoning.
11. Add the chicken with its juices. Cook until done.
12. Add sun-dried tomatoes, remaining black pepper powder and stir.
13. Add brown sugar and mix well.
14. Serve hot.

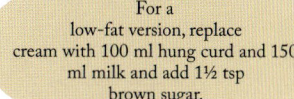

For a low-fat version, replace cream with 100 ml hung curd and 150 ml milk and add 1½ tsp brown sugar.

SERVINGS

BAKED SPICY YOGHURT CAULIFLOWER STEAKS ON A BED OF ROASTED VEGETABLES (Serves 4)

- Cauliflower: 500 gm
- Yoghurt: 180 ml
- Cumin powder: ½ tbsp
- Kashmiri chilli powder: ½ tbsp
- Red chilli powder: ½ tbsp
- Curry powder: ½ tsp
- Salt: 1 tsp
- Black pepper powder: ½ tsp
- Lemon juice: 1 tbsp
- Olive oil: 1 tbsp
- Garlic paste: 1 tbsp
- Cream: 1 tbsp (optional)

1. Wash cauliflower head thoroughly and remove leaves.
2. Cut into thick steaks along with the stem.
3. Blanch cauliflower in hot water for 3–4 minutes. Drain in a colander.
4. Mix all the other ingredients, except oil, to form a smooth marinade.
5. Check seasoning and spice levels. Add 1 tbsp cream, if too spicy.
6. Dip the cauliflower steaks in the marinade and coat all over.
7. Marinate for 2 hours at room temperature and then transfer to a baking tray.
8. Cover the cauliflower-laden tray with foil.
9. Bake in a preheated oven at 180°C for 10 minutes.
10. Further bake uncovered for 15–20 minutes.
11. The cauliflower steaks will have a nice brownish skin on it.

Roasted Vegetable Bed

- Red bell pepper: 1 roasted in a pan and chopped with skin
- Yellow bell pepper: 1 diced
- Cherry tomatoes: 12–15
- Spring onion bulbs: 6–8 halved and roasted in a pan
- Fresh basil leaves: 6–8
- Olive oil: 1 tbsp
- Garlic: 4 cloves sliced
- Salt: ¾ tsp
- Chilli flakes: ½ tsp
- Mixed herbs: 1 tsp
- Brown sugar: ½ tsp

1. Heat oil and sauté garlic. Add cherry tomatoes and let them soften. Add salt.

2. Add yellow bell pepper and roasted red bell pepper.
3. Add chilli flakes, mixed herbs, brown sugar and basil leaves.
4. Add spring onions, cover and cook till done.
5. Place the baked cauliflower steaks on the bed of vegetables before serving.

SPINACH AND COTTAGE CHEESE CASSEROLE
(Serves 4)

- Cooked spinach: ½ cup recipe below
- Cottage cheese: ¾ cup
- Potatoes: ¾ cup mashed smooth
- Butter: 1 tbsp
- Chilli flakes: ½ tsp
- Salt: 1 tsp
- Black pepper powder: ½ tsp
- Milk: 2–3 tbsp
- Cheddar cheese/Cheese slices: 50 gm grated/2

1. Mash potatoes. Add ½ tsp salt and black pepper powder. Add milk and mix till smooth.
2. Transfer to an ovenproof pie dish.
3. Brush a layer of melted butter on top and bake in a preheated oven at 160°C for 15–20 minutes or until golden.
4. Smoothen cottage cheese with your fingers or a whisk, and add the cooked spinach to it gradually. Check seasoning and add remaining salt.
5. Layer the spinach and cottage cheese mix over the baked mashed potatoes.
6. Top with grated Cheddar cheese or cheese slices cut into rectangles.
7. Bake in a preheated oven at 160°C for 15–20 minutes until the top is set and the cheese has melted. Serve hot.

Cooked Spinach

- Spinach: 500 gm
- Garlic: 3–4 cloves
- Green chilli: 1
- Onion: 1 medium chopped
- Tomatoes: 2 medium chopped
- Ginger paste: ½ tsp
- Garlic paste: 1 tsp
- Coriander powder: ½ tsp
- Cumin powder: ½ tsp

- Vegetable stock cube: ¾ cube dissolved in water
- Salt: 1½ tsp
- Milk: 150 ml
- Refined oil: 1½ tsp

1. Boil spinach leaves with garlic cloves and green chilli till soft.
2. Strain and keep aside. Cool and purée.
3. In a pan, heat oil and sauté onions with ½ tsp salt until pink. Add ginger and garlic paste and cook.
4. Add coriander powder, cumin powder, remaining salt and sauté. Add tomatoes.
5. Cook until oil separates and add spinach. Mix well and cook for 8–10 minutes.
6. Add stock cube dissolved in water. Add milk.
7. Cook for 5–7 minutes. Check seasoning and remove from flame.

KEEMA SCOTCH EGGS (Serves 6)

- Mutton mince: 400 gm
- Eggs: 6 hard boiled and peeled
- Onion: 1 large chopped
- Ginger paste: 1 tsp
- Garlic paste: 1 tsp
- Salt: 1 tsp
- Paprika: 1 tsp
- Coriander leaves: 1 tbsp chopped
- Mint leaves: 1 tsp chopped
- HP sauce: 2½ tbsp
- Refined oil: 1½ tbsp + to deep fry
- Eggs: 2 whisked with a pinch of salt
- All-purpose flour: 100 gm
- Panko bread crumbs: 150 gm

1. Soften mince with your fingers.
2. Heat oil in a non-stick pan, and sauté onion with salt until translucent.
3. Add ginger and garlic paste and sauté further.
4. Add paprika, mix well and remove from flame.
5. Add coriander leaves and mint leaves. Let the mixture cool.
6. Add the mixture to the mince along with HP sauce and mix well.
7. Grind the mixture for a minute in the blender.

8. To test, cook a tiny pinch of the mince in a pan at this stage, in order to check the taste.
9. Remove mince from blender and divide into 6 portions.
10. Place a portion on a cling film square.
11. Place a boiled egg in the middle and bring the corners together.
12. Twist the corners to tighten the mince around the egg.
13. Ensure mince is properly wrapped around the egg. Place in the freezer for 15 minutes.
14. Take out from the refrigerator and remove the cling film.
15. Dust eggs with seasoned flour all over.
16. Spread panko or breadcrumbs on a plate.
17. Dip mince wrapped eggs in whisked eggs.
18. Toss in panko or breadcrumbs to coat.
19. Place eggs in your palm and shape again.
20. Place in the freezer on a plate for an hour.
21. At this point, refrigerate to store or deep fry in hot oil.
22. Serve halved with tomato ketchup.

VEGETARIAN BREAD ROLLS   (Serves 6)

(Measuring cup size: 250 ml)

Starter Dough (Tangzhong)

- All-purpose flour: 2 tbsp
- Milk: 3 tbsp
- Water: 3 tbsp

1. Cook all the ingredients in a non-stick pan to make a paste.
2. Remove from flame and keep aside.

Dough

- Active dry yeast: 1 tbsp
- Sugar: ⅙ cup
- Milk: ½ cup
- Milk powder: 2 tbsp
- Baking powder: ¾ tsp
- All-purpose flour: 2½ cups
- Butter: ¼ cup
- Yoghurt: ¼ cup

1. Bloom yeast in lukewarm milk mixed with sugar for 8 minutes.
2. Sieve flour and baking powder together and add milk powder.
3. Mix all the dry ingredients together.
4. Add the starter dough and the bloomed yeast.
5. Add yoghurt to the dough.
6. Knead for 15–20 minute by hand or for 8–10 minutes if using a stand mixer.
7. Add butter and knead further. The dough should be elastic.
8. Transfer to a greased bowl and proof in a warm place for 90 minutes.
9. Wrap the bowl in a moist cloth.
10. Transfer dough from the bowl onto a flour-dusted slab. Knock and stretch the dough lightly.
11. Divide into 12 portions, approximately 50 gm each.
12. Shape into balls. Place a ball on the counter, cup your palms and gently apply pressure from above to get the exact shape.
13. Place in a parchment-lined baking tray.
14. Proof for 50 minutes.
15. Preheat oven to 175 °C for 10 minutes.
16. Brush the tops of the rolls with milk.
17. Bake for 20 minutes.
18. Apply warm melted butter on top.
19. Allow the rolls to cool and transfer to a wire rack.

RUSSIAN SALAD (Serves 4)

Mayonnaise

- Egg yolk: 1 large
- Refined oil: 125 ml
- Dijon mustard: 1 tbsp
- Salt: ¼ tsp
- Black pepper powder: ¼ tsp
- Lime juice: 1 tsp

1. Whisk egg yolk with mustard, salt and black pepper powder.
2. Add oil one drop at a time until the yolk and oil emulsify.
3. Continue adding oil gradually and keep whisking.

SERVINGS

4. Add lime juice and whisk further.
5. This can be refrigerated for up to 3 days.

- Carrot: ¼ cup diced
- Beans: ¼ cup diced
- Peas: ¼ cup shelled
- Boiled potato: 1 diced
- Powdered sugar: ½ tsp (optional)

Adding pineapple and boiled shredded chicken is optional.

1. Parboil carrots, beans and peas in salt water.
2. Drain and chill in the refrigerator.
3. Mix all vegetables with mayonnaise, check seasoning, add powdered sugar if required and serve cold.

Fruit Fool

What's not to love when all things sweet – fruit, custard and cake – come together? The trifle evolved from a dessert called fool. The modern trifle saw an inclusion of gelatin jelly. Versions of this dessert have used biscuits, macaroons and cakes of all kinds as layers. Beautiful large glass bowls have also been created specifically for this dessert. This recipe has jam and patisserie crème, instead of jelly and regular custard. It really adds another dimension to the cake. It is diet friendly too, since it has no butter, but only when ignoring all the sugar that is used in it. Quite like the diet potato chips story!

Researching the history of this dessert led me to discover a Scottish version, called Tipsy Laird, where Drambuie or whisky is infused – probably the reason why this was called Tipsy Pudding in a certain boarding school!

If making the sponge cake a day prior, transfer to a ziplock bag and store at room temperature. This will prevent the sponge cake from drying.

SERVINGS

MIXED FRUIT TRIFLE CAKE LAYERED WITH PATISSERIE CRÈME (Serves 8)

Basic Sponge

- All-purpose flour: 150 gm
- Eggs: 6
- Sugar: 150 gm
- Hot water: 1½ tbsp
- Vanilla essence: 1 tsp

1. Line two 10 inch cake pans with parchment.
2. Whisk sugar and eggs in a bowl for 5 minutes.
3. Add vanilla essence, followed by hot water, and whisk until it forms soft peaks. This will take at least 10 minutes. Fold in flour.
4. Divide the batter into both pans. Preheat oven to 200 °C and bake for 10–12 minutes.
5. Insert a toothpick in the centre of the cake to check if done. It should come out clean.
6. Leave the oven door a little ajar and let the sponge cool in it for another 5 minutes.
7. Remove from oven, cool in the pan and then transfer to a wire rack.

Patisserie crème

- Egg yolks: 3
- Castor sugar: 65 gm
- Milk: 250 ml
- Vanilla essence: ¾ tsp
- Cornflour: ¾ tsp
- All-purpose flour: ¾ tsp

1. Whisk egg yolks and castor sugar until creamy and pale yellow.
2. Add cornflour and flour and whisk further. Boil milk in a thick-bottom saucepan.
3. Let the milk cool and then add it to the egg yolk mixture and mix well.
4. Pour the mixture back in the saucepan and cook over a low flame, stirring continuously.
5. Add vanilla essence and remove from flame once the mixture is smooth and thick.
6. Let it cool and then place it in the refrigerator.

Placing the saucepan in which the patisserie crème is being cooked over pan of boiling water (double boiler method) is safer.

Cake

- Mixed fruit: 1 can
- Canned orange juice: 100 ml
- Seasonal fruit: 1 cup
- Orange or apricot jam: 4 tbsp

1. Strain the canned fruit and retain the syrup for sponge layers. Chop the canned fruit into cubes.
2. Mix orange juice and the strained syrup together.
3. Divide the individual sponge cakes horizontally into two layers using a thread or a knife.
4. Place a sponge layer on the cake board/stand.
5. Spread a few spoons of fruit syrup all over the sponge, ensuring that the edges are moist.
6. Apply jam and place another layer of sponge on it.
7. Again spread a few spoons of fruit syrup over the sponge evenly.
8. Now apply a layer of patisserie crème and place half the quantity of canned fruit cubes over it.
9. Place another layer of sponge. Spread some syrup over it. Sandwich this with a layer of jam and then place the last sponge layer over it.
10. Spread a few spoons of fruit syrup over the layer.
11. Spread the remaining patisserie crème on the top and sides of the cake and refrigerate for 1–2 hours.
12. Top with remaining canned and fresh fruit and serve sliced.

Photo on p. 118 (Clockwise): Creamy mustard chicken with sun-dried tomatoes, Russian salad, Vegetarian bread rolls, Keema scotch eggs, Spinach and cottage cheese casserole, Baked spicy yoghurt cauliflower steaks on a bed of roasted vegetables; Photo on p. 123: Mixed fruit trifle cake layered with patisserie crème.

For the Love of Food
(Suggested Menu Plan)

LET'S PARTY
Starters

Shrimp in Garlic and Parsley	p. 327
Chicken Mince Tartlets	p. 382
Asparagus Cottage Cheese Tartlets	p. 383
Fruity Cheese Board	p. 69

Mains

Chicken Escalopes	p. 354
Creamy Vegetables	p. 354
Spinach and Cottage Cheese Casserole	p. 117
Nandini's Ratatouille as a Potpie	p. 426
Swati's Rocket and Strawberry Salad	p. 427
Mansi's Cheese Filled Garlic Parsley Braided Wreath Bread	p. 334

Dessert

Fruit Fool – Mixed Fruit Trifle Cake Layered with Patisserie Crème	p. 124

FAMILY TIME

Creamy Mustard Chicken with Sun-dried tomatoes	p. 115
Spiced Hassleback Potatoes	p. 415
Broccoli in Cheese Chilli Sauce	p. 415
Green Apple Salad in Vinaigrette	p. 40
Mixed Flour Spiced Soda Bread	p. 345

Dessert

Lemon Pound Cake	p. 332

A Blast from the Past!

Mughlai food is rich, aromatic and delectable. It is a blast from the past. In fact, the etymology of most Mughlai dishes can be traced to Persian origins. In the 1400s, the arrival of the Mughals in India ensured the spread of this cuisine in North India and some other parts of the country, like Hyderabad and Bhopal. The cooking techniques are all about retaining aroma and the recipes have been passed down generations.

In Delhi, a dear friend's family with roots in Chitli Qabar of Purani Dilli has often sent us food and each dish has always been perfect in flavour and texture. I have used her recipes as the base for some of the dishes.

Most dishes in this cuisine have a backstory. For instance, 'yakhni' comes from the word 'akhin' which means broth or soup. The stories of this dish can be traced back to an Afghan king who once visited an army barracks and found his men undernourished. Cooks were instructed to create a dish which infused bone broth in the pulao, thus adding more nutrition. There are many versions of the yakhni pulao. The first version I cooked in college had yoghurt, but the recipe here does not. Murgh musallam is yet another delightful dish, the sheer delight when one cuts through the chicken is unmatchable, with the firm yolks of the eggs used in the stuffing visible and intact.

After cooking the spectacular meal, I had the urge to use a set of serving dishes which are a treasured hand-me-down from my mother. These are brass and plated with heavy silver. They were made to order in the late 1970s in Moradabad, which then had a thriving brass industry with a major focus on exports. Today, most factories have stopped manufacturing these serving dishes leaving one with no option but to use steel and glass versions.

ARSHI'S MURGH MUSALLAM (Serves 4)

- Whole chicken: 1 kg without skin

Stuffing

- Eggs: 2 boiled, fried whole in oil
- Cashew nuts, pistachios and almonds: a fistful, fried and crushed slightly
- Gravy: 75 ml

Gravy

- Onions: 500 gm
- Ghee: 2 tbsp
- Refined oil: 1 tbsp
- Cloves: 2
- Green cardamoms: 3
- Poppy seeds: 1 tbsp
- Ginger paste: 1 tsp
- Garlic paste: 1 tsp
- Kashmiri chilli powder: 1½ tsp
- Red chilli powder: ½ tsp
- Coriander powder: 4 tsp
- Yoghurt: 250 ml
- Water: 150 ml + 250ml
- Salt: 1 tsp
- Fried sliced onion: 3 tbsp for garnish

1. Soak poppy seeds in water for 1 hour. Strain and grind to a paste.
2. Grind onions to a paste.
3. Heat ghee and oil in a thick-bottom pan.
4. Add whole spices and let them crackle.
5. Add onion paste. Let it sweat a little and then add ginger and garlic paste. Add poppy seed paste and let it cook.
6. Add all the spice powders and a little salt.
7. Cook on a low flame for 1½ hours until the onions are brown and the oil separates.
8. Add whisked yoghurt and cook for another 15 minutes.
9. Add 150 ml water and cook further until the gravy is done.

Assembling

1. Stuff the chicken with the mixture of gravy, nuts and boiled eggs.
2. Seal the opening of the chicken with thread and let it rest for 15 minutes.
3. Heat ghee in a heavy-bottom pot. Toss the stuffed chicken in it, turning it on all sides so it can brown a little. Remove the chicken and keep aside.
4. Add the gravy to the pan with 250 ml water. Place the chicken and cook until it is well coated with the gravy.
5. Cover with a tight lid and then wrap the lid with a cloth for the process of dum or slow cooking. Place the pot on a tawa. Cook for 15 minutes on a low flame.
6. Open the pot, flip the chicken and cover again with both the lid and cloth for another 10 minutes.
7. Remove the cloth and the lid. Coat the chicken with gravy. Simmer for a bit. Put a knife through the middle to see if it is cooked. Untie the thread from the chicken.
8. Serve the chicken topped with gravy and some fried onions.

PURANI DILLI YAKHNI PULAO (Serves 4)

Yakhni

- Mutton: 1 kg medium pieces
- Onion: 1 large sliced
- Green cardamoms: 5
- Cloves: 5
- Black cardamoms: 2
- Cinnamon: 2 inch stick
- Black peppercorns: 4–5
- Coriander seeds: 4 tsp
- Garlic: 1 whole large (crushed whole with the skin on)
- Ghee: 1 tbsp
- Refined oil: 1 tbsp
- Salt: 1½ tsp
- Water: 1 litre

1. Heat a thick-bottom pan, add ghee and oil.
2. Add all the whole spices. Let them crackle, then add the garlic and stir.
3. Add onions with salt and let them sweat and turn translucent.
4. Add mutton and cook for 10 minutes until it is slightly brown.

5. Add water, cover with a lid, and tightly wrap the lid with a cloth. This is the process of dum.
6. Dum for 60–75 minutes.
7. Remove the mutton pieces and reserve.
8. Remove all whole spices before straining the stock.
9. While straining mash the garlic and onions to extract their juices.

Pulao

- Basmati Rice: 450 gm soaked in water for 30 minutes
- Salt: 1 tsp or as per taste
- Green cardamoms: 3
- Cloves: 2
- Black cardamom: 1
- Cumin seeds: 1 tsp
- Black peppercorns: 6–7
- Mace: a pinch
- Nutmeg: a pinch
- Garlic paste: 1 tsp
- Ginger paste: 1 tsp
- Green chillies: 2 slit
- Yakhni stock: 1100 ml (to make desired quantity add lukewarm water to yakhni)
- Saffron: ½ tsp dissolved in 50 ml lukewarm milk
- Ghee: 2 tbsp
- Fried sliced onion: 3 tbsp for garnish

1. Heat ghee in a thick-bottom pot.
2. Add whole spices and let them crackle . Add mace and nutmeg.
3. Add reserved mutton pieces and stir fry, then add ginger and garlic paste and cook.
4. Add slit green chillies and sauté mutton till light brown in colour.
5. Add strained, soaked rice, lightly stir fry for 5 minutes until it is well coated with ghee.
6. Add stock, cover with a lid, and tightly wrap the lid with a cloth.
7. Place the pot on a tawa and let the pulao cook.
8. After 15 minutes, remove the cloth and the lid and pour saffron milk along the sides.
9. Cover again with the lid, wrap the cloth again and cook for 15 minutes or until done.
10. To check whether pulao is done, insert a knife – it should come out dry.
11. Using a flat serving spoon toss the pulao in the pot.
12. Finish with fried onions, transfer to a platter and serve.

Photo on p. 133 (Clockwise): Purani dilli yakhni pulao, Arshi's murgh musallam, Laal paneer with hari badi mirch, Moradabadi dahi ki phulki and Rawa laccha paratha.

MORADABADI DAHI KI PHULKI (Serves 6)

Pakodas (Makes 16–18 pakodas)

- Gram flour: 150 gm
- Red chilli powder: ¾ tsp
- Carrom powder: ½ tsp
- Salt: 1½ tsp
- Chaat masala: 1 tsp
- Water: 150 ml
- Baking powder: a pinch
- Refined oil: to deep fry

Dahi

- Yoghurt: 500 ml
- Water: 150–200 ml
- Garlic: 4 cloves pounded
- Yellow chilli powder: ¾ tsp
- Roasted cumin seeds: 1 tsp
- Salt: 1½ tsp

Tempering

- Ginger: 1½ inch julienned
- Green chillies: 2–3 slit
- Refined oil: 1 tsp

1. Whisk yoghurt with garlic, yellow chilli powder and roasted cumin seeds.
2. Add water to give the yoghurt a pouring consistency.
3. Add salt and let dahi chill in the refrigerator.
4. To make the pakodas, put all the dry ingredients in a bowl and gradually add water.
5. Whisk well. Let the mixture rest for an hour. Whisk again. Heat oil in a wok/kadai.
6. Shape the batter into balls with your fingers and drop into the oil, and fry till golden brown.
7. Remove pakodas from oil and transfer to a bowl filled with lukewarm water for 30 seconds.
8. Take out and press between your palms to remove excess water.
9. Put pakodas in the dahi.
10. To temper, heat oil in a pan, then gently toss in ginger juliennes and green chillies.
11. Pour temper over dahi–pakoda mixture before serving.

RAWA LACCHA PARATHA   (Serves 4)

(Measuring cup size: 250 ml)

- All-purpose flour: 2½ cups
- Salt: 1 tsp
- Sugar: 1–2 tsp (depending on preferred sweetness)
- Milk: 1 cup
- Semolina: 4–5 tbsp
- Refined oil/Ghee: 4–5 tsp

1. Mix flour, salt, sugar, semolina and make a dough.
2. Add milk gradually while kneading.
3. Let the dough rest for an hour.
4. Divide into 8–9 equal balls.
5. Roll out each ball into a disc.
6. Cut a line with a knife from the centre to the edge.
7. Roll dough from one side to form a cone.
8. Turn the cone inwards to make a ball.
9. Roll out again into a disc and cook on a hot tawa with a little oil/ghee and serve.

LAAL PANEER WITH MOTI HARI MIRCH   (Serves 4)

- Paneer (cottage cheese): 650 gm (cut into cubes)
- Onions: 2 large grated
- Tomatoes: 3 large blanched, peeled and puréed
- Garlic paste: 1 tsp
- Ginger paste: 1 tsp
- Turmeric powder: ½ tsp
- Kashmiri chilli powder: 1½ tsp
- Coriander powder: 1½ tsp
- Cumin powder: 1 tsp
- Garam masala powder: 1 tsp
- Moti hari mirchi: 6 slit into half and deseeded

- Refined oil: 1–2 tbsp
- Kasuri methi: 1 tbsp
- Cream: 2–3 tbsp
- Salt: 1–1½ tsp

1. Heat oil in a pan, fry moti hari mirch, take out from the pan and keep aside.
2. In the same pan, add grated onions, ½ tsp salt and cook for 5 minutes.
3. Add turmeric powder, ginger and garlic paste and cook. Now add Kashmiri chilli powder, garam masala powder, cumin powder and coriander powder.
4. Cook till onions turn golden brown. Add tomato purée and cook until the oil separates.
5. Add paneer, moti hari mirch and 150 ml of water. Simmer and add remaining salt. Once the gravy is cooked top with kasuri methi rubbed between the palms.
6. Add cream to finish and serve.

A Royal Tribute

Baking with nut flours is tricky because of their high fat content which can create a crumbly cake. Balancing proportions is the key to a moist yet firm product. Some of my attempts to bake with nut flours have been a complete disaster. But this time around, it worked!

The accompanying cream is my version of the Middle Eastern Muhallabelia cream and is dedicated to those who love Rooh Afza. This cake is a great dessert for a Mughlai or Middle Eastern meal.

PISTACHIO CAKE (Serves 8)

- All-purpose flour: 75 gm
- Shelled pistachios: 135 gm
- Sugar: 200 gm
- Butter: 135 gm
- Eggs: 4
- Milk: 50 ml
- Baking powder: ¾ tsp
- Green edible food colour: a few drops
- Cardamom essence: ½ tsp
- Vanilla essence: ½ tsp

1. Blitz the pistachios along with sugar in a food processor to a fine powder. Do not let it become a paste.
2. Sieve flour with baking powder.
3. Whisk pistachio mix, sugar powder with butter till smooth and shiny.
4. Add eggs and whisk further.
5. Add both essences and colour. Add milk.
6. Add flour gradually, mix and fold.
7. Pour into a 10 inch greased and parchment–lined baking pan.
8. Gently tap the pan on the table to remove air pockets.
9. Preheat the oven for 5 minutes to 175 °C.
10. Place the baking pan and bake for 35–40 minutes.
11. Remove and let cake cool in the pan. Then transfer to a wire rack and cool for an hour.
12. Remove parchment midway through the cooling process.
13. Slice and serve with Rose Muhallabelia cream.

The quantities of the ingredients can be halved and the cake can be baked in a 6 inch diameter cake pan as well.

ROSE MUHALLABELIA CREAM

- Cream: 75 ml
- Milk: 125 ml
- Condensed milk: 75 ml
- Rooh Afza: 2 tbsp
- Cornflour: 1 heaped tbsp dissolved in 2 tbsp cold milk

1. In a thick-bottom sauce pan, heat cream, milk and condensed milk on a low flame for 5–7 minutes. Add cornflour and keep whisking as it thickens. Add the Rooh Afza to the mixture. Whisk again for a minute. It should have a pouring consistency as it will thicken further on cooling.
2. Remove from flame and let it cool.
3. Transfer to a pouring jug.

Photo on p. 136: Pistachio cake accompanied, Rose muhallabelia cream.

For the Love of Food
(Suggested Menu Plan)

LET'S PARTY

Starters

Mansi's Bihari Boti Wings	p. 85
Makhmali Gulabi Boti	p. 62
Hara Bhara Cheesy Kebab	p. 64
Quick Fix Dahi ke Kebab	p. 87

Mains

Arshi's Kabuli Pulao	p. 424
Chukandar ka Saalan	p. 426
Arshi's Murgh Musallam	p. 129
Paneer Takatak	p. 82
Raita of Choice	
Rawa Laccha Paratha	p. 134

Dessert

Pistachio Cake	p. 135
Rose Muhallabelia Cream	p. 137

FAMILY TIME

Purani Dilli Yakhni Pulao	p. 130
Moradabadi Dahi ki Phulki	p. 132
Hyderabadi Lauki Paneer ke Kofte	p. 246
Ulta Tawa Naan	p. 312

Dessert

Pratima's Pineapple Sheera	p. 31

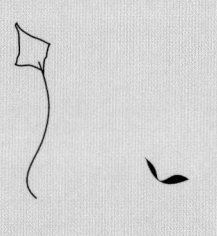
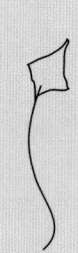
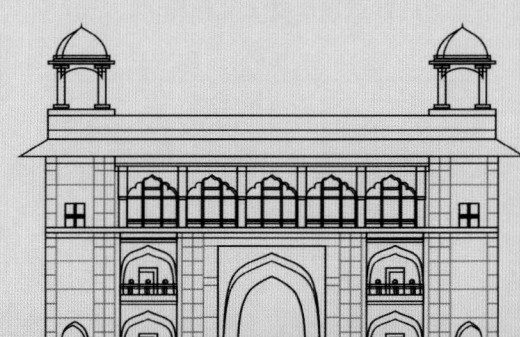

KOLKATA CHRONICLES

Summer in Kolkata

Summer in Kolkata for me is a vision of women in beautiful Dhakai sarees, sipping sherbet and cooking aesthetic, light meals. Reality check: the sweltering heat and humidity aren't the easiest to deal with and the kitchen is certainly the last place you want to find yourself in. I think that may be the reason for sleeveless blouses making an appearance as well as embroidered petticoats in white visible under the muslin of Bengali sarees, a sharp contrast to their otherwise conservative sartorial sense!

In the colonial era, Bengali cookbook writing was a phenomenon and added another dimension to the way the cuisine was treated. The cookbooks offered recipes and also provided knowledge about how an ideal kitchen could be maintained with details on hygiene, organization and equipment. A very progressive kitchen was introduced to the modern educated Bengali woman. I've been lucky enough to get my hands on one such cookbook, albeit a photocopy.

Bengali food uses a lot of seasonal vegetables and the use of vegetables in fish dishes is very common. Not everything is about making gravies with large doses of onions and garlic – rather it is about actually creating flavours from simple spices like cumin, mustard seeds and of course the panch phoran which is a mix of five spices; cumin, fennel, fenugreek, onion seeds and mustard seeds. Dairy products are commonly used in the dishes and mustard oil is the medium of cooking.

Historically, Bengal has never grown lentils. Hence fish was treated as the primary protein. Widows – who were sometimes very young girls, due to the prevailing tradition of young girls being married off to older men – were not allowed to eat meat and that led to the creation of an interesting vegetarian dimension to the cuisine. A 'Bong Odiya' friend's recipe for phulkobir malai curry is one such addition. When you don't eat the 'crawlies', you still enjoy your meal!

LAAL MASOOR DAL (Serves 4)

(Measuring cup size: 150 ml)

- Masoor dal: ½ cup lightly roasted on a pan for 5 minutes
- Water: 375 ml
- Panch phoran: 1 tsp
- Yellow mustard seeds: ½ tsp
- Kashmiri chilli powder: 1 tsp
- Onions: 4 tbsp heaped chopped
- Ginger–garlic paste: 1 tbsp
- Tomatoes: 2 medium cut into quarters
- Green chillies: 2 slit
- Mustard oil: 1–2 tbsp
- Salt: 1½ tsp

1. Boil water in a pot. Add roasted dal and ½ tsp salt. Cook till more than three-fourths done, ensuring the lentils remain whole.
2. Heat oil in a pan. Add mustard seeds and panch phoran and let them crackle.
3. Add onions with a little salt and cook till pink.
4. Then add ginger–garlic paste and cook well.
5. Add tomatoes and let them soften.
6. Add green chillies and Kashmiri chilli powder. Sauté for 2–3 minutes.
7. Now add the boiled dal with remaining salt and mix thoroughly.
8. Let it boil for 5–8 minutes.
9. Remove from the flame. Serve hot.

KODHAISHUTIR CHENNA BHAPA (Steamed Cottage Cheese and Pea Mash in Mustard Paste) (Serves 4)

- Chenna: 150 gm
- Green peas: 100 gm
- Tomatoes: 2 medium puréed
- Mustard oil: 3 tbsp
- Turmeric powder: ½ tsp
- Kashmiri chilli powder: ½ tsp
- Green chillies: 3–4 slit
- Yoghurt: 75 ml
- Coriander leaves: 1 tbsp chopped
- Salt: 1½–2 tsp

Masala Paste

- Yellow mustard seeds: 1 tbsp
- Black mustard seeds: 1 tbsp
- Coconut: 2 tbsp grated
- Poppy seeds: 1 tbsp

1. Soak both mustard seeds and poppy seeds in water for 20 minutes. Strain.
2. Grind all the ingredients for the masala paste together in a mixer and keep aside.
3. Boil peas till soft, strain and mash roughly.
4. Preheat the oven with a tray filled with water to 180 °C for 15 minutes.
5. Heat 1 tbsp of mustard oil in a pan.
6. Cook the masala paste in the oil with 2 green chillies and turmeric powder.
7. Add puréed tomatoes and cook with 1 tsp salt. Add Kashmiri chilli powder.
8. Add the mashed peas, ½ tsp salt and cook well for 4–5 minutes.
9. Remove from flame and let it cool.
10. Soften chenna until crumbly and mix with cooked peas, yoghurt, 2 tbsp mustard oil, remaining green chillies and coriander leaves. Check seasoning.
11. Give it a light mix and place in an ovenproof dish. Cover the dish with foil.
12. Place the dish in a water bath in the oven for 20–25 minutes.
13. Remove from the oven and serve hot.

SHEEM, BODI DIYE JEERA, AADA RUI MAACH (Broad Beans, Dried Lentil Dumplings and Rohu Fish in a Light Ginger–Cumin Gravy) (Serves 4)

- Rohu fish: 5–6 pieces (round curry cut)
- Potatoes: 2 cut into wedges (soaked in water)
- Broad beans (sheem): 8 halved
- Dried Lentil dumplings (bodi): 10
- Ginger: 1 inch
- Cumin seeds: 1½ tsp
- Nigella seeds: ½ tsp
- Green chillies: 2 slit
- Garlic: 1 tsp minced

- Bay leaves: 1–2
- Turmeric powder: ½ tsp +1 tsp
- Kashmiri chilli powder: ½ tsp
- Refined/Mustard oil: 4–5 tbsp
- Tomatoes: 1½ medium cut into quarters
- Salt: 1½–2 tsp

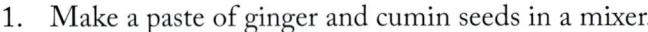

1. Make a paste of ginger and cumin seeds in a mixer.
2. Marinate fish with ½ tsp salt and ½ tsp turmeric powder for 30 minutes.
3. Heat oil in a wide non-stick pan, and add lentil dumplings. Fry and drain on a paper towel.
4. Lightly pan fry fish in the same pan for 2 minutes on each side.
5. Remove fish from pan and keep aside.
6. Put onion seeds in the same pan followed by garlic and sauté. Add potatoes and broad beans and stir fry lightly for 7–8 minutes.
7. Add ginger–cumin paste and cook well.
8. Add tomatoes, lightly toss and let them soften.
9. Add bay leaves, green chillies, remaining turmeric powder, Kashmiri chilli powder, salt and stir.
10. Gently place fish, followed by 250 ml water. Add dried lentil dumplings.
11. Cover the pan with a lid and simmer for 5–8 minutes, flipping the fish gently once in between. Check seasoning and remove from flame and serve hot.

SHAILASHREE'S PHULKOBIR MALAI CURRY
(Cauliflower Coconut Cream Curry) (Serves 4)

- Cauliflower: 350 gm
- Onion: 1 large
- Ginger: 1 inch
- Garlic: 4 large cloves
- Cinnamon powder: 1 tsp dissolved in a tsp of water
- Red chilli powder: ½ tsp
- Refined oil: 5 tbsp
- Fresh coconut chopped: ¾ cup
- Water: 250 ml
- Canned coconut cream: 8 tbsp
- Green chillies: 2 slit
- Salt: 1 tsp

1. Cut cauliflower into large florets.
2. Pound ginger and garlic together in a mortar and pestle until smooth and add the dissolved cinnamon powder to it.
3. Roughly chop onion and grind to a paste in a mixer.
4. Chop and grind coconut pieces with a little water. Add remaining water and pass the mixture through a muslin cloth to get fresh coconut milk.
5. In a pan heat 3 tbsp of oil and lightly fry the cauliflower until half done. Remove and keep aside. In the same pan, heat the remaining oil, add the onion paste with ½ tsp salt and allow it to cook.
6. Midway through the process, add the ginger–garlic–cinnamon paste and cook further.
7. The cooking process will take 15 minutes.
8. Add red chilli powder followed by cauliflower and cook for 7–8 minutes.
9. Add the coconut milk, coconut cream and slit green chillies. Simmer for another 8–10 minutes. Do not cover with a lid as the cauliflower should not be overcooked.
10. Serve hot.

LAMBA BEGUN BHAJA (Spiced Shallow Fried Brinjal)
(Serves 4)

- Long purple brinjal: 4 cut vertically with the stem
- Turmeric powder: 1¼ tsp
- Red chilli powder: ¾ tsp
- Salt: ½ tsp
- Sugar: ½ tsp
- All-purpose flour: 1½ tsp
- Mustard oil: 2–3 tbsp

1. Marinate brinjal in turmeric powder, salt, red chilli powder and sugar for 15–20 minutes. Sprinkle flour on top.
2. Heat mustard oil on a low flame in a non-stick pan.
3. Cook the brinjals on both sides till well done.
4. Serve immediately.

Photo on p. 143 (Clockwise): Kodhaishutir channa bhapa, Shailashree's phulkobir malai curry, Sheem, bodi diye jeera ada rui maach, Lamba begun bhaja and Laal masoor dal.

Colonial Hangover

This dessert is dedicated to the 'bhadralok' who truly make the city of Kolkata. Old-world bakeries like Nahoum's in New Market and Flury's on Park Street bring forth their versions of popular Western patisserie products.

'Bhapa' literally means steam. Steaming a carrot cake with a yoghurt blend makes a nice medley of a creamy mousse and moist cake. My love for carrot cake with a cream cheese frosting was the fulcrum of this dessert.

BHAPA CARROT CAKE AND DOI MEDLEY
(Serves 6)

- Carrot cake: 4–5 slices
- Yoghurt: 500 ml
- Condensed milk: 120 ml
- Green cardamom powder: ½ tsp

1. Hang the yoghurt in a muslin cloth for 2–3 hours.
2. Cut the cake slices into small pieces. Fill ramekins with cake pieces until one-third full. Press down gently with a spoon.
3. Whisk hung yoghurt and condensed milk until smooth. Add cardamom powder.
4. Top cake with the yoghurt mix, dividing equally between 6 small ramekins.
5. Cover ramekins with foil. Preheat oven to 180 °C for 10 minutes.
6. Place ramekins on a tray filled with hot water. The water level should be such that one-third of the ramekins are immersed.
7. Place the tray carefully in the oven and bake for 20 minutes.
8. Remove ramekins from the oven, cool and refrigerate.
9. Serve chilled.

Photo on p. 146: Bhapa carrot cake, Doi medley.

For the Love of Food
(Suggested Menu Plan)

LET'S PARTY

Starters
Beetroot Chop	p. 72
Spinach Momos with Spicy Chutney	pp. 221, 216
Khira Chingudi Saha Tentuli Paga	p. 172
Mutton Chop	p. 73

Mains
Amba Soriso Chicken	p. 171
Mama's Patrapoda Maccha	p. 190
Shailashree's Phulkobir Malai Curry	p. 144
Lamba Begun Bhaja	p. 145
Niramish Aloo Dum	p. 26
Pooris	
Steamed Rice	

Dessert
Bhapa Carrot Cake and Doi Medley	p. 147

FAMILY TIME
Aloo Chop	p. 406
Laal Masoor Dal	p. 141
Tankapani Soriso Manso	p. 159
Chenna Stuffed Pumpkin Flower Fritters	p. 181
Lamba Begun Bhaja	p. 145
Steamed Rice	

Dessert
Baked Rasabali	p. 209

ODISHA

True-Blue Katki's Love...

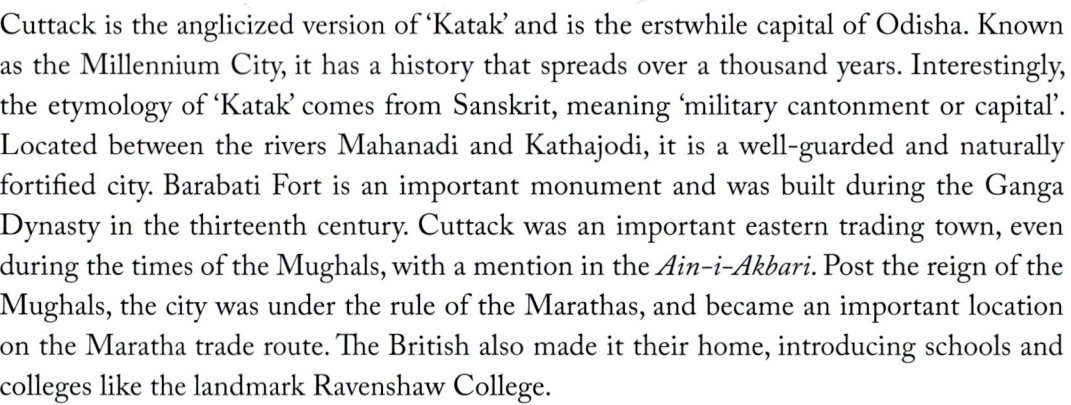

Cuttack is the anglicized version of 'Katak' and is the erstwhile capital of Odisha. Known as the Millennium City, it has a history that spreads over a thousand years. Interestingly, the etymology of 'Katak' comes from Sanskrit, meaning 'military cantonment or capital'. Located between the rivers Mahanadi and Kathajodi, it is a well-guarded and naturally fortified city. Barabati Fort is an important monument and was built during the Ganga Dynasty in the thirteenth century. Cuttack was an important eastern trading town, even during the times of the Mughals, with a mention in the *Ain-i-Akbari*. Post the reign of the Mughals, the city was under the rule of the Marathas, and became an important location on the Maratha trade route. The British also made it their home, introducing schools and colleges like the landmark Ravenshaw College.

Cuttack is an amalgamation of British developments like Civil Lines and Cantonment Road and pre-existing villages and settlements called *sahis*. Among friends we have often sat down and talked about the names and characteristics of these *sahis* areas like Peyton Sahi, Kathagada Sahi, Gauda Sahi and Khat Bin Sahi. The names are certainly different and probably either reflected the trade or the community living there. Today, next to Barabati Fort, stands a stadium known by the same name where various national and international events are held.

Growing up, Cuttack was where we as a family spent our summer vacations at my grandparents' homes. Both my grandfathers were in the police service, having served under the British, and post Independence under the Government of India. My parents moved back to Cuttack after my father retired, bidding adieu to his naval uniform. Visits home meant eating all the street food available from ten gupchups or golgappas for a rupee to eating chaat at Gouri Shankar Park. I have no idea how our stomachs handled the not-so-clean plates and spoons, but I guess they were 'immunity builders'!

But ask any Katki what their favourite meal is and most probably pat will come the response 'Dahi Bara Aloo Dum' or DBAD. The thought of mixing dahi vada with potato curry and dry pea curry isn't what one considers normal. But the delicious end result is what made it a winner at the National Street Food Festival held in Delhi in 2020.

I have been looking out for the perfect recipe for this, and it finally came from someone who has lived there for years. Rinku's dahi baras are perfect and she knows each vendor and his traits and timings – the famous ones being Raghu, Eshwara and Bhagi.

An interesting detail she mentioned was that Bhagi only ventures out in the morning and has an educational route to sales from colleges to schools! The others appear only in the evening. Queuing up and waiting for their arrival is an added experience! The aloo dum was a researched trial-and-error recipe and the recipe for ghugni comes from a roadside vendor in Bhubaneswar.

RINKU'S DAHI BARA (Serves 4)
(Measuring cup size: 150 ml)

Bara (Makes 15 baras)

- White urad dal: 1 cup
- Water: 60 ml
- Oil: to deep fry

1. Soak dal in water for 4–5 hours. Strain.
2. Grind dal to a paste with 60 ml water.
3. Now using your hands like a whisk, mix the batter in a circular motion for 4–5 minutes, and let it to rest for 10 minutes.
4. Repeat the process of whisking for another 4–5 minutes and let the batter rest for 45 minutes.
5. Whisk the batter for 5 minutes. It would have increased in volume.
6. Heat oil in a deep wok/kadai on a medium flame.
7. Moisten your hands. Make balls with the batter and drop into the hot oil

8. Remove baras once they attain a light golden colour and drop into lukewarm salt water. If making in advance, do not add salt to this water.
9. Squeeze out the water and use immediately or refrigerate plain baras.

Dahi Bara

- Yoghurt: 350 ml
- Water: 750 ml
- Green chillies: 2 finely chopped
- Roasted cumin powder: 1 tsp
- Salt: 1½ tsp
- Roasted red chilli powder: 1 tsp
- Ginger: 1 tsp grated
- Mint leaves: 1 tbsp chopped

Tempering

- Mustard: ½ tsp
- Cumin seeds: ½ tsp
- Curry leaves: a few
- Dried red chillies: 1–2
- Refined oil: 1 tsp

1. Mix yoghurt and water with green chillies, roasted cumin powder, salt, roasted red chilli powder, ginger and mint leaves. Add 10 baras to the yoghurt.
2. Heat oil in a pan and add all the ingredients for tempering. Let them crackle.
3. Pour tempering over the baras.

Meetha Bara

- Sugar: 2½–3 tbsp
- Salt: ¾ tsp
- Red chilli powder: ½ tsp
- Water: 500 ml

Tempering

- Mustard seeds: ½ tsp
- Cumin seeds: ½ tsp
- Curry leaves: a few
- Dried red chillies: 1–2
- Refined oil: 1 tsp

1. In a saucepan boil sugar and water till it dissolves into a thin syrup.
2. Add salt and red chilli powder. Add 5 baras and keep aside.
3. Heat oil in a pan and add all the ingredients for tempering. Let them crackle and pour over the baras.

ALOO DUM (Serves 4)

- Baby potatoes: 750 gm
- Turmeric powder: ½ tsp
- Red chilli powder: ½ tsp
- Salt: ¾ tsp

1. Prick potatoes and boil in salt water until three-fourths done. Strain and keep aside.
2. Let potatoes cool then peel.
3. Marinate in turmeric powder and red chilli powder for 2–3 hours.

- Onions: 2 large chopped
- Tomatoes: 2 large grated (do not chop)
- Green chillies: 1–2 chopped
- Garlic: 8 cloves chopped
- Ginger: 2 inches chopped
- Mustard oil: 3–4 tbsp
- Black cardamom: 1
- Dried red chillies: 2
- Cinnamon: 2 inch stick
- Bay leaves: 2 small
- Kashmiri chilli powder: 1 tsp
- Roasted red chilli powder: 1 tsp
- Turmeric powder: ½ tsp
- Salt: 1½ tsp
- Roasted cumin powder: ½ tsp
- Curry powder/Meat masala: 1–1¼ tbsp
- Home-made garam masala: 1 tsp
- Coriander leaves: 1–2 tbsp chopped
- Water: 250 ml

1. Heat oil in a pan over a medium flame.
2. Add all the whole spices and let them crackle.
3. Add onions and sauté until golden brown.
4. Add ginger, garlic and green chillies. Sauté for 3–4 minutes.
5. Add all the spice powders, except the home-made garam masala.
6. Add tomatoes, salt, and cook until the oil separates and the mixture is smooth.
7. Add potatoes and fry well on a high flame.
8. The mixture should turn a dark, glossy, reddish brown.
9. Cover and cook for 3–5 minutes.
10. Add desired quantity of water and boil the gravy.
11. Add home-made garam masala and coriander leaves.

GHUGNI (Serves 4)

(Measuring cup size: 250 ml)

- Dried peas: 1 cup
- Turmeric powder: ½ tsp
- Salt: 1½ tsp
- Water: 600 ml

1. Soak dried peas overnight in water and strain.
2. Boil water with ½ tsp turmeric powder and 1½ tsp salt.
3. Add peas, cover and cook for 35–40 minutes until soft.
4. Remove one-fourth quantity of the peas.
5. After another 15 minutes, remove half the quantity of the remaining peas.
6. Leave the rest of the peas in the pot.

- Tomatoes: 2 large grated
- Ginger: 1 inch grated
- Green chillies: 2 grated
- Red chilli powder: 1 tbsp (combine Kashmiri chilli and roasted red chilli powder)
- Roasted cumin powder: 1 tsp
- Coriander powder: 1 tbsp
- Cumin seeds: ½ tsp
- Turmeric powder: ½ tsp
- Mustard oil: 1 tbsp
- Home-made garam masala powder: 1 tsp
- Coriander leaves: 1 tbsp
- Salt: ½ tsp

1. Heat oil in a pan, add cumin seeds and let them crackle.
2. Add dry spices, except coriander powder and home-made garam masala.
3. Add tomato, ginger, green chillies and cook over medium heat for 5–7 minutes.
4. Add coriander powder, salt and cook until the oil separates.
5. Add all the peas including the last batch. Reserve the pea water.
6. Add home-made garam masala powder and coriander leaves.
7. Cover and cook until the peas soften.
8. Add reserved pea water and more warm water as needed.
9. Serve over dahi bara.

> Eat separately, sprinkled with chopped onions, coriander powder, cumin powder, chilli powder and tamarind paste.

Photo on p. 153: DBAD - Dahi bara aloo dum and ghugni; **Photo on p. 156:** Peda.

Assembling

- Sev: 4 tbsp
- Onions: 4 tsp chopped
- Coriander leaves: 2 tbsp chopped
- Green chillies: 2 chopped
- Roasted cumin powder: ½ tsp
- Red chilli powder: 1 tsp

1. In a bowl, put 2-3 of the dahi baras and add 1-2 meetha baras.
2. Top with a large spoon each of aloo dum and ghugni.
3. Top with sev, onions, coriander leaves, green chillies, roasted cumin powder and red chilli powder.

Sweet Saviour

For some relief after the fiery DBAD, the spice levels usually require a soother to stop the tongue from burning. The peda is the solution! That is my association with the peda, but it is a popular sweet all over the country. In India the best-known peda is the Mathura peda, as it is one of the main delicacies in the Chappan Bhog or the 56 food items served to Lord Krishna on Janmashtami, the day of his birth. Mathura is also his birthplace. Food historians say that the art of making pedas dates back to the 1800s.

However, the Odisha peda is a slightly caramelised version with the colour ranging from creamy beige to a light brown. The larger quantity of sugar in this version of the peda is added after the entire cooking process. This was the only clue I gathered from an article in a local newspaper. The rest of the recipe and the process of its making was an attempt at combining ingredients from my experience of tasting them. This sweet comes with a warning – be ready for an arm workout!

PEDA (Serves 8)

- Cow milk: 1½ litre
- Liquid ghee: 90–100 ml + a little to grease palm
- Granulated sugar: 4 tsp
- Cardamom powder: ¼ tsp
- Powdered Sugar: ¼ cup

1. Pour milk in a thick-bottom wok/kadai and let it thicken while stirring for 1¼ hour over a medium flame. The end result will be a soft and smooth-textured mass called khoya.
2. Heat 70 ml ghee in a wok/kadai. Add granulated sugar and let it caramelize.
3. Add the khoya and let it combine to a smooth ball. You should be able to make a soft
4. shiny ball with a portion of the mixture.
5. Add cardamom powder and remove from flame.
6. Once the mixture is lukewarm, add powdered sugar and knead for at least 20 minutes.
7. The sugar will dissolve further as you knead.
8. Add remaining 30 ml of ghee gradually and check if it shapes into a ball. Then, divide
9. the mixture into 20 gm portions.
10. Grease your palms with a touch of ghee.
11. Shape the balls into at discs, use a design stamp on them or leave them plain.
12. Let them harden a little at room temperature before serving.
13. Refrigerate in an airtight container. The pedas will last for 2–3 days.

'Home'

The in-laws are a very large extended family in Bhubaneshwar and their homes are referred to by the areas they are located in and not by the people living there. Each family consists of many members or what we call a 'joint family.' It is quite like community living as some of these households comprise four or five families.

There are many lessons to learn from them; from being patient, to being there for each other, to dealing with mood swings and the rules and regulations, to the many sessions of laughter when everyone gathers together and of course the rituals that are part of traditional homes.

One such ritual is a 4 a.m. wake-up for four consecutive Thursdays in the Margasira Masa or the ninth month in the Hindu calendar for Lakshmi Puja. One sits down for prayers, all bathed and hair washed, midway through the reading of the scriptures one can hear my mother in-law sweetly asking God for forgiveness, as all of us are only partially awake, with only one overpowering thought in our heads – 'Give me my coffee!' I have to admit, though, that over the years, many strict rituals have given way to simplified versions, with blurred boundaries.

Each household cooks their specialities and obviously, all the 'aunts in-law' and nanas (cooks) are happy to teach the ones willing to learn. Of course, there are stories of the exceptionally good quality of mutton provided to satisfy cravings. A vegetarian by choice from my twenties, there are times when the abundance of non-vegetarian food on the table leaves me wondering if there's anything left alive to eat! But Odiya food does have a great balance for herbivores and carnivores. All of it is accompanied with warm rice, ghee and a pitha sometimes.

Like most other pithas, the chitau pitha is also given as an offering to Lord Jagannath on Chitau Amavasya, the New Moon day in the Shravan month which is the fifth month in the Hindu calendar. There is also a ceremony at my in-laws in the fifth month of pregnancy which is called Chitau Khiya. During this time chitau pitha or rice crepes are made and five young boys are invited and fed, resonating with the orthodox blessing 'May you be the mother of a hundred sons'.

TANKAPANI SORISO MANSO (Mutton Cooked in Mustard Gravy) (Serves 4)

- Mutton: 1 kg curry cut

Marinade:

- Black mustard seeds: 4 tbsp
- Red chillies: 2
- Ginger: 2 inches
- Garlic: 6
- Yoghurt: 3 tbsp
- Salt: ½ tsp

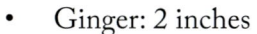

Photo on p. 160 (Clockwise): Nayapalli janhi chatu tatiya basa, Tankapani soriso manso, Nayapalli posto bara, Nadiya rasa bhaja chenna tarkari, Abhi nana's ou khatta and Chitau pitha.

1. Soak mustard seeds, garlic, ginger and dried red chillies in water for 30 minutes.
2. Strain and grind to a paste.
3. Strain the mixture to remove the skin of the mustard seeds.
4. Add yoghurt, salt and mix well.
5. Marinate meat in this mixture for 1 hour at room temperature.

Gravy

- Sugar: ½–1 tsp
- Onions: 3 medium
- Tomatoes: 2 medium chopped
- Mustard oil: 2 tbsp
- Green chillies: 2 slit
- Curry leaves: 1 sprig
- Home-made garam masala powder: 1 tsp
- Turmeric powder: ½ tsp
- Salt: 1 tsp

1. Heat mustard oil in a thick-bottom pan, add sugar and let it caramelize.
2. Add onions and fry until golden brown. Add slit green chillies and curry leaves.
3. Add chopped tomatoes and cook until the oil separates.
4. Add marinated mutton, salt and turmeric powder.
5. Add garam masala powder and let the mutton cook over a low flame.
6. Add water as required as this has to be a thick gravy.
7. Cover with a lid and stir occasionally. This will take 45 minutes to an hour to cook.
8. Check salt and remove from flame. Serve hot.

NAYAPALLI JANHI CHATU TATITYA BASA (One Pot Ridge Gourd and Mushrooms) (Serves 4)

- Ridge gourd: 900 gm
- Mushrooms: 250 gm
- Mustard seeds: 1 tbsp
- Garlic: 2 cloves
- Dried red chillies: 2
- Ginger: 1 inch
- Dry mango kernels: 1–2 soaked in water
- Onion: 1 medium quartered
- Tomatoes: 1 medium quartered
- Salt: 1 tsp
- Turmeric powder: 1 tsp

SERVINGS

- Mustard oil: 2–3 tbsp
- Red chilli powder: ½ tsp
- Green chillies: 2 slit

1. Soak mustard seeds, garlic, ginger, dried red chillies in water for 30 minutes. Grind to a paste and pass through a strainer.
2. Peel, deseed and chop ridge gourd into large cubes.
3. Remove stems of the mushrooms and halve them.
4. Take a large wok/kadai and put all the vegetables in it along with the strained mustard paste, salt, turmeric powder, red chilli powder, slit green chillies, soaked dry mango kernels and mustard oil. Give it a good mix with your fingers.
5. Place the wok/kadai over a medium flame and cover tightly with another dish overturned (see image above.)
6. Cook over a low flame for 30–40 minutes until the vegetables soften.
7. Check seasoning and serve hot.

Diced potatoes can also be added to this dish.

NADIYA RASA BHAJA CHENNA TARKARI (Fresh Cottage Cheese Cubes in Coconut Gravy) (Serves 4)

- Chenna: 250 gm
- Refined oil: to deep/pan fry

1. Place moist chenna in a muslin cloth.
2. Flatten into a disc and place a heavy weight on it.
3. After 20 minutes remove chenna from muslin and cut into squares.
4. Heat oil in a pan and pan fry/deep fry chenna.

Gravy

- Baby potatoes: 8 small
- Tomatoes: 3 puréed
- Onions: 2 chopped
- Ginger: 1 tsp
- Garlic: 1 tsp
- Sugar: 1 tsp

- Grated coconut: 3 tbsp
- Poppy seeds: 1 tbsp
- Green chillies: 2
- Coconut milk: 100 ml
- Cinnamon: 1½ inch stick
- Green cardamoms: 2
- Bay leaf: 1
- Cloves: 2
- Kashmiri chilli powder: 1 tsp
- Red chilli powder: ½ tsp
- Turmeric powder: ½ tsp
- Home-made garam masala powder: ½ tsp
- Refined oil: 2–3 tbsp
- Ghee: 1 tbsp
- Salt: 1 tsp

1. Soak poppy seeds in water for 20 minutes. Strain and grind with grated coconut and green chillies to a fine paste.
2. Pound ginger and garlic together.
3. Heat oil and ghee in a non-stick pan. Toss the potatoes until they are cooked through.
4. Remove potatoes and keep them aside.
5. In the pan used earlier add remaining oil and ghee, add sugar and let it dissolve.
6. Add all the whole spices and let them crackle.
7. Add onions and ½ tsp salt. Let it cook until soft and golden brown.
8. Add pounded ginger and garlic and sauté. Add ground coconut paste and cook.
9. Add puréed tomatoes, both chilli powders, turmeric powder and garam masala powder.
10. Cook until the oil separates, and add a little water, followed by coconut milk.
11. Add the fried chenna cubes, potatoes and remaining salt.
12. Let it simmer for 15–20 minutes. The gravy should be thin.
13. Serve hot.

ABHI NANA'S OU KHATTA (Elephant Apple Chutney)
(Serves 6)

- Elephant apple: 200 gm
- Jaggery: 150 gm
- Refined oil: 35 ml
- Curry leaves: 2 sprigs
- Panch phoran: ½ tsp
- Dried red chillies: 2

- Asafoetida powder: ¼ tsp
- Roasted cumin powder: 1 tsp
- Roasted fenugreek powder: ¼ tsp
- Red chilli powder: ½ tsp
- Salt: 1 tsp
- Turmeric powder: ½ tsp
- Cornflour: 1 tsp

1. Peel and slice elephant apple. Gently crush each piece.
2. Heat oil in a non-stick pan.
3. Add panch phoran and dried red chillies and let them crackle.
4. Add asafoetida powder, curry leaves and stir gently.
5. Add elephant apple and stir fry for 5–7 minutes.
6. Add salt, turmeric powder, followed by jaggery.
7. Boil for 10 minutes over a low flame till the elephant apple softens.
8. Mix 1 tsp cornflour in 50 ml of boiling water and add.
9. Let it cool and top with the roasted cumin powder, red chilli powder and roasted fenugreek powder. Serve at room temperature.

NAYAPALLI POSTO BARA (Poppy Seed Patty) (Serves 6)

- Poppy seeds: 100 gm
- Onion: 1 medium chopped
- Green chillies: 4 chopped
- Salt: 1 tsp
- Garlic: 7–8 cloves chopped
- Refined oil: 1–2 tbsp

1. Soak poppy seeds for an hour in water.
2. Strain and grind to a smooth paste.
3. Add all the other ingredients except oil and mix well.
4. Divide mixture into 12 equal portions.
5. Heat oil in a non-stick flat pan over a low flame.
6. With wet palms, shape the mixture into flat discs and place in the pan.
7. Gently cook for 2 minutes till brown and flip to cook the other side.
8. Cook each side further for 2–3 minutes by pressing down gently. Serve hot.

CHITAU PITHA (Rice and Coconut Crepes) (Serves 4)

- Raw rice: 150 gm
- Fresh grated coconut: 100 gm
- Salt: 1 tsp
- Water: 100 ml

1. Soak rice in water for 2½ hours and strain.
2. Add grated coconut and grind to a paste.
3. Add water and salt to make a smooth, thin batter.
4. Heat a non-stick appam pan over a low flame.
5. Add a ladle of the batter and swirl gently so that the batter spreads along the sides of the pan.
6. Cover with a lid so that a lacy pattern forms and cook for 2–3 minutes.
7. Remove the pitha to a platter and serve warm.

Caramel Rasagolas

A war of words usually breaks out over the origin of the rasgulla or rasagola. Many Odiya and Bengali food enthusiasts and historians have argued over its birthplace. The 'Odisha Rasagola' did get the GI (Geographical Indication) tag in 2019 under this name.

This sweet is unique in colour and texture and is offered at the Jagannath temple on the last day of the Ratha Yatra, which is the tenth day. Folklore says that it was offered to Lord Jagannath's wife Goddess Lakshmi who, upset at her husband who left without her consent and stayed away for nine days, shut the doors on him after his return from the Yatra.

While the argument on who made this sweet first still continues, I decided to turn *gudiya* which is what the sweetmeat makers or halwais are called in Odiya. Of course, reaching out to an actual one to learn was part of the process.

The pale rust-red colour of this rasagola sets it apart from the other rasagolas available. One of the popular spots to savour this delicacy is Pahala, a village between Cuttack and Bhubaneswar. Memories from my childhood include stopping at a roadside stall to eat one fresh from a large pot. The ₹5 rasagola was a jumbo-sized speciality in those days!

ODISHA RASAGOLA (Serves 6)

Syrup 1

- Sugar: 60 gm
- Water: 90 ml

1. Heat a wok/kadai and caramelize 2 tsp of sugar till dark brown.
2. Add remaining sugar and water.
3. Let it boil until it is sticky and turns into a syrup.
4. Remove from flame and keep aside for 18–24 hours.

The addition of syrup 1 gives a unique flavour and a depth of colour. Traditionally, the leftover syrup from the previous day's rasagola is used.

Syrup 2

- Sugar: 275 gm
- Water: 850 ml
- Green cardamoms: 2 whole

1. Add sugar and water to syrup 1 and boil over a high flame.
2. Add whole cardamoms and boil until sticky but not thick.
3. Ensure a thin syrup. Remove from flame and keep aside.

Rasagola Balls

- Cow milk (full fat): 1 litre
- Semolina: 4 gm
- Lime juice: 2–3 tbsp
- All-purpose flour: 1 gm (optional)
- Green cardamom powder: ¼ tsp

1. Boil milk in a heavy-bottomed pot.
2. After a few quick boils, add lime juice. Turn off the flame and let the milk curdle.
3. Place a muslin cloth on a strainer and strain the curdled milk through it.

SERVINGS

Photo on p. 167: Caramel rasagolas - Odisha rasagolas; Photo on p. 168: The process of making the rasagolas.

4. Bring the ends of the muslin cloth together and twist tightly to squeeze out excess water to get 150–175 gm of chenna.
5. Pour water over the muslin wrapped chenna and not on the chenna directly, to remove all traces of lime.
6. Wrap the chenna again tightly and squeeze the muslin to drain out excess water. Let this hang for 1½ hours.
7. Knead the chenna with your palm on a kitchen slab for 8–10 minutes till smooth.
8. Add semolina and cardamom powder. Knead further for 8–10 minutes.
9. Ensure the semolina dissolves completely. The chenna should be smooth and soft and your palms mildly greasy. Add all-purpose flour if desired and knead.
10. Divide the chenna mixture into 12 parts and roll them into small smooth balls. The smoother the surface, the fewer the cracks.
11. Boil Syrup 2 in a wok/kadai on a high flame and add the chenna balls.
12. Cover the wok and boil the chenna balls on high for 8 minutes until the balls expand, after which lower the flame to medium heat.
13. Remove the lid and turn the balls gently. Cover and boil again for 5 minutes. After this, they should have doubled in size. Remove the cover.
14. Simultaneously, heat 300 ml of water in another wide thick-bottom pot. Once the water boils, turn the flame off.
15. While the second pot of water boils, separately pour another 100 ml of boiling water gently along the sides of the wok/kadai with the chenna balls. The syrup needs to be thin for the balls to expand.
16. Keep turning the chenna balls to ensure a uniform colour. Also move the syrup over them for another 15 minutes.
17. Transfer the cooked chenna balls carefully to the second pot of water, which will be warm but not hot at this point.
18. Let the rasagolas cool in the pot to room temperature.
19. Transfer the water from the pot with the chenna balls gradually into Syrup 2, leaving the chenna balls and about 100 ml of the water in the pot.
20. Boil Syrup 2 for 3–4 minutes. Let it cool to lukewarm.
21. Squeeze the chenna balls to remove a little water and transfer to Syrup 2.
22. Rasagolas are best served warm or at room temperature but you can serve them cold as well.

Tips

- Overkneading the chenna will result in balls decreasing in size on cooling.
- Use a wide wok/kadai so that the chenna balls have enough space to expand.
- Ensure that the flame is at medium as the liquid boils.
- The syrup should not be too thick as it will flatten the balls.
- The balls should be covered in syrup as well, otherwise they will flatten.
- The transfer to the second pot with warm water ensures that the balls do not flatten.
- To ensure a transparent syrup, add 75 ml milk to the boiling syrup. A frothy impure surface will form. Discard the same. Do this before you add the cooled and cooked chenna balls.

'Odisha Canvas'

Odia cuisine is fairly undiscovered by the world. Since I belong to this beautiful state, it has only been natural to gravitate towards using the local produce creatively. Odia food is simple and yet there is a complexity in the processes, ingredients and flavour. The local produce is outstanding and the variety available baffling. I was really surprised to find unique ingredients at the 'Adisha' Store, which is an attempt by the state government to promote tribal produce. This includes locally grown products like coffee and black rice.

I have often come across families of Odia cooks, where generations who have been in the profession have moved to neighbouring Bengal adding to their repertoire of food. Many believe that the introduction to pithas, the rasagola or even gondhoraj in Bengali cuisine came from Odia cooks. This is probably why we can see a huge overlap in the cuisines of the two states. Cooking with less oil and using techniques like grilling, steaming and poaching are popular.

The Kalinga Dynasty boasts of a 2000-year-old maritime history. Ships sailed out from the coast of Odisha via Burma and Cambodia. Caravans went overland to Malaysia, making their way to Indonesia. There is commonality in these countries in the use of ingredients like coconut, turmeric, chillies, tamarind and jaggery and also in the cooking methods like the use of leaves to steam food, along with roasting and smoking meats wrapped in leaves placed in clay ovens. Today, we improvise on techniques in our modern kitchens and find ways to retain flavour.

The recipes in the following pages cross borders, from Bengal to the routes these ships sailed, and also other continents. Fusing cuisines is always interesting. Often, what is in one's head doesn't translate on to the plate, but when it does, you can pat yourself on the back and entertain a dream or two of participating in MasterChef! I often wonder why the designation of 'chef' is used so casually. In reality, chefs are trained professionals, proficient in all aspects of food preparation and create magical recipes from scratch that you can taste.

AAMBA SORISO CHICKEN (Chicken Cooked with Pickled Mangoes and Mustard) (Serves 4)

Bengalis use aam kasundi as an accompaniment and bottled versions can be found of the same. This recipe uses local raw mangoes and a quick pickling method to create flavours that go well with the chicken dish.

Aamba Soriso Paste

- Raw mangoes: 150 gm skin removed and cubed
- Green chilli: 1
- Garlic: 2 large cloves
- Black mustard seeds: 20 gm
- Sugar: 1 tsp
- Salt: ½ tsp
- Mustard oil: 2 tbsp

1. Add salt to the mangoes. Place for 15 minutes on a muslin and let the water drain out.
2. Grind all the ingredients along with the mangoes together to a paste except for mustard oil. Place in a jar. Top with mustard oil, cover and leave overnight.

Photo on p. 173: Aamba soriso chicken.

Marination

- Chicken: 1 kg curry cut and pierced with a fork)
- Garlic: 2 tbsp
- Turmeric powder: 1 tsp
- Green chillies: 1–2 chopped
- Kashmiri chilli powder: 1 tsp
- Salt: 1 tsp level

1. Pierce the chicken pieces with a fork and marinate with all other ingredients and the aamba soriso paste for 4–6 hours.

Gravy

- Mustard oil: 1 tbsp
- Poppy seeds: 1 tbsp
- Turmeric powder: ¾ tsp
- Sugar: 1½ tsp
- Salt: 1 tsp
- Ginger paste: 1 tsp

1. Soak poppy seeds in water for 20 minutes. Strain and grind to a paste.
2. Heat oil in a pan and then lower the flame.
3. Sauté the poppy seed paste and ginger paste until it turns light brown.
4. Add turmeric powder and sugar. Stir and then add the marinated chicken and juices.
5. Let it cook, uncovered, over a low flame, tossing the chicken until the masala cooks well. This will take 20–25 minutes. Add salt.
6. Turn up the flame to medium and add hot water.
7. Let the chicken simmer to a thickish gravy.
8. Check spice and seasoning.
9. Serve hot.

KHIRA CHINGUDI SAHA TENTULI PAGA (Milk Prawns with Tamarind Dipping Sauce) (Serves 4)

(Measuring cup size: 150 ml)

The Chinese use evaporated milk to create buttermilk prawns; this version uses milk powder and the popular 'checha' or pounding of ingredients to create a distinct flavour. Butter is substituted for ghee. 'Paga' is a sour liquid mix, made with souring agents like yoghurt, dried mango kernels and tamarind.

Khira Chingudi

- Prawns: 300 gm with tail
- Salt: ½ tsp + ½ tsp
- Turmeric powder: ½ tsp
- Red chilli powder: ½ tsp
- Rice flour: 1 tbsp
- Refined oil: to pan fry
- Ghee: 2 tbsp
- Black mustard seeds: 1 tsp
- Curry leaves: 2 sprigs
- Kashmiri chilli powder: ½ tsp
- Shallots: 6–7
- Garlic: 3–4 large cloves
- Green chillies: 2–3
- Milk powder: ½ cup
- Hot water: 1½ cups

1. Marinate prawns for 15 minutes at room temperature with ½ tsp salt, turmeric powder and red chilli powder. Add rice flour and mix.
2. Heat oil in a non-stick pan and pan fry prawns for 2–3 minutes. Flip and fry further for 2–3 minutes.
3. Remove and drain on a paper towel.
4. Pound shallots, garlic and green chillies together using a mortar and pestle.
5. In a bowl, mix milk powder with boiling water. Ensure that there are no lumps.
6. In another pan, heat ghee, add mustard seeds and curry leaves and let them crackle. Add Kashmiri chilli powder and sauté.
7. Add the pounded mixture and cook until it turns light brown.
8. Add milk mixture and let it thicken to a sauce-like consistency on a medium flame.
9. Add prawns and coat well with the sauce. Add ½ tsp salt and check seasoning.
10. Cover and cook for 3–4 minutes. Serve with the tentuli paga.

Tentuli Paga

- Ghee: 1 tsp
- Cumin seeds: 2 tsp
- Dried red chillies: 2–3
- Curry leaves: 1 sprig
- Tamarind: 30 gm
- Hot water: ½ cup + 1 cup
- Coconut sugar: 25 gm
- Salt: ½ tsp
- Red chilli powder: ½ tsp

1. Soak tamarind in ½ cup hot water for 20 minutes, after which strain and extract the juice.

2. Dissolve coconut sugar in the remaining hot water.
3. In a saucepan, boil tamarind extract and coconut sugar together till it thickens.
4. Meanwhile, in a non-stick pan, heat ghee and temper cumin seeds, dried red chillies and curry leaves.
5. Add the temper to the tamarind sauce and let it simmer.
6. Add salt and red chilli powder.
7. Boil to a medium thick sauce. Serve hot with prawns.

POI PUTULI AND COCONUT BLACK RICE
(Malabar Spinach Parcels) (Serves 4)
(Measuring cup size: 250 ml)

As mentioned earlier, steaming in leaves is a popular method of cooking. The poi leaf or malabar spinach leaf is usually cooked with vegetables and shrimp. This dish where the leaf is made into a vegetable parcel is a visually appealing version.

It is served with black rice or kalibati dhana, which is native to Odisha and was produced in larger quantities 50–70 years ago. The emergence of other varieties of paddy led to a decline in kalibati farming. However, in recent times, it has made a comeback and is grown in the district of Sambalpur. Black rice was known as 'forbidden rice' in ancient China for its prohibitive cost. It has high medicinal value and is good for diabetes and cancer patients. The recipe here is a savoury version of the popular breakfast porridge from Indonesia.

Parcels

- Malabar spinach leaves: 12 large
- Pumpkin: 125 gm peeled, deseeded and chopped
- Potato: 1 large chopped
- Button mushrooms: 6 chopped
- Snake beans: 4 chopped
- Green chillies: 1–2 finely chopped
- Onion: ½ large chopped
- Tomato: 1 large chopped
- Ginger paste: ½ tsp
- Garlic paste: ½ tsp
- Panch phoran: ¼ tsp
- Turmeric powder: ¼ tsp

SERVINGS

- Salt: ½–¾ tsp
- Mustard oil: 3 tbsp

1. Heat oil in a non-stick pan. Toss in the potatoes with ¼ tsp salt and cook until slightly soft and light brown then remove from the pan.
2. In the same pan, add panch phoran. Let it crackle and then add turmeric powder, ginger and garlic paste and sauté till light brown.
3. Add chopped onions, ¼ tsp salt and cook until translucent and pink.
4. Add tomatoes and cook until soft, followed by all other chopped raw vegetables. Toss, add ¼ tsp salt and then cover with a lid and cook on a low flame for 5–7 minutes.
5. Remove lid, add potatoes, green chillies and check seasoning.
6. Cook for another 5 minutes.
7. Using tongs, gently place the Malabar spinach leaves over an open flame for 30 seconds. This helps the leaves soften and makes them easy to fold.
8. Take 2 leaves at a time, placing one across the other on a flat surface. Place 2–3 tsp of the vegetable mixture and fold into a parcel. Tie with a string.
9. Boil water in a steamer and place the parcels in the basket.
10. Steam for 10 minutes and keep them warm in the steamer basket.
11. Remove thread.

Gravy

- Yellow mustard seeds: 4 tsp
- Poppy seeds: 1 tsp
- Dried red chillies: 2–3
- Garlic: 4 cloves large
- Ginger paste: ½ tsp
- Green chillies: 1–2 slit
- Tomatoes: 3 medium chopped
- Onion: 1½ grated
- Salt: ¾–1 tsp
- Coriander powder: ½ tsp
- Turmeric powder: ¼ tsp
- Mustard oil: 2–3 tbsp
- Water: 250–300 ml

1. Soak mustard seeds, poppy seeds, dried red chillies and garlic in ½ cup water for 10 minutes.
2. Strain and grind to a paste. Add ¼ cup water after grinding.

3. Heat oil in a non-stick pan. Add turmeric powder and onions and cook until translucent with ½ tsp salt.
4. Add ginger paste and cook.
5. Add the mustard–poppy paste and cook on low heat.
6. Add tomatoes, slit green chillies and coriander powder. Add remaining salt and allow the sauce to cook.
7. Add water gradually and simmer till it attains a sauce-like consistency.
8. Transfer hot gravy to the serving dish and place warm/hot parcels on the gravy.
9. Serve immediately.

> Adding 10–12 pounded small shrimps along with the vegetables while cooking is also an option

Coconut Black Rice

- Black rice: 1 cup
- Canned coconut milk: 2 cups
- Water: 2 cups
- Ghee: 1 tbsp
- Onion: 1 medium chopped
- Garlic: 5 cloves sliced
- Curry leaves: 1 sprig
- Dried red chillies: 1–2
- Salt: to taste

1. Wash and soak rice in water for 30 minutes. Strain and keep aside.
2. In a thick-bottom saucepan, heat ghee. Add garlic and stir fry.
3. Add curry leaves and dried red chillies.
4. Add onions, salt and sauté.
5. Add coconut milk and water. Let it boil.
6. Add the rice and let it cook till done.
7. Serve hot.

Photo on p. 174: Khira chingudi saha tentuli paga; Photo on p. 177: Poi putuli with Coconut black rice.

CHENNA STUFFED PUMPKIN FLOWER FRITTERS
(Serves 4)

Italians often use zucchini flowers to make fritters, sometimes stuffed with local cheese. This variant uses the easily available pumpkin flowers and is stuffed with fresh cottage cheese, coated and fried. Usually in Odia cuisine these flowers are batter fried in rice flour.

- Pumpkin flowers: 10
- Onion: 1 large chopped
- Green chillies: 2 chopped fine
- Coriander leaves: 1–2 tbsp chopped
- Cheddar cheese: 60 gm grated
- Cream: 2 tbsp
- Chenna: 110 gm
- All-purpose flour: 1 cup
- Chilled club soda: 1 cup
- Salt: 1¼ tsp
- Red chilli powder: ¼ tsp
- Turmeric powder: ¼ tsp
- Refined oil: to deep fry

1. Clean pumpkin flowers. Wash and dry on a paper towel.
2. Mix chopped onions, coriander leaves, green chillies, chenna, Cheddar cheese and cream together to make a smooth mix. Add ½ tsp salt.
3. Stuff the inside of the flowers with 1½ tsp cheese mixture and twist the top.
4. Do not overstuff.
5. Heat oil in a wok/kadai over a medium flame.
6. Meanwhile, mix together flour, chilled club soda, ¾ tsp salt, red chilli powder and turmeric powder to make a smooth batter.
7. Dip the stuffed flowers into the batter. Glide flowers along the edges of the bowl to remove excess batter.
8. Drop in hot oil and gently fry till golden.
9. Serve hot.

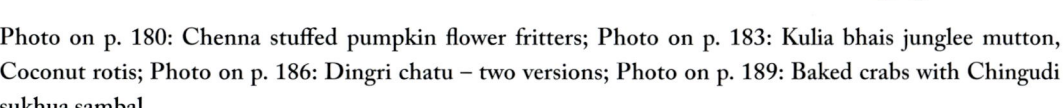

Photo on p. 180: Chenna stuffed pumpkin flower fritters; Photo on p. 183: Kulia bhais junglee mutton, Coconut rotis; Photo on p. 186: Dingri chatu – two versions; Photo on p. 189: Baked crabs with Chingudi sukhua sambal.

KULIA BHAI'S JUNGLEE MUTTON AND COCONUT ROTIS (Serves 4)
(Measuring cup size: 150 ml)

Junglee mutton is a four-ingredient meat dish which is made often by my brother-in-law. He slow cooks it on a wood fire. However this version is an attempt to replicate the recipe sans the woodfire. The accompanying coconut rotis are popular in Sri Lanka as well. Interestingly the Sinhalese have their origins in Odisha.

Junglee Mutton

- Mutton: 1 kg rib and pieces
- Dried red chillies: 15 deseeded
- Ghee: 100 ml
- Salt: 1 tsp
- Hot water: 75–100 ml
- Wood charcoal: 1 piece

1. Heat ghee just till it melts in a thick-bottom wok/kadai. Add mutton.
2. Sauté mutton for 3–4 minutes and then add dried red chillies.
3. Reduce flame and let the mutton simmer for 2–2½ hours with salt.
4. Cover for some time at intervals.
5. Add warm water gradually as it simmers to ensure that the meat softens.
6. Once the meat is nearly cooked, on another flame, heat a piece of wood charcoal until it glows red and place on a foil shaped like a katori (small bowl).
7. Place the heated coal in the centre of the wok/kadai and pour a few spoons of the ghee from the cooked mutton on it and let it smoke.
8. Cover tightly with a lid for 3 minutes.
9. Remove the foil with the coal but mix the coal-infused ghee back into the mutton.
10. Remove from flame and serve with coconut rotis.

Coconut Roti

- All-purpose flour: 1½ cups
- Fresh grated coconut: ½ cup
- Salt: ½ tsp
- Green chillies: 2 finely chopped
- Onion: 1 medium finely chopped
- Canned coconut milk: ½ cup
- Ghee: as required

1. Make a dough with all the ingredients except ghee. Adding coconut milk gradually.
2. Divide the dough into 6 equal portions.
3. Roll each ball into 6 inch diameter discs.
4. Heat a flat non-stick pan.
5. Rub the pan with a little ghee.
6. Cook rotis on the pan, 3 minutes on each side.
7. Apply a dab of ghee when flipping.
8. Serve hot.

DHINGRI CHATU – TWO VERSIONS (Buttermilk Mushrooms and Mushroom Koftas in Coriander–Coconut Gravy)

(Measuring cup size: 250 ml)

Buttermilk Dhingri Chatu

- Mushrooms: 8
- Spice buttermilk: 1 cup
- Rice flour: ½ cup
- Water: ⅔ cup
- Red chilli powder: ¼ tsp
- Kashmiri chilli powder: ¼ tsp
- Ginger paste: ½ tsp
- Garlic paste: ½ tsp
- Refined oil: 2–3 tbsp

1. Soak mushrooms in buttermilk for 5–7 minutes.
2. Mix rice flour, both chilli powders, ginger paste and garlic paste with water to make a smooth batter.
3. Heat a non-stick flat pan and brush with oil.
4. Coat mushrooms in batter and place on the pan.
5. Cook each side for 2–3 minutes. Remove from flame.
6. Serve hot.

Dhingri Chatu Koftas

- Mushrooms: 300 gm stems removed and chopped finely
- Onion: 1 medium chopped
- Turmeric powder: ¼ tsp
- Green chillies: 2 chopped
- Garlic paste: ½ tsp
- Coriander leaves: 1 tbsp chopped
- Salt: ½ tsp
- Rice flour: 3 tbsp
- Mustard oil: 1 tbsp
- Refined oil: for deep frying

1. In a non-stick pan, place chopped mushrooms with ¼ tsp salt, once the water dries out remove from flame and keep aside.
2. Heat mustard oil. Lightly sauté onions with ¼ tsp salt until translucent.
3. Add garlic paste, turmeric powder, green chillies and coriander leaves.
4. Lightly stir fry for 3–4 minutes.
5. Add mushrooms and cook for 3–4 minutes.
6. Let the mixture cool, add rice flour and mix well.
7. Divide into 8 equal portions and shape into balls.
8. Deep fry the balls and keep aside to add to the gravy.

Coriander Masala

- Coriander seeds: 1 tsp
- Cumin seeds: 1 tsp
- Cloves: 3
- Dried Kashmiri chillies: 2
- Garlic: 3 big cloves
- Coriander leaves: 10 gm

1. In a dry non-stick pan, roast all the dry spices.
2. Grind to a paste with coriander leaves and a few teaspoons of water until smooth.

Gravy

- Coconut: 150 gm grated
- Mustard oil: 2 tbsp
- Ginger paste: 1 tsp
- Onion paste: 100 gm
- Brown sugar: 1 tsp
- Canned coconut milk: 1 cup
- Salt: 1¼ tsp
- Green chillies: 3 slit
- Coriander leaves: 60-65 gm
- Water: ½ cup + ¼ cup

1. Grind grated coconut with ½ cup water and strain to extract milk.
2. Heat oil in a non-stick pan. Add brown sugar and let it caramelize.
3. Add ginger paste and stir fry. Add onion paste and ½ tsp salt.
4. Cook for 15–20 minutes till light brown.
5. Add coriander masala and cook further.
6. Add coconut extract and canned coconut milk. Simmer for 10 minutes.
7. Add slit green chillies and coriander leaves. Simmer for 10 minutes.
8. Add remaining salt, ¼ cup water and let the gravy boil.
9. Then add the mushroom koftas and simmer for a few minutes.
10. Serve hot.

BAKED CRABS WITH CHINGUDI SUKHUA SAMBAL
(Dried Shrimp Sambal) (Serves 4)

The ever popular baked crabs with bechamel sauce in a new avatar, cooked with a coconut milk emulsion and an addition of local dried shrimp as a sambal. This was a refined second attempt as the first recipe with just pounded shrimp and a larger quantities of coconut milk left a pungent after taste. The use of dried shrimp is commonly seen in Asian cuisine.

Chingudi Sukhua Sambal

- Dried Shrimp: 25 gm
- Whole Kashmiri chillies: 4
- Dried red chillies: 4
- Garlic cloves: 6 sliced
- Shallots: 4 sliced
- Pink salt: 1½ tsp
- Tamarind paste: 2–3 tsp
- Coconut sugar: 1 tsp heaped
- Refined oil: 100 ml
- Salt: ½ tsp

1. Soak dried shrimp in hot water for 20 min. After which strain and wash thoroughly.
2. Grind in a mixer with 1 tbsp of water.
3. Soak both chillies in water for 30 min. Strain and chop.

SERVINGS

4. Heat 2 tbsp of oil in a pan. Add sliced shallots and fry till translucent with 1/2 tsp salt.
5. Add garlic and stir fry till golden.
6. Add tamarind paste and cook.
7. Add coconut sugar and cook.
8. Add both varieties of chopped chillies and cook for 15 min.
9. Remove from flame. Cool and grind in a mixer till smooth and transfer to a jar.
10. Heat remaining oil till it smokes and pour over the chilli paste.
11. Store in the refrigerator and use as needed.

Stuffing

- Crab shells: 2–3
- Crab meat: 250 gm chunks
- Coconut cream: 50 ml
- Refined oil: 35 ml + 1 tbsp
- Mustard powder: ¼ tsp
- Black Pepper powder: ¼ tsp
- Pink salt: 1–1¼ tsp
- Shallots: 3–4 sliced
- Curry leaves: 1–2 sprigs
- Green chillies: 1–2 chopped
- Turmeric powder: ¼ tsp
- Lemon juice: 2 tsp
- Rice flour: 1 tbsp heaped

1. Whisk chilled coconut cream with mustard powder, black pepper powder and ½ tsp pink salt.
2. Gradually add 35 ml oil to the coconut cream, add 1 tsp of lemon juice and whisk till it emulsifies.
3. Heat oil in a pan add shallots with ½ tsp salt till translucent.
4. Add curry leaves and green chillies and cook.
5. Add crab meat and mix gently ensuring the chunks are intact. Add turmeric powder.
6. Add 2–3 tsp of the chingudi sukhua sambal, mix gently.
7. Add rice flour and mix, turn off flame.
8. Add 4–5 tbsp of coconut cream mixture made earlier. Mix lightly.
9. Check seasoning and add 1 tsp lemon juice.
10. Transfer stuffing into boiled and cleaned shells.
11. Preheat oven at 180 °C for 10 min.
12. Place stuffed crab shells and bake for 15 min. After which grill for 5 min.
13. Serve hot with extra sambal and lemon wedges.

MAMA'S PATRAPODA MAACHA BHAATA (Steamed Yoghurt Fish with Rice) (Serves 4)

(Measuring cup size: 250 ml)

My mom's version of yoghurt fish is delightful. Teaming it with rice and steaming it all together makes for a great one pot meal, ofcourse you can choose to make it without the rice. She has always preferred using yellow mustard seeds over the black variety as the flavour is more subtle and there is less of an aftertaste. The ingredients are simple, very quick to prep with the final cooking just before you plate. It is a finger-licking meal!

- Rohu: 4 large round thick slices
- Mustard oil: 4 tbsp
- Yellow mustard seeds: 1 tbsp
- Poppy seeds: 1 tbsp
- Lime juice: 1 tbsp
- Garlic: 4 large cloves
- Green chillies: 2
- Yoghurt: 150 ml
- Turmeric powder: 1 tsp
- Salt: 2 tsp
- Red chilli powder: ½ tsp
- Coriander leaves: 1 tbsp chopped
- Basmati rice: ½ cup
- Banana leaves: 4–6 large pieces
- Tomatoes: 4 tbsp diced
- Ginger: 1 inch juliennes
- Green chillies: 2 slit
- Coriander leaves: 1–2 tbsp chopped

1. Soak mustard seeds, poppy seeds, garlic and 2 green chillies in water for 15 minutes, strain and place them in a mixer with 1 tbsp yoghurt. Grind to a smooth paste.
2. Add ½ tsp turmeric powder, red chilli powder, 1½ tsp salt, 1 tbsp chopped coriander leaves, the remaining yoghurt and 2 tbsp mustard oil to the paste. Mix well and keep this aside.
3. Marinate fish slices in lime juice, ½ tsp salt and ½ tsp turmeric powder for 30 minutes.
4. Soak rice in water for an hour and boil till three-fourths done. Strain and keep aside.
5. Heat 2 tbsp mustard oil in a non-stick flat pan over a low flame. Place the fish slices in the pan and cook for 3 minutes on each side and remove from flame and keep aside.
6. Pour the mustard–yoghurt paste made earlier over the fish pieces. Coat well and let them rest for 10 minutes.

7. Gently heat the banana leaves on an open flame to soften them. Lay them flat on the counter.
8. On each banana leaf, shiny side up place a few tablespoons of rice, a piece of fish and sufficient yoghurt paste, top with a tablespoon of tomatoes, a few juliennes of ginger, some coriander leaves and pieces of slit chillies.
9. Fold the banana leaves inwards. Tie with a string to make a parcel and place on a plate which fits in the steamer.
10. Boil water in the lower compartment of the steamer. Place the fish parcels in the upper compartment and steam for 10–15 minutes.
11. Remove the fish rice parcels and serve hot.

DALMA BELA (Dalma Bowl) (Serves 4)
(Measuring cup size: 250 ml)

Dalma is the mother of all food in Odisha. It is a basic dish of lentils cooked with vegetables, simple, wholesome and fuss-free. The origin of this dish dates back to the eleventh century when it was offered as prasad to Lord Jagannath in his temple at Puri. With the passing of time there has been an addition of onions and tubers, which is ususaly not a temple offering. The original recipe was made with chana dal but now arhar and moong dal are also used.

World over a one-pot version of popular dishes exists. This is an attempt to create a bowl, or bela as we Odiyas call it, which smells and tastes of everything home. A version that brings to mind the ever popular khow suey or even a donburi.

Dalma

- Arhar dal (pigeon peas): 200 gm
- Turmeric powder: ½ tsp
- Salt: 1 tsp
- Bay leaf: 1
- Ginger: 1 inch crushed
- Onion: 1 medium chopped
- Tomatoes: 1 large chopped
- Dried red chillies: 4
- Panch phoran: 1 tsp
- Refined oil: 1 tbsp

- Roasted cumin powder: ¾ tsp
- Roasted chilli powder: ½ tsp
- Sugar: ½ tsp
- Potato: 1
- Pumpkin: 125 gm
- Brinjal: ½ medium size
- Raw banana: ½
- Raw papaya: 150 gm
- Yam: 100 gm optional
- Water: 900 ml
- Ghee: 1 tbsp
- Cumin seeds: ¼ tsp

1. Boil 900 ml water in a deep pot. Add dal, turmeric powder, bay leaf and salt.
2. Boil for 15–20 minutes till soft.
3. Cut all vegetables into big squares, except onions and tomatoes which have to be chopped.
4. Add all the vegetables except onions and tomatoes to the dal and add crushed ginger. Cook till vegetables soften.
5. Meanwhile, heat oil in another wok/kadai.
6. Add panch phoran, 2 dried red chillies and let them crackle.
7. Add onions and sauté until golden.
8. Add tomatoes and sauté.
9. Add boiled dal and vegetables, followed by roasted cumin powder and chilli powder.
10. Add sugar and mix well. Check seasoning. and add tempering.
11. For tempering, heat ghee in a small pan.
12. Add 2 dried red chillies, cumin seeds and let them crackle.
13. Pour tempering over the dalma.

Aloo Jhuri (Fried Potato Sticks)

- Potatoes: 400 gm
- Curry leaves: 1 sprig
- Refined oil: to deep fry
- Salt: ½ tsp
- Chaat masala: ½ tsp
- Red chilli powder: a pinch
- Black peppercorns: 8 crushed
- Black salt: ½ tsp

1. Grind peppercorns.
2. Peel potatoes and slice into thin roundels.
3. Soak in water with ½ tsp salt and wash out all the starch.

4. Dry between two paper towels and allow the roundels to dry further for 15 minutes after removing the top paper towel.
5. Cut into thin juliennes.
6. Heat oil in a deep wok/kadai on a high flame.
7. Lower the flame, deep fry curry leaves and keep aside.
8. Add potatoes in batches to the wok/kadai and fry until golden.
9. Drain in a colander lined with a paper towel.
10. Transfer to a bowl and toss in curry leaves.
11. Add chaat masala, red chilli powder, crushed black peppercorns and black salt.
12. Toss well.

Crackling Saaga (Amaranth Leaves)

- Amaranth leaves: 50 gm
- Salt: a pinch
- Dried red chillies: 1–2
- Refined oil: to deep fry

1. Separate amaranth leaves from stem and wash thoroughly.
2. Spread on a paper towel and dry for 30 minutes.
3. Chop the leaves roughly.
4. Heat oil in a deep wok/kadai.
5. Fry dried red chillies, and keep aside.
6. Gently drop the amaranth leaves in the oil in batches and fry until crisp.
7. Drain in a colander lined with a paper towel.
8. Transfer to a serving dish.
9. Season with salt and add fried red chillies.
10. Serve immediately.

Photo on p. 191: Mama's Patrapoda Maacha Bhaata; Photo on p. 194: Dalma bela with all its accompaniments – Fried garlic, crackling saaga, gondharaj lemon salsa, aloo jhuri, chingudi checha and smoked mustard oil red chilli paste.

SERVINGS

Fried Garlic

- Garlic: 15 cloves
- Refined oil: to deep fry

1. Peel the garlic cloves.
2. Slice finely.
3. Heat oil in a deep wok/ kadai on a high flame.
4. Lower the flame, add the garlic slices and deep fry until golden brown.

Gondhoraj Lemon Salsa

- Onion: 1 large chopped
- Tomato: 1 large chopped
- Coriander leaves: 35 gm
- Green chilli: 1 chopped
- Gondhoraj lemon juice: ½ lemon
- Salt: ¼ tsp

1. Mix all of the ingredients to make a salsa.

Chingudi Checha Popcorn (Pounded Shrimp Popcorn)

- Shrimp: 175 gm
- Turmeric powder: ½ tsp
- Salt: 1 tsp
- Red chilli powder: ½ tsp
- Lime juice: 1½ tsp
- Ginger paste: ¾ tsp
- Garlic paste: 1 tsp
- Mustard oil: 1½ tbsp
- Onion: 1 small chopped
- Green chillies: 1–2 chopped
- Garlic: 2 large cloves
- Rice flour: 3½ tbsp
- Refined oil: to deep fry

1. Marinate shrimp with turmeric powder, salt, red chilli powder, lime juice, ginger paste and garlic paste for 2 hours.
2. Heat mustard oil in a non-stick pan and lightly fry the shrimp until golden.
3. Using a mortar and pestle, gently pound together the cooked shrimp with chopped onions, garlic and green chillies.
4. Transfer to a bowl and mix with rice flour.
5. Divide into small portions and shape roughly.
6. Heat refined oil in a deep wok/kadai on a high flame.

7. Lower the flame and deep fry the shrimp balls until golden.
8. Drain on a paper towel and serve hot.

Smoked Red Chilli Chutney

- Dried red chillies: 5–6
- Mustard oil: 2 tbsp
- Salt: ¼ tsp

1. Grind red chillies to a paste with a little water preferably on a grinding stone and transfer paste to a bowl.
2. Heat mustard oil to smoking point.
3. Add smoked oil to the ground chillies. Add salt and mix well.

To Assemble the Bowl

- Cooked Gobind bhog rice: 2 cups
- Fried peanuts: a fistful

1. At the bottom of the bowl, place a few spoons of warm rice.
2. Top with hot dalma, followed by crackling saaga, aloo jhuri and chingudi checha popcorn.
3. Add gondhoraj lemon salsa, along with some fried garlic, fried peanuts and smoked red chilli chutney.

Generations of Love

Growing up, there would be annual visits to Odisha with time spent at both sets of grandparents' homes. Those summer memories at my maternal abode rekindle a plethora of food stories. One such memory is of the kakra or the kakara pitha – since my Odia to English spellings need work! Aai, my maternal grandmother, was a fabulous cook and ensured that every grandchild's cravings were taken care of.

Kakara pitha is made as an offering to the Gods and it usually has semolina in it. But this recipe is cooked with whole wheat flour that creates a lovely texture. After Aai passed away and our annual visits to Odisha no longer took place, my mother makes these for us and till date, I get a box every few months. I got creative and wanted to see if savoury versions of this pitha could be made as a nice add-on for a tea table or a starter for an Odia meal. Mother to daughter, love does keep us alive!

TRADITIONAL KAKARA PITHA (Serves 6)
(Measuring cup size: 250 ml)

Filling

- Sugar: 75 ml
- Grated coconut: 1 cup
- Green cardamom powder: ¼ tsp

1. Place a deep wok/kadai over a medium flame. Add sugar and let it dissolve.
2. Add grated coconut and mix well with sugar, and cook until golden brown. Add cardamom powder and mix well.
3. Remove wok/kadai from flame and let the mixture cool.

Outer Cover

- Whole wheat flour: 1 cup
- Jaggery powder: ¼ cup
- Water: 200 ml
- Salt: a pinch

- Ghee: ½ tbsp
- Refined oil: to deep fry

1. Heat water in a deep wok/ kadai over a medium flame.
2. Add jaggery powder and boil a little.
3. Add whole wheat flour, and salt. Blend to a smooth semi-soft mixture with a spatula.
4. Remove from flame and transfer to a plate.
5. Cool, add ghee and knead gently.
6. Divide into 12 equal portions.
7. Flatten dough ball between the palms.
8. Shape with fingers to make a bowl-like shape.
9. Place 1½ tsp filling in the centre and close the edges to make a smooth ball with minimum cracks.
10. Heat oil in a deep wok /kadai and deep fry the balls until golden.
11. Drain excess oil from the balls on a paper towel.
12. Serve at room temperature.

Photo on this page: The Process of filling a Kakara pitha; Photo on p. 201: Traditional kakara pitha, Phulkobi kakara pitha, Chicken kakara pitha.

SERVINGS

PHULKOBI KAKARA PITHA AND CHICKEN KAKARA PITHA (Makes 12)

(Measuring cup size: 250 ml)

Chicken Filling

- Boneless chicken breast: 2 minced roughly
- Ginger: 3 inches
- Garlic: 3–4 big cloves
- Onion: 1 medium chopped
- Green chillies: 1–2
- Meat masala powder: ½ tsp
- Sugar: a pinch
- Salt: ¼ tsp
- Refined oil: 1 tbsp

1. Crush ginger, garlic and green chillies using a mortar and pestle.
2. Heat oil in a non-stick pan.
3. Add a little sugar and let it caramelize.
4. Add crushed ginger, garlic, and green chillies. Sauté lightly.
5. Add chopped onions and sauté until golden.
6. Add chicken and sauté with meat masala and salt.
7. Cook till chicken is done.
8. Remove pan from flame and keep aside.

Cauliflower Filling

- Cauliflower florets: 200 gm chopped finely
- Potatoes: 100 gm chopped into little cubes
- Ginger: 3 inches
- Onion: 1 medium chopped
- Green chillies: 2–3
- Salt: ½ tsp
- Oil: 2 tbsp
- Red chilli powder: ½ tsp
- Cheddar cheese: 75 gm

1. Crush ginger and green chillies using a mortar and pestle.
2. Heat oil in a non-stick pan.
3. Add crushed ginger and green chillies. Sauté lightly.
4. Add chopped onions and gently sauté until golden.
5. Add cauliflower and potatoes. Sauté with red chilli powder and salt.
6. Cover and cook until the cauliflower and potatoes are done.

7. This will take 5–7 minutes.
8. At this stage, add grated cheese and mix well.
9. Remove pan from flame and keep aside.

Outer Cover

- Whole wheat flour: 1 cup
- Roasted fennel seeds: ½ tsp crushed
- Water: 1 cup
- Salt: a pinch
- Black pepper powder: ½ tsp
- Ghee: ½ tbsp
- Refined oil: to deep fry

1. Heat water in a deep wok/kadai over a medium flame.
2. Add whole wheat flour, fennel powder, black pepper powder and salt. Blend to a smooth semi-soft mixture with a spatula.
3. Remove from flame and transfer to a plate. Cool. Add ghee and knead gently.
4. Divide into 12 equal portions.
5. Flatten dough ball between palms.
6. Shape with fingers to make a bowl-like shape.
7. Place 1½ tsp of either chicken or cauliflower filling in the centre and close the edges to make a smooth ball with minimum cracks.
8. Heat oil in a deep wok/kadai to deep fry the balls until golden.
9. Drain excess oil from the balls on a paper towel.
10. Serve with a roasted tomato salsa or chutney of choice.

PANIYA GUDA ATTA CAKE (Serves 4)

Liquid jaggery is a common accompaniment with pithas or rice cakes. A whole wheat tea cake made with this golden ingredient ticks all the boxes.

SERVINGS

- Butter: 50 gm
- Paniya guda (liquid jaggery): 65 ml
- Honey: 1½ tbsp
- Egg: 1
- Whole wheat flour: 85 gm
- Baking powder: ½ tsp
- Baking soda: ¼ tsp
- Green cardamom powder: ¼ tsp
- Cinnamon powder: ¼ tsp
- Dried ginger powder: ½ tsp
- Orange zest: ½ tbsp
- Vanilla essence: ½ tsp
- Milk: 1 tbsp
- Brown sugar: 1 tsp
- Orange slices: 3–4 to top (optional)

1. Ensure butter and egg are at room temperature.
2. Preheat oven to 180 °C for 10 minutes.
3. Grease and line a 5 x 3 inch loaf pan with parchment.
4. Sieve whole wheat flour with baking soda and baking powder.
5. With an electric mixer whisk the butter.
6. Add liquid jaggery and honey. Whisk at a low speed.
7. Add the egg and whisk. Add sieved flour followed by cardamom powder, cinnamon powder and dried ginger powder.
8. Cut and fold the batter. Add orange zest, vanilla essence and milk.
9. Pour the batter into the pan. Tap the pan on the counter to remove air pockets.
10. Sprinkle the top with brown sugar and bake for 25–27 minutes.
11. Insert a toothpick in the centre to check if the cake is done.
12. Remove from oven and cool in the pan for 10 minutes.
13. Take the cake out of the pan, remove the parchment and cool on a wire rack.
14. Decorate with orange slices and serve.

KORAPUT COFFEE FLAVOURED CHENNA BURNT BASQUE AND SALTED JAGGERY CARAMEL SAUCE

(Measuring cup size: 250 ml)

Odisha produces its own coffee in the tribal district of Koraput. Located at 3000 feet above sea level, the weather makes it ideal for coffee plantations.

The crop was introduced 90 years ago by the erstwhile royals of Jeypore. State Government initiatives under the Tribal Cooperative Board of Odisha have led to the promotion of the brand Koraput coffee. The coffee has a distinct flavour, it is medium roasted, dark-bodied and as it grows in the wild, it has organic value.

A coffee lover like me had to use it to create a delectable dessert somewhere between the traditional chenna podo and the Western cheesecake.

Burnt Basque

- Chenna: 175 gm
- Cream cheese: 30 gm
- Cream: 1 cup
- Granulated sugar: 100 gm
- Eggs: 2
- All-purpose flour: 15 gm
- Koraput coffee extract: 4 tbsp (5 heaped tsp in a filter with 125 ml water)
- Milk powder: 2 tbsp
- Vanilla essence: ½ tsp
- Salt: ⅙ tsp

1. Whip chenna with cream cheese, alternating with cream and granulated sugar.
2. Add milk powder and eggs one at a time, followed by vanilla essence, salt and Koraput coffee extract.
3. Fold in the flour.
4. Let the smooth batter rest for 20 minutes.
5. Preheat oven to 250°C for 12 minutes.
6. Meanwhile, grease and line a 7 inch diameter cake pan with parchment extending above the rim of the pan. Press along the edges to get a neat bottom edge. Grease the parchment with butter.
7. You can double line with parchment as well.
8. Pour in the batter and gently tap the pan on the counter.
9. Bake in the oven for 20 minutes at 250°C and then at 190°C for 5 minutes.
10. The centre will be wobbly and the top will have a burnt, shiny appearance.
11. Let the cheesecake rest at room temperature. The centre will drop rapidly and there will be a cracked appearance.
12. Chill in the refrigerator for an hour.
13. Serve with warm salted jaggery sauce and berries of choice.

Salted Jaggery Sauce

- Jaggery powder: 75 gm
- Salted butter: 45 gm
- Cream: 75 ml
- Koraput coffee extract: 2 tbsp
- Pink salt: ¾ tsp

1. In a heavy-bottom saucepan, place butter and jaggery powder. Whisk on a low flame until smooth.
2. Remove from flame, add cream and whisk.
3. Place the saucepan back on the flame, whisking continuously. Add the Koraput coffee extract and pink salt. Cook until it attains a sauce-like consistency.
4. Serve warm.

CHATUA PEANUT BUTTER COOKIES (Serves 6)

Chatua is a popular breakfast cereal made with Bengal gram. Popular versions in Odisha contain peanut powder and milk powder as well. This cereal does make a nice cookie to accompany your tea.

- Chatua: 100 gm
- Baking powder: ½ tsp
- Peanut butter: 2 tbsp heaped
- Jaggery powder: 50 gm
- Pink salt: ¼ tsp
- Ghee: 3 tbsp
- Chopped pistachios: a few

1. Preheat oven to 170°C for 10 minutes.
2. Sieve chatua and baking powder.
3. Add peanut butter and pink salt.
4. Mix jaggery powder and ghee together to form a smooth mixture and add to the chatua mix.
5. Divide mixture into 12 smooth balls of 20 gm each.
6. Flatten tops and press chopped pistachios on it. Bake for 25 minutes.
7. The cookies will harden on cooling.

BAKED RASABALI (Serves 4)

Most desserts in Odisha began as offerings to God. Rasabali originated in the district of Kendrapara, as an offering at the Baldev Jew temple. This is also offered at the Jagannath temple in Puri as a part of the Chhappan Bhog or 56 food items offered to the Lord.

The rasabali is a semi-flat deep fried ball of farmer's cottage cheese or chenna put into rasa or sweetened milk. This is a baked version, an attempt to simplify the process and avoid a few calories. I live in the hope that the gods are kind and the routine morning weigh-in doesn't show an increase on the scales!

Baked Bali

- Chenna: 300 gm (recipe on p. 166)
- Semolina: 1¼ tbsp
- Powdered sugar: 1½ tbsp
- Ghee: 1½ tbsp
- Granulated sugar: 1½ tbsp for caramel
- Green cardamom powder: ¼ tsp

1. Ensure chenna is soft.
2. Preheat oven to 180 °C for 20 minutes.
3. Using your hands lightly mix together chenna, semolina, powdered sugar and green cardamom powder.
4. Line a 6 inch square baking pan with parchment.
5. Apply ghee on the parchment.
6. In a non-stick pan, heat granulated sugar and let it caramelize.
7. Pour the caramel on to the parchment.
8. Now put the chenna mixture on it, patting with a spatula.
9. Apply a little ghee on the surface.
10. Place another parchment paper on top of the chenna mixture.
11. Bake for 30 minutes and remove the top parchment.
12. Shift the oven to grill option and bake for another 10 minutes.
13. Let the mixture cool in the oven then remove from oven and take it out of the tin.
14. Once it attains room temperature, refrigerate for 30 minutes to an hour.
15. Cut into cubes.

SERVINGS

Rasa

- Milk: 750 gm
- Condensed milk: 100 ml
- Cornflour: ¾ tsp dissolved in 2 tsp of water
- Cashew nuts: 8
- Raisins: 10–12
- Milk powder: 1 heaped tbsp dissolved in 2 tbsp of water
- Ghee: 1 tbsp
- Green cardamom: 3
- Salt: a pinch
- Saffron: a few strands

1. Heat ghee in a pan and stir fry cashew nuts and raisins until brown.
2. Heat milk in a pot. Let it reduce to three-fourths the quantity, then add condensed milk and cardamom pods.
3. Once it thickens a little, add milk powder. Let it simmer and then add cornflour to thicken just a little more as this is meant to be a thin rabri.
4. Add cashew nuts, raisins and salt.
5. Add the baked balis and let them simmer for 8–10 minutes.
6. Add saffron strands.
7. Remove from flame. Cool and then refrigerate.
8. Serve chilled.

Photo on p. 202: Paniya guda atta cake; Photo on p. 205: Koraput coffee in a chenna burnt baque with a salted jaggery caramel sauce; Photo on p. 208: Chatua peanut butter cookies; Photo on p. 211: Baked Rasabali.

For the Love of Food
(Suggested Menu Plan)

LET'S PARTY
Starters

Kulia Bhai's Junglee Mutton	p. 182
Khira Chingudi Saha Tentuli Paga	p. 172
Aloo Chop	p. 406
Phulkobi Kakara Pitha with Chutney of Choice	p. 200

Mains

Aamba Soriso Chicken	p. 171
Mama's Patrapoda Maacha	p. 190
Nayapalli Janhi Chatu Tatitya Basa	p. 161
Poi Putuli	p. 176
Nayapalli Posto Bara	p. 164
Abhi nana's Ou Khatta	p. 163
Crackling Saaga	p. 195
Steamed Rice	
Coconut Rotis	p. 182

Dessert

Baked Rasabali	p. 209

FAMILY TIME

Chenna Stuffed Pumpkin Flower Fritters	p. 181
Tankapani Soriso Manso	p. 159
Nadiya Rasa Bhaja Chenna Tarkari	p. 162
Chitau Pitha	p. 165

Dessert

Peda	p. 157

DARJEELING DAIRIES

Calling on the Queen of the Hills

Darjeeling is an idyllic hill station with tea plantations, colonial buildings, a toy train and warm people. I have been lucky to have folks from this town as an integral part of our home. Tea and tourism are Darjeeling's two main avenues of revenue. The original inhabitants are Lepchas, but the majority are Gorkhas, with a few Tibetans and some Bengalis. The local food reflects a melting pot of flavours.

Momos, a Tibetan addition to the cuisine, are popular and can be found in every nook and corner of the town. The popularity of momos can be attributed to the many vendors selling it on carts in every city of India. There now exists a Punjabi version too, called 'tandoori momos'!

Thaipo, the obese cousin of the momo, is distinct in size and has a flat bottom and is easier to shape. Eating one is equal to eating four regular momos! Shaphalay, on the other hand, is the fried stuffed pancake-style dumpling quite like a fried momo, but larger in size. After all, big is beautiful, right? You can't think skinny all the time!

The fillings, chutney and soup with most dishes are similar. The variants depend only on taste and different techniques of shaping. The spinach momo is an attempt to make the momo different. So just get the basics right and keep twisting and rolling to create a range of food!

CLEAR SOUP

Chicken Stock

- Chicken breast: 2
- Water: 500 ml
- Onion: 1 sliced
- Garlic: 5 cloves
- Salt: ½ tsp

1. Boil water in a deep pot.
2. Add all the ingredients and boil for 20 minutes.
3. Strain the liquid and keep aside.
4. Chicken can be shredded and used.

Vegetable Stock

- Potatoes: 300 gm peeled and quartered
- Onions: 100 gm peeled and quartered
- Garlic: 4 cloves
- Water: 500 ml

1. In a pressure cooker put potatoes, onion, garlic and water.
2. Pressure cook for two whistles.
3. Cool and strain.
4. Do not mash the potatoes, onions or garlic while straining.

Making the Soup

1. To make the soup, use the required quantity of stock.
2. Add vegetables or meat of choice and boil.
3. Check seasoning and add a dash of soy sauce.
4. Top with spring onions and coriander leaves.

SPICY CHUTNEY

- Tomatoes: 2
- Dried red chillies: 3
- Kashmiri chillies: 3
- Sesame seeds: 1 tbsp
- Salt: ½ tsp

1. Microwave or boil tomatoes till soft.
2. Roast sesame seeds and both varieties of chillies.
3. Grind all the ingredients with salt, in a mixer till smooth.

THAIPO, MOMO AND SHAPHALAY FILLING

Chicken Filling

- Chicken mince: 250 gm
- Onions: 130 gm chopped
- Ginger: 1 tbsp minced
- Garlic: 4 cloves minced
- Spring onions: 20 gm white portion
- MSG/vegetable stock cube: ½ tsp/ ½ cube
- Salt: ½–¾ tsp
- Black pepper powder: ½ tsp
- Refined oil: 3 tbsp
- Dark soy sauce: 1 tbsp

1. Mix all the ingredients to make a smooth mixture.
2. Use it raw for momos and thaipo.

Vegetable Filling

- Carrots: 80 gm
- Cabbage: 80 gm
- Onions: 80 gm
- Cottage cheese: 80 gm
- Salt: 1 tsp
- MSG/vegetable stock cube: a pinch/ ½ cube
- Butter: 80 gm

1. Chop all the vegetables finely.
2. Add salt, butter, MSG/vegetable stock cube dissolved in 1 tbsp water and mix.

Stir Fried Potato Filling

- Potatoes: 2 large boiled
- Onion: 1 large chopped
- Garlic: 4 cloves
- Coriander leaves: 1½ tbsp chopped
- Vegetable stock cube: ½
- Refined oil: 2 tbsp
- Salt: ½ tsp

1. Heat oil in a pan.
2. Stir fry onions and garlic.
3. Crush boiled potatoes and add.
4. Add stock cube dissolved in a 1 tbsp water.
5. Add coriander leaves and salt. Mix well and remove from flame.

THAIPO (Serves 4)

- All purpose flour: 250 gm
- Active dry yeast: 1 tsp
- Lukewarm water: 175 ml

1. Bloom yeast in 100 ml of lukewarm water for 8 minutes.
2. Make a well in the flour, add yeast and remaining water.
3. Knead dough well and let it proof for 1½ hours.
4. After which knock down the dough and give it a stretch.
5. Divide into 6 balls.

To Make Thaipo Buns

- Vegetable/Chicken filling: recipe on p. 216

1. Divide filling into 6 portions.
2. Roll out the dough balls keeping the centre thick and thinning the sides.
3. Now flatten the centre mound.

4. While the disc is on the tabletop, place the chicken/vegetable filling in the centre then start pleating from one side till the entire bun is pleated.
5. The bottom of the bun has to be flat.
6. Twist the top and push down towards the centre.
7. Heat a steamer with water in the bottom pan.
8. Apply a little oil on the surface of the perforated upper compartment to prevent the buns from sticking. Steam for 15 minutes or till the buns are done. Serve hot.

Thaipo is best eaten smeared with chutney and dipped in a vegetarian/non-vegetarian soup.

SHAPHALAY (Deep Fried Stuffed Pancake) (Serves 4)

- All-purpose flour: 150 gm
- Water: 80 ml
- Salt: ½ tsp
- Refined oil: to deep fry

1. Make a dough with flour, salt and water like you would for rotis.

Stuffed Pancake

- Stir Fried Potato/Chicken Filling: recipe on pp. 214, 215

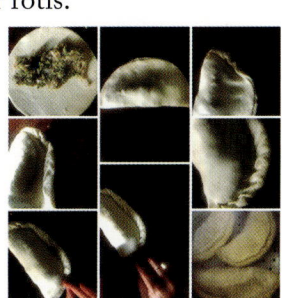

1. Divide the dough into 4 balls.
2. Roll into discs around 5–6 inches in diameter.
3. Place cooked mixture on one half of the circle and cover with the other half.
4. Pinch the dough from one end and turn it inward to secure the filling.
5. After this, continue pinching till the end.
6. Heat oil in a pan and deep fry the shaphalay.
7. Serve hot with chutney.

Stir fry chicken/potato filling in a little oil.

Photo on p. 217: The process of making Thaipo; Photo on p. 218: Thaipo with spicy chutney; Photo on p. 219: The process of making the shaphalays.

SPINACH MOMOS (Serves 6)

- Spinach: 100 gm
- All-purpose flour: 300 gm
- Salt: ¾ tsp

1. Purée spinach with a pinch of salt.
2. Mix purée with flour to make a soft dough.
3. Add water to the dough only if required while kneading.
4. Divide the dough into 24 small balls.
5. Roll each ball into small discs, approximately 3 inches, ensuring the disc is thin.
6. Place 1½ tsp of vegetable mixture in the centre.
7. Fold disc upwards in half and make a pleat at the corner to seal.
8. Continue making pleats until you reach midway.
9. Join the plain back of the disc to the pleated front. Pinch the ends tight and inwards.
10. Fill the bottom compartment of the steamer with water and boil. Place the momos on the upper compartment of the steamer and steam until done.
11. Serve with chutney and thukpa.

THUKPA (Serves 2)

- Vegetable/Chicken stock: 400 ml
- Noodles: 60 gm boiled and drained
- Tomato: ½ large chopped
- Cabbage: 30 gm sliced
- Mushroom: 30 gm sliced
- Carrot: 30 gm julienned
- Capsicum: 15 gm sliced
- Beans: 15 gm
- Spring onion: 15 gm chopped
- Green chilli: 1
- Ginger: 1 inch
- Garlic: 1 clove
- Salt: ½ tsp
- Turmeric powder: ⅛ tsp
- Soy sauce: 1 tsp
- Home-made Chinese chilli paste: ¾ tsp
- Vinegar: 1 tsp
- MSG: a pinch (optional)
- Refined oil: ½ tbsp
- Coriander leaves: 2 tbsp chopped

SERVINGS

1. Using a mortar and pestle, pound ginger, garlic and green chillies.
2. Heat oil in a non-stick pan.
3. Sauté the chilli–ginger–garlic mixture, add tomatoes and let it soften.
4. Add salt and turmeric powder.
5. Add beans and mushrooms and let them cook. Add carrot and capsicum.
6. Add stock followed by soy sauce and MSG if desired.
7. Add cabbage, noodles boil for 4–5 minutes and add vinegar and home-made chinese chilli paste.
8. Top with spring onions and coriander leaves. Serve hot.

If making chicken thukpa, use chicken stock and follow the same procedure with the addition of chicken pieces while stir frying.

PLAIN MOMOS (Serves 6)

- All-purpose flour: 300 gm
- Water: 150 ml
- Salt: ¾ tsp

1. Knead all the ingredients into a soft dough.
2. Divide into 24–26 balls. Roll into thin discs.
3. Place ½ tsp of the vegetable/chicken filling in the centre.
4. Pleat as per choice.
5. Fill the bottom compartment of the steamer with water and boil.
6. Place the momos on the upper compartment of the steamer and steam till done.
7. Serve with chutney and thukpa.

Photo on p. 220: Shaphalays; Photo on p. 223: Thukpa and Spinach momos.

SERVINGS

Tea and Cake

Darjeeling First Flush Tea is considered to be one of the finest in the world as it has a brisk floral aroma with a light hue. However, even the other leaf teas are as good. The tea stalls at the Chowrasta are a paradisal setting to sample how the locals drink their chai! The masala chai cake is a celebration of the flavour of Darjeeling tea. The combination of a few Indian spices infused in it enhances the flavour. I have come across recipes in the past which offer a frosting to give an additional flavour but this cake works really well without it. Brown sugar also gives it a darker hue.

DARJEELING MASALA CHAI CAKE (Serves 4)

- All-purpose flour: 150 gm
- Baking powder: 1 tsp
- Eggs: 2 large (room temperature)
- Powdered sugar: 120 gm
- Brown sugar: 50 gm
- Butter: 110 gm
- Tea leaves: 2 tsp
- Tea dust: 1 tsp
- All spice powder: ¼ tsp
- Dried ginger powder: ½ tsp
- Green cardamom powder: ½ tsp
- Vanilla/Cardamom essence: ½ tsp
- Milk: 60 ml
- Water: 75 ml

1. Ensure eggs and butter are at room temperature. Sieve flour and baking powder together.
2. Boil tea leaves and tea dust in 75 ml water for 4–5 minutes.
3. Strain and add 60 ml milk. Let it cool.
4. Preheat oven to to 175 °C for 8–10 minutes.
5. Measure 80 ml of the milk tea and keep aside, discarding the rest.
6. Whisk butter and both the sugars together until creamy.
7. Add eggs and whisk further. Add all the spice powders.
8. Add vanilla/cardamom essence and milk tea. Add sieved flour.
9. Fold flour mixture into the batter.and transfer into a 9 inch parchment-lined pan.
10. Bake for 30–35 minutes. Insert a toothpick in the centre it should comes out clean.
11. Cool in the pan and tranfer to a wire rack. Remove parchment from cake.
12. Serve with a dusting of powdered sugar.

Photo on p. 225: Darjeeling masala chai cake.

For the Love of Food
(Suggested Menu Plan)

LET'S PARTY

Starters

Chicken Momos with Spicy Chutney	pp. 222, 216
Spinach Momos with Spicy Chutney	pp. 221, 216
Bhai's Asian Dry Red Chilli Prawns	p. 75
Salt and Pepper Tofu with Simple Chinese Dipping Sauce	p. 76

Mains

Soya Nugget Balls in Barbecue Sauce	p. 417
Chilli Long Beans	p. 418
Twice-Fried Lotus Stem	p. 420
Steamed Asian Chicken with Chilli Oil	p. 444
Soy Ginger Salmon	p. 441
Cucumber Salad	
Steamed Rice	

Dessert

Gingernut, Coconut and Lime Cheesecake	p. 304

FAMILY TIME

Thaipo with Clear Soup	pp. 217, 215
or	
'Chindese' Chopsuey	p. 475

Dessert

Darjeeling Masala Chai Cake	p. 224

KONKAN EXPRESS

The Four S Trail

There is no denying my love for South Indian food. Having friends from the Konkan region who have opened their homes and hearts to us is an added benefit. This is yet another story of recipes passed down from a mother. One phone call to Mangala Aunty and I received not just the recipes but a carton full of masalas and goodies! I truly believe sharing recipes is like sharing your table. Late night chats with her daughter, Chaitra, who is a dear friend herself despite us living in different time zones, helped me learn the right texture and technique of cooking their cuisine, sometimes with video call demonstrations.

Konkanis originated on the banks the of Saraswati river and hence were called Saraswats. Later, they moved to settle down across Goa, Western Maharashtra and Karnataka, known as the Konkan belt. Their cuisine was influenced by the local produce of the region as well as by traders from other lands like the Portuguese and the Dutch. As a result of this, the food of this region has the 4 S's – sweet, spicy, sour and salt. It is sweet by virtue of jaggery and coconut, spicy because of fiery chillies, ginger and garlic, and sour from the use of kokum and tamarind. Seafood and meat are an integral part of the cuisine.

The story behind the food photograph add another colourful dimension, taking me back to a time when I was running out of props like serviettes and kitchen towels in different colours. The second lockdown in India, and stores being shut, led to DIY experiment with tie-and-dye, using turmeric and spinach as natural colours on basic cotton fabric. It was all about food there too!

* 228

MANGALA AUNTY'S GREEN MUTTON CURRY

(Serves 4)

(Measuring cup size: 250 ml)

- Mutton: 1 kg curry cut

Masala Paste

- Green chillies: 3–4
- Black peppercorns: 2 tsp
- Coriander seeds: 1 tsp
- Cumin seeds: 1 tsp
- Ginger: 2 inches chopped
- Garlic: 1 clove
- Cloves: 6–8
- Cinnamon: 2 inch stick
- Poppy seeds: 2 tsp
- Coriander leaves: ½ cup chopped
- Onion: 1 chopped
- Refined oil: 1½ tbsp

1. Heat oil in a pan, add all the whole spices and poppy seeds. Sauté.
2. Add ginger, garlic, onion and sauté. Remove from flame and cool.
3. Add coriander leaves, green chillies and grind to a paste in a mixer.

Mutton Gravy

- Onions: 3 chopped
- Tomatoes: 3 puréed
- Fenugreek leaves: ¾ cup
- Refined oil: 2–3 tbsp
- Salt: 1 tsp
- Coriander leaves: 2 sprigs chopped (optional)

1. Heat oil in a pressure cooker and sauté onions with ¼ tsp salt till brown.
2. Add fenugreek leaves and cook.
3. Add masala paste made earlier and cook well.
4. Add puréed tomatoes and remaining salt. Cook for 15 minutes.
5. Add mutton and cook in the masala for 15 minutes, add 150 ml water and pressure cook for two whistles. Open pressure cooker.
6. Let the mutton simmer for 20 minutes.
7. Garnish with chopped coriander leaves (optional) and serve hot.

Photo on p. 231 (Top to bottom): Red chutney, Mangla aunty's green mutton curry, Chaitra's pan polo, Potato saagu, Chaitra's alasande upkari, Mangalorean ghassi with lobia and spinach.

MANGALOREAN GASSI WITH LOBIA AND SPINACH (Serves 4)

(Measuring cup size: 150 ml)

Masala Paste

- Coriander seeds: 1½ tsp
- Fenugreek seeds: a pinch
- Mustard seeds: ¼ tsp
- Cumin seeds: ¼ tsp
- Dried red chillies: 2
- Refined oil: 1½ tbsp
- Onion: 1 large sliced
- Turmeric powder: ¼ tsp
- Garlic: 3–4 cloves chopped
- Tamarind paste: 1 tsp
- Grated coconut: 4 tbsp heaped

1. Dry roast coriander seeds, cumin seeds, fenugreek seeds, mustard seeds and dried red chillies in a pan on a low flame and reserve. Heat oil and sauté onions till brown.
2. Add turmeric powder, garlic, grated coconut and tamarind paste, cook for 5–7 minutes.
3. Turn off the flame and let the mixture cool.
4. Grind the onion and coconut mixture with the reserved roasted spices to a fine paste.

Gassi

- Black-eyed kidney beans (lobia): 1 cup
- Spinach: 1 cup roughly chopped
- Salt: 1 tsp
- Turmeric powder: ½ tsp
- Onion: 1 sliced
- Tomatoes: 1½ finely chopped
- Coconut milk: 1 cup
- Refined oil: 1½ tbsp
- Curry leaves: 1 sprig
- Cinnamon: 1 inch stick
- Carom seeds: ¼ tsp
- Water: 400 ml

1. Soak black-eyed kidney beans overnight in water. Wash and add 400 ml water.
2. Pressure cook with ½ tsp salt and turmeric powder for 3–4 whistles.
3. Strain black-eyed kidney beans and reserve water. Heat oil in a wok/kadai, add carom seeds, followed by cinnamon and curry leaves. Let them crackle.
4. Add sliced onions and fry them for 3–4 minutes, then add masala paste and cook for 10 minutes. Add remaining salt.

5. Add tomatoes and cook until the oil separates.
6. Add black-eyed kidney beans, spinach and mix well.
7. Add reserved water from the boiled black-eyed kidney beans.
8. Add coconut milk and simmer for 20 minutes until done. Serve hot.

POTATO SAAGU (Serves 4)

- Potatoes: 4 boiled
- Turmeric powder: ½ tsp
- Mustard seeds: 1 tsp
- Salt: 1 tsp
- Refined oil: 1½ tbsp
- Green chillies: 1–2 slit
- Asafoetida powder: ¼ tsp
- Curry leaves: 1 sprig
- Warm water: 75 ml
- Coriander leaves: ½ cup chopped

1. Heat oil in a pan and crackle mustard seeds, curry leaves. Add turmeric powder.
2. Roughly crush the potatoes and add along with asafoetida powder, green chillies and salt.
3. Cook for 3–4 minutes and then add 75 ml warm water.
4. Give the potatoes a quick mix.
5. Serve hot garnished with chopped coriander.

RED CHUTNEY
(Measuring cup size: 250 ml)

- Coconut: ¼ cup grated
- Tamarind paste: 1 tsp
- Coriander seeds: 1½ tsp
- Cumin seeds: ½ tsp
- Clove: 1
- Cinnamon: 1 inch stick
- Dried red chillies: 2
- Salt: ¾–1 tsp
- Jaggery: ½ tsp (optional)

> This spicy chutney can be spread on a dosa before adding the potato saagu as a filling.

1. Dry roast whole spices and dried red chillies on a pan and grind with grated coconut, tamarind paste, jaggery and a few tablespoons of water in a mixer till smooth.
2. Add salt and mix well. Transfer to a bowl and serve.

CHAITRA'S ALASANDE UPKARI (Yard-long Beans and Peanut Masala) (Serves 4)

(Measuring cup size: 250 ml)

- Barbati (Yard-long beans): 2 cups
- Raw peanuts: ½ cup
- Refined oil: 1 tbsp
- Mustard seeds: ½ tsp
- Chana dal: ½ tsp
- Urad dal: ½ tsp
- Asafoetida powder: a pinch
- Green chillies: 2–3 slit
- Salt: 1 tsp
- Grated coconut: 2 tsp heaped

1. Wash beans, trim the ends and cut beans into inch-sized pieces.
2. Heat oil in a pan. Add mustard seeds, chana dal, urad dal and peanuts.
3. Sauté on a low flame to ensure that the ingredients do not burn.
4. Add a pinch of asafoetida powder followed by green chillies.
5. Add beans, ¼ cup water and salt. Cover and cook for 8–10 minutes on a medium flame.
6. When the water has dried up and the beans are cooked, turn off the flame and garnish with grated coconut and serve.

CHAITRA'S PAN POLO (Rice Pancakes) (Serves 4)

(Measuring cup size: 150 ml)

- Sona masoori rice: 2 cups
- Coconut: 1½ cups grated
- Water: 500–550 ml
- Salt: 1–1½ tsp

SERVINGS

1. Wash rice thoroughly and soak in water for 3–4 hours.
2. Strain and grind the rice with a little water till semi-smooth.
3. Add grated coconut and grind till smooth. Transfer to a bowl.
4. Add remaining water gradually and mix batter thoroughly after adding salt.
5. Heat a wide flat pan which has a rim on a high flame.
6. Pour a ladle of batter and let it spread on the pan evenly.
7. The batter will become lacy. Cover with a lid and cook for 2 minutes.
8. Remove lid and cook further for a minute. Fold into a triangle and serve.

Aambe Phool

MANGO CUSTARD MINI PIES TOPPED WITH RASAYAN (Serves 6)

- Puff pastry: 7 inch square
- Ghee: to brush moulds lightly
- Mango purée: 100 ml
- Mango jam: 1 tbsp heaped
- Powdered sugar: 1 tbsp
- Milk: 125 ml
- Custard powder: 3 tbsp
- Cornflour: 2–3 tsp
- Salt: a pinch
- Cashew nuts: a few fried

Filling

1. Dissolve custard powder in milk in a thick-bottom pan.
2. Add powdered sugar and salt. Cook on a medium flame till thick.
3. Add jam and mix well. Then add cornflour dissolved in a tablespoon of water.
4. Let the custard thicken a little.
5. Remove from flame and let the custard cool. Add mango purée and mix with a spatula till smooth.
6. Transfer to a thick-bottom saucepan and give it a boil and let the mixture thicken to piping consistency.
7. Keep mango custard aside and cool.

SERVINGS

Flowers

1. Grease 12 moulds of a mini muffin pan with ghee.
2. Preheat oven to 200 °C for 10 minutes.
3. Roll puff pastry to a rectangle 7 x 21 inches approximately and cut into 12 equal squares.
4. Place each puff pastry square into the moulds and press down in the middle.
5. Pipe mango filling into each puff pastry square.
6. Fold the edges of the puff pastry squares inwards over the filling to make a flower.
7. Brush over with a little ghee. Bake in oven for 18–20 minutes till golden.
8. Remove from the mould and top each flower with fried cashew nuts.
9. Serve hot with rasayan.

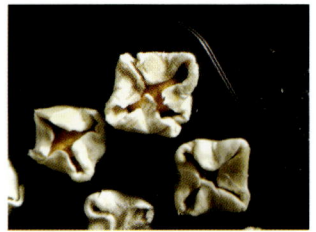

Rasayan

- Ghee: 2 tsp
- Cashew nuts: 6
- Coconut milk: 300 ml
- Condensed milk: 2 tbsp
- Jaggery powder: 2 tbsp
- Cinnamon powder: ½ tsp
- Green cardamom powder: ½ tsp
- Black pepper powder: ½ tsp
- Salt: a pinch

1. Heat ghee in a pan and fry cashew nuts. Remove from pan, cool and chop.
2. In the same pan, add condensed milk and let it cook in the remaining ghee.
3. Add coconut milk and keep stirring.
4. Add all the spice powders and salt.
5. Add jaggery powder and let the rasayan thicken to a coating consistency and a light brown colour. Serve at room temperature with mango custard filled flowers.

Photo on pg 235: Aambe phool; Photos on pg 236: The process of making the aambe phool.

For the Love of Food
(Suggested Menu Plan)

LET'S PARTY

Starters

Vegetable Paniyaram	p. 22
Hurida Koli	p. 98
Mushroom Pepper Fry	p. 260
Egg Roast	p. 79

Mains

Spicy Rasam	p. 94
Vadas	p. 96
Mangala Aunty's Green Mutton Curry	p. 229
Anju's Prawn Green Mango Curry	p. 259
Chaitra's Alasande Upkari	p. 233
Potato Saagu	p. 232
Steamed Rice	
Papad	

Dessert

Mango Custard Mini Pies Topped with Rasayan	p. 234

FAMILY TIME

Mangalorean Gassi with Lobia and Spinach	p. 230
Anju's Nadan Kozhi Curry	p. 255
Chaitra's Pan Polo	p. 233
Red Chutney	p. 232

Dessert

Unniyappam with Indian Tres Leche	p. 264

HYDERABADI CUISINE

Eid Mubarak - Dastarkhan

I am all for celebrating festivals. Come Eid each year, a meal befitting the occasion has to be made and then I hope that some sevaiyan comes from a friend's home. Dastarkhan is a traditional meal in Deccani or Hyderabadi cuisine, usually a five-course meal laid out on a cloth on the floor and eaten with your fingers.

Hyderabad became an independent state when one of the viceroys of the Mughal Empire, Asaf Jah, broke away. His descendants called themselves Nizams. Modern Hyderabadi cuisine evolved under the Nizams. They were extremely wealthy and to date the Nizam's jewels are considered to be some of the rarest. The city developed its own unique cultural and culinary heritage with a strong Indo-Muslim integration. Hyderabadi Hindi is an example of that and something I have always enjoyed listening to. The Nizam's kitchen by itself created 49 varieties of biryani. This was the result of the re-creation of Turkish and Arabic dishes with regional influences.

Interestingly, the cuisine crossed the boundaries of royalty and was adapted by the middle classes as well. Dalcha is a popular Hyderabadi dish which is also commonly cooked in a lot of Odia Muslim homes – probably because some of these families are from Berhampur, a district in Odisha which shares its borders with Andhra Pradesh. This recipe is an adaptation from one such home. Dried mango kernels are used as a souring agent in Odia cuisine and the same has been adapted by them here as well. 'Korma' is the Urdu word for braising – a cooking technique which involves lightly frying the main ingredient and then stewing it in a gravy in a sealed container. There are many ways of making this dish and multiple experiments have led to my version.

Peanuts, desiccated coconut and tamarind are also used in this cuisine, a South Indian adaptation. The perfect picture of national integration on the table!

ALI FAMILY DALCHA (Serves 4)

- Chana dal: 175 gm
- Turmeric powder: ½ tsp
- Salt: ½ tsp

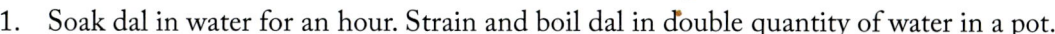

1. Soak dal in water for an hour. Strain and boil dal in double quantity of water in a pot.
2. Add turmeric powder and salt.
3. Boil the dal till soft but not mushy.
4. Mash the dal gently and keep aside.

An increase in the quantity of dal up to 350 gm is an option, but water, spices and seasoning will have to be adjusted. The end product will be more yellow in appearance and watery.

- Mutton: 1 kg curry cut
- Onions: 2 large sliced
- Ginger–garlic paste: 2 tsp
- Tomatoes: 4 medium chopped
- Brinjals: 2 long cut into thick roundels
- Green chillies: 4 slit
- Coriander leaves: 1 small bunch chopped
- Refined oil: 3 tbsp
- Red chilli powder: 1 tsp
- Kashmiri chilli powder: 1 tsp
- Coriander powder: 2 tsp
- Salt: 1½ tsp
- Tamarind paste: 4 tsp
- Dry mango kernels: 2 soaked in water

1. Heat oil in a thick-bottom pan. Add sliced onions, ½ tsp salt and sauté till brown.
2. Add ginger–garlic paste. Cook further and add coriander powder and both chilli powders.
3. Add mutton, 1 tsp salt and cook until brown.
4. Cover and cook on a medium flame for 45 minutes to 1 hour, stirring occasionally and adding a little water as required so that it does not stick to the bottom of the pan. (For a quicker version, pressure cook for two whistles and simmer.)
5. Once the mutton is cooked, add tomatoes and cook till the oil separates. This will take 15–20 minutes.
6. Add brinjals and let them cook, then add green chillies.
7. Add 250–350 ml of water gradually, followed by the mashed chana dal.
8. Add tamarind paste and the soaked mango kernels and let the dalcha simmer for some time until dal and mutton blend together. It should not become a thick gravy.
9. Check seasoning, add more salt if needed. Serve hot, garnished with coriander leaves.

MURGH KORMA (Serves 4)

- Chicken: 1½ kg curry cut
- Ghee: 3–4 tbsp
- Onions: 4 sliced
- Black peppercorns: 6–7
- Cloves: 6–7
- Black cardamoms: 2
- Green cardamoms: 4
- Ginger paste: 1½ tsp
- Garlic paste: 1½ tsp
- Coriander powder: 4 tsp
- Red chilli powder: 1 tsp
- Salt: 1½ tsp
- Home-made garam masala: 1 tsp
- Yoghurt: 350 gm
- Cream: 75 ml
- Almonds slivers: 2 tbsp

1. Heat ghee in a non-stick pot.
2. Fry onions till brown. Remove onions and keep aside.
3. Mix fried onions with yoghurt and grind in a mixer.
4. In the pot used earlier, add the whole spices and let them crackle.
5. Add ginger–garlic paste and sauté.
6. Add chicken and sear with some salt until brown.
7. Add all the spice powders and sauté the chicken further.
8. Add onion–yoghurt paste and remaining salt, mix well.
9. Cover with a lid tightly, cook for 25–30 minutes on a low flame till done.
10. Finish with whipped cream and almond slivers.

BAGHARA RICE (Serves 4)

- Ghee: 3 tbsp
- Rice: 275 gm
- Onions: 2 large
- Black cardamom: 1
- Green cardamoms: 2
- Cinnamon: 2 inch stick
- Cloves: 3–4
- Black peppercorns: 6–8
- Cumin seeds: ¼ tsp
- Water: 600 ml
- Almonds: 50 gm
- Cashew nuts: 50 gm
- Peanuts: 50 gm
- Salt: to taste

1. Soak rice in water for 30 minutes strain and keep aside. Slice onions into thin roundels.
2. In a deep pot, heat 2 tbsp ghee, add onions and sauté till brown.
3. Remove onions and let cool till crisp.
4. In the same pot, add all the whole spices and let them crackle. Add rice and a little salt, stir fry and add water.
5. Cover the pot with a lid, place a muslin cloth over the lid and knot it tightly. Slow cook for 10 minutes.
6. Open the lid, and use a fork to fluff the rice.
7. In a separate pan, heat 1 tbsp ghee. Add almonds, cashew nuts and peanuts and let them brown. Let nuts cool and crisp up.
8. Transfer rice to a serving platter and top with nuts and fried crisp onions. Serve hot.

MIRCH BHINDI KA SAALAN (Serves 4)

- Saalan mirch: 200 gm
- Bhindi (Okra): 100 gm
- Refined oil: 2 tbsp
- Salt: ½ tsp

1. Heat oil in a pan, add saalan mirch with ¼ tsp salt. When the skin softens remove from pan and keep aside. In the same pan fry okra with ¼ tsp salt and keep aside.

Paste

- Desiccated coconut powder: 2 tbsp
- Peanuts: 2 tbsp
- Sesame seeds: 2 tbsp
- Cumin seeds: 2 tsp
- Coriander seeds: 2 tsp
- Onion: 1 large sliced
- Refined oil: 1 tsp
- Turmeric powder: ¾ tsp
- Salt: ¾ tsp

1. Dry roast desiccated coconut powder, peanuts, sesame seeds, cumin seeds and coriander seeds.

SERVINGS

2. Grind to a paste with onion, oil and a little water till smooth.
3. Add turmeric powder and salt, keep aside.

Gravy

- Refined oil: 3 tbsp
- Nigella seeds: 1 tsp
- Mustard seeds: 1 tsp
- Fenugreek seeds: 1 tsp
- Ginger–garlic paste: 2 tsp
- Tamarind paste: 2 tsp
- Tomato: 1 large sliced
- Jaggery: ½ tsp
- Hot water: 400 ml

1. Heat oil in a pan.
2. Add nigella seeds, mustard seeds and fenugreek. Let them crackle.
3. Add ginger–garlic paste. Cook well and then add the ground paste made earlier.
4. Let it cook until the oil separates, then add 100 ml water.
5. Add tamarind paste and cook.
6. Add tomato and jaggery.
7. Cover and cook for 7–8 minutes.
8. Add 300 ml of hot water and boil. Add fried saalan mirch and okra.
9. Let the gravy simmer for 10 minutes.
10. Serve hot.

Photo on p. 245 (Clockwise): Ali Family Dalcha, Murgh Qorma, Arshi's Sabut Gobi ka Musallam, Hyderabadi Lauki Paneer ke Kofte, Baghara Rice and Mirch Bhindi ka Saalan.

HYDERABADI LAUKI PANEER KE KOFTE (Serves 4)

Kofta

- Bottle gourd: 120 gm (peel, grate and squeeze to remove water)
- Cottage cheese: 75 gm
- Gram flour: 30 gm
- Coriander chopped: 2 tbsp
- Turmeric powder: ¼ tsp
- Red chilli powder: ¼ tsp
- Salt: ¼ tsp
- Refined oil: to deep fry

1. Mix all the ingredients well.
2. Rub a little oil on your palms.
3. Divide the mixture into 8 balls and deep fry.

White Paste

- Desiccated coconut powder: 2 tbsp
- Charmagaz: 3 tbsp
- Almonds: 6
- Poppy seeds: 3 tsp

1. Soak almonds in water overnight and peel.
2. Add all the remaining ingredients to the almonds and grind to a paste.

Gravy

- Yoghurt: 200 ml
- Sugar: 1½ tsp
- Tomato purée: 3 tbsp
- Onion: 1 large sliced and fried golden
- Refined oil: 1–2 tbsp
- Cinnamon: 2 inch stick
- Green cardamoms: 2
- Ginger–garlic paste: 2 tbsp
- Red chilli powder: ½ tsp
- Kashmiri chilli powder: ½ tsp
- Green chillies: 2 slit
- Turmeric powder: ¼ tsp
- Coriander leaves: 1 tbsp chopped
- Mint leaves: 1 tbsp chopped
- Salt: 1–2 tsp

1. Mix fried onions with the yoghurt. Add sugar and grind in a mixer to make a smooth brown paste.

2. Heat oil in a non-stick pan.
3. Add whole spices and let them crackle. Add ginger–garlic paste and stir.
4. Add white paste and cook for 5 minutes after which add turmeric powder, both chilli powders, green chillies and cook.
5. Add tomato purée and cook until the oil separates.
6. Now, add brown onion paste and cook on a low flame.
7. Add coriander leaves and mint leaves. Add salt.
8. Once the gravy is cooked, add koftas and toss gently.
9. Add desired quantity of water and let the gravy simmer.
10. Check seasoning and remove from flame. Serve hot.

ARSHI'S GOBI MUSALLAM (Serves 4)

- Cauliflower: 750 gm, remove leaves
- Cottage cheese: 125 gm mashed
- Cumin seeds: ½ tsp
- Onion: 1 medium chopped
- Ginger paste: 1 tsp
- Garlic paste: 1 tsp
- Turmeric powder: ¼ tsp
- Red chilli powder: ¼ tsp
- Garam masala powder: ½ tsp
- Raisins: 40 gm
- Cashew nuts: 40 gm
- Salt: ¾ tsp
- Ghee: 1 tbsp

1. Soak the whole cauliflower in boiling water with ¼ tsp salt for 5 minutes.
2. Drain and keep aside.
3. Heat ghee in a pan lightly fry raisins and cashew nuts drain and keep aside.
4. Add cumin seeds and let them crackle, followed by ginger–garlic paste and chopped onion. Sauté with a little salt until translucent.
5. Add turmeric powder and red chilli powder. Cook for 5 minutes, add mashed cottage cheese, ½ tsp salt and mix well.
6. Add garam masala powder and remaining salt.
7. To the mixture, add fried raisins and cashew nuts.

SERVINGS

8. Stuff cauliflower with the cottage cheese mixture from the stem side, making insertions if needed.
9. Keep aside.

Gravy

- Onions: 250 gm
- Ghee: 1 tbsp
- Refined oil: ½ tbsp
- Clove: 1
- Green cardamoms: 2
- Poppy seeds: ½ tbsp
- Ginger paste: ½ tsp
- Garlic paste: ½ tsp
- Kashmiri chilli powder: ¾ tsp
- Red chilli powder: ½ tsp
- Coriander powder: 2 tsp
- Yoghurt: 125 ml
- Water: 75 ml + 175 ml
- Onions: 2 tbsp sliced and fried
- Salt: ¾–1 tsp

1. Grind onions to a paste.
2. Soak poppy seeds in water for 30 minutes strain and grind to a paste.
3. Heat ghee and oil in a thick-bottom pot.
4. Add whole spices and let them crackle.
5. Add onion paste, let it sweat a little and then add ginger–garlic paste and cook. Add poppy seed paste and cook and then add all the spice powders and a little salt.
6. Cook on a low flame for 45 minutes until onions are brown and the oil separates.
7. Add whipped yoghurt and cook for another 15 minutes.
8. Add 75 ml water and cook until the gravy is done.
9. Place the stuffed cauliflower in the gravy. Add 175 ml of water gradually.
10. Cover pot with a lid and cook the cauliflower turning it over occasionally. Prick the stem and check if cooked.
11. Garnish with fried onions and serve.

SERVINGS

Skinny Yet Double

During the holy month of Ramadan, fasts are broken after sunset, with a spread of savouries and sweets. Shahi tukda is very often seen at iftari. The Hyderabadi cousin is 'double ka meetha' made similarly though fluffier. 'Double roti' is what a loaf of white bread is called.

In the past, I have made this by frying bread slices in ghee, dipping them in sugar syrup and then pouring delicious rabri over them. However, now that every calorie counts, I have adapted it to a baked version. I call it 'Skinny Double ka Meetha' since I'm trying to ensure that doubling on the scale does not happen!

SKINNY DOUBLE KA MEETHA (Serves 4)

Rabri

- Milk: 1 litre
- Green cardamom powder: 1 tsp
- Sugar: 100 gm
- Rose water: 1 tsp
- Saffron: a few strands dissolved in 2 tsp milk

1. Boil milk with cardamom powder till it reduces to half.
2. Add sugar followed by rose water and saffron milk.
3. Stir and let it thicken to a sauce-like consistency.
4. Remove from flame and keep aside.

Double

- Bread: 6 slices cut into 12 triangles
- Ghee: 3–4 tbsp
- Almonds: 1½ tbsp chopped thick
- Pistachios: 1½ tbsp

1. In a pan heat 1 tbsp ghee and fry almonds and pistachios.
2. Apply a little ghee to both sides of the bread with a teaspoon.
3. Heat a non-stick flat pan on a low flame and place bread slice on it.
4. Lightly brown bread triangles on both sides for 3–4 minutes each.

Assembling the Dessert

1. Preheat oven to 180 °C for 10 minutes. Spread a thin layer of rabri at the base of a shallow, rectangular baking dish.
2. Overlap the bread triangles (refer image on p. 249) alternating with a spoon of rabri.
3. Pour remaining rabri over and cover with a foil. Bake for 20 minutes then remove foil and bake for another 4–5 minutes.
4. Serve at room temperature, topped with fried nuts.

Photo on p. 249: Skinny Double Ka Meetha

For the Love of Food
(Suggested Menu Plan)

LET'S PARTY

Starters
Paneer Takatak with Sheermal	pp. 82, 84
Aloo Chop	p. 406
Mutton Chop	p. 73
Chutney Pomfret	p. 430

Mains
Murgh Korma	p. 242
Pudina Keema	p. 84
Mirch Bhindi ka Saalan	p. 243
Arshi's Gobi Musallam	p. 247
Madras Kathal Masala	p. 421
Baghara Rice	p. 242
Parathas of Choice	

Dessert
Skinny Double ka Meetha	p. 250

FAMILY TIME
Ali Family Dalcha	p. 241
Laal Paneer with Moti Hari Mirchi	p. 134
Chukandar ka Saalan	p. 426
Sheermal	p. 84
Baghara Rice	p. 242

Dessert
Tutti Frutti Pound Cake with Vanilla Ice Cream	p. 398

MALABAR SADHYA

Backwaters Beckon

Kerala conjures up images of coconut palms, gorgeous rain showers and breathtaking backwaters. It is literally 'God's Own Country,' which is also, coincidentally, the tagline for one of the best-run tourism campaigns our country has seen.

Cochin (now Kochi) is where I spent a few years of my childhood. As with most other cuisines that I have been introduced to, this, too, was my mother's doing. She always learnt from the local domestic help and those recipes became a part of our table. Rice pancakes like appams, and iddiyapams, coconut-based curries and the use of coconut oil make the base of this cuisine, with large doses of meat and seafood.

Kerala's spice trade goes back 5000 years, which is why whole spices are an integral part of the food culture. The arrival of the Portuguese explorer Vasco da Gama on the Malabar coast in 1548 is seen as the beginning of European colonization. Historians believe that the Jews arrived in Cochin as early as 1 BC. The appam, a lacy pancake, originated in Jewish homes and was popularized by the Syrian Christians. Kochi's Jewish Town has a beautiful synagogue, but unfortunately only one 'pardesi Jewish' family now lives there, all the others have either migrated to Israel is what one gathers from the locals.

A recent trip to Kochi had me salivating over the food. The best meal was on a houseboat in the backwaters of Alleppey. Being with a great set of friends only added to the joy. Like always, a local family friend, Anju was kind enough to share recipes. From them, each year, we receive the best tin box of Christmas cake, pure sin! Interestingly, Kerala is where the first Christmas cake was made in India, in the town of Thalassery in 1880, at a humble bakery called Mambally's Royal Biscuit Factory. I stopped trying to bake a Christmas cake once I ate the Kerala version. I am incapable of getting it that right!

Coconut oil is my go-to, whether for moisturizing, removing makeup or for hair treatment. When cooking Kerala food, it is the oil I prefer to use – albeit, the extra virgin variety to ensure that it does not overpower the flavours of the other ingredients.

MAMA'S APPAMS (Serves 4)

(Measuring cup size: 150 ml)

- Raw rice: 2½ cups
- Cooked rice: ½ cup
- Finely grated coconut: 2 cups
- Salt: 1 tsp
- Sugar: 1 tsp
- Active dry yeast: 1 tsp level
- Water: ¼ cup + 250 ml

1. Soak raw rice in water for 5–6 hours. Strain and grind soaked rice with ¼ cup water.
2. Add cooked rice and grind further.
3. Transfer to a bowl and add grated coconut, salt, sugar and yeast.
4. Leave the batter to ferment at room temperature for 4 hours in the summer or 6 hours in the winter.
5. Add about 250 ml water to make a pouring consistency.
6. Heat appam pan (chattu) on a medium flame.
7. Pour a ladle of the batter in the centre of the pan and swirl the pan around so that a thin layer spreads along the sides of the pan.
8. Cover and steam for 2–3 minutes. Lacy edges would have formed.
9. Open the pan and leave for 1 minute. Remove from pan and serve.

> For the egg appam, break an egg with the yolk intact after the lacy edges of the appam have formed. Sprinkle a little salt and pepper over it and cover for 1–2 minutes.

ANJU'S NADAN KOZHI CURRY (Serves 4)

- Coconut oil: 2–3 tbsp
- Onions: 2 large chopped
- Chicken: 750 gm curry cut
- Garlic: 8 cloves
- Ginger: 1 inch
- Green chillies: 3
- Kashmiri chilli powder: 1–2 tsp
- Coriander powder: ½ tsp
- Turmeric powder: ¼ tsp
- Fennel powder: ¼ tsp
- Green cardamoms: 2–3
- Cinnamon: 1 inch stick
- Cloves: 4–5
- Salt: 1½ tsp
- Water: ½ cup + ½ cup
- Coconut cream: ½ cup

SERVINGS

1. Dry grind cardamom, cinnamon and cloves. Keep aside.
2. Heat coconut oil in a wok and sauté the onions with ½ tsp of salt.
3. Using a mortar and pestle pound together garlic, ginger and green chillies. Add to onions in the wok. Sauté till light brown.
4. Add Kashmiri chilli powder, coriander powder, turmeric powder, fennel powder and the ground masala powder made earlier.
5. Add remaining salt, chicken pieces and cook until golden brown. Add coconut cream and ½ cup water.
6. Let the chicken cook and let the gravy thicken till it turns a reddish brown.
7. Add another ½ cup water and let the gravy boil.

Tempering

- Shallots: 6 thickly sliced or halved
- Curry leaves: 2 sprigs
- Dried red chillies: 2
- Ghee: 1 tbsp
- Salt: a pinch

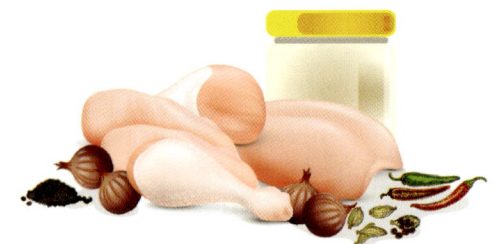

1. Heat ghee in a pan, add sliced shallots and salt. Cook until golden brown. Add curry leaves, dried red chillies and let them crackle.
2. Pour over the curry before serving.

MAMA'S VEGETABLE STEW (Serves 4)
(Measuring cup size: 250 ml)

- Carrot: ½ cut into batons
- Peas: ¼ cup
- Beans: 5–6 cut into batons
- Potato: 1 large cut into cubes
- Fox nuts (makhana): 10
- Chopped coconut pieces: 2 tbsp
- Onion: 1 medium to large sliced
- Ginger: ¾ tbsp juliennes
- Green chillies: 1–2 slit
- Curry leaves: 1 sprig

SERVINGS

- Cinnamon: 1 inch stick
- Black peppercorns: 4–5
- Green cardamoms: 2
- Cloves: 3
- Coconut oil: 1½ tbsp
- Refined oil: 2 tbsp
- Salt: 1 tsp
- Coconut milk: 200 ml
- Water: 150 ml
- Coconut cream: 75 ml

1. Heat oil in a thick-bottom pan over a low flame.
2. Add the whole spices and let them crackle.
3. Add onions, ginger, curry leaves and green chillies with a little salt.
4. Cook till onions are soft and pink.
5. Add all the vegetables beginning with harder ones, let them soften. Do not cover.
6. Add coconut milk, followed by 150 ml water.
7. Cook for 5–7 minutes.
8. Add fox nuts and coconut pieces.
9. Boil for 2–3 minutes and add remaining salt.
10. Add coconut cream, adjust seasoning and remove from flame and serve.

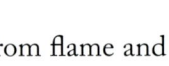

RAJU BHAIYA'S RED CHILLI CHUTNEY

- Refined oil: 1 tsp
- Dried red chillies: 5
- Kashmiri chilli powder: 1 tsp
- Boiling water: 4–5 tbsp
- Salt: ½ tsp

1. Heat oil in a pan on a low flame, add dried red chillies and sauté.
2. Add salt and Kashmiri chilli powder, ensuring it does not burn.
3. Add boiling water.
4. Cook for a few minutes and then remove from flame.
5. Serve at room temperature.

Photo on pg 257: (Clockwise) Anju's nadankozhi curry, Mama's Appams, Raju bhaiya's red chilli chutney and Mama's vegetable stew.

ANJU'S PRAWN GREEN MANGO CURRY (Serves 4)

Prawns

- Prawns: 12 large
- Shallots: 8–10
- Ginger: 2 inch roughly chopped
- Garlic: 8 cloves
- Sugar: ½ tsp (optional)
- Coconut oil: 1 tbsp

1. Heat oil in a pan on a medium flame.
2. Add sugar and let it caramelize.
3. Add half the quantity of shallots, garlic and ginger. Stir fry for 2 minutes.
4. Add prawns and cook for 8–10 minutes until the colour changes, remove from flame and keep aside.
5. Crush the remaining shallots, garlic and ginger using a mortar and pestle and reserve.

Curry

- Green chillies: 2 slit
- Kashmiri chilli powder: 4 tsp
- Turmeric powder: ½ tsp
- Salt: 1 tsp
- Coconut milk: 400 ml
- Water: 150 ml
- Raw mango: 6–7 thick peeled long slices

1. In a heavy-bottom pan, mix all the ingredients except raw mango slices.
2. Place on medium flame and simmer.
3. Add the crushed shallots, ginger and garlic mixture reserved earlier.
4. Let the curry boil while stirring continuously. Add cooked prawn mixture and raw mango slices.
5. Let the curry cook for 15–20 minutes on a low flame. Adjust seasoning.

Tempering

- Coconut oil: 1 tsp
- Mustard seeds: 1 tsp
- Dried red chillies: 2–3
- Curry leaves: 1 sprig

1. Heat oil in a pan, add curry leaves, mustard seeds and dried red chillies. Let them crackle. Pour over the curry before serving.

MUSHROOM PEPPER FRY (Serves 4)

- Mushrooms: 500 gm
- Refined oil: 2 tbsp
- Ginger: 2 tsp chopped
- Garlic: 3 tsp chopped
- Onions: 2 chopped
- Tomatoes: 1½ medium chopped
- Curry leaves: 2 sprigs
- Coriander powder: 2 tsp
- Turmeric powder: ½ tsp
- Red chilli powder: ¾ tsp
- Salt: 1½ tsp
- Green chillies: 2–3 slit
- Black peppercorns: 25 crushed

1. Cut and halve mushrooms. Wash and strain.
2. Heat oil in a non-stick pan, sauté ginger and garlic. Add green chillies.
3. Add onions and cook till light brown, then add curry leaves.
4. Add tomatoes and cook till soft. Add red chilli powder, coriander powder, turmeric powder and salt. Add mushrooms.
5. Let the mushrooms cook till dry, then add crushed peppercorns.
6. Remove from flame and serve hot.

MAMA'S AVIAL (Serves 4)

(Measuring cup size: 250 ml)

- Potatoes/Elephant yam: 100 gm
- Beans: 100 gm
- Flat beans: 100 gm
- Ash gourd: 100 gm
- Drumsticks: 100 gm
- Peas: 100 gm
- Raw banana: 1
- Yoghurt: 1 cup slightly sour
- Curry leaves: 15
- Turmeric powder: ¼ tsp
- Salt: 1½ tsp
- Ghee: 1 tsp
- Coconut oil: a few drops

Paste

- Coconut: ½ grated
- Raw rice: 1 tsp
- Cumin seeds: 1 tsp lightly roasted
- Green chillies: 4

1. Grind paste ingredients together in a mixer and keep aside.
2. Cut all vegetables into batons.
3. Soak raw bananas and potatoes in water to prevent discoloration.
4. In a pan heat 1½ cups water and add the hard vegetables with turmeric. Cook till three-fourths done, then remove and keep aside.
5. Now add the soft vegetables and cook till three-fourths done.
6. Strain the vegetables and reserve the water.
7. Heat 1 tsp ghee in a pan and add parboiled vegetables.
8. Add paste made earlier, stir and cook.
9. Whisk yoghurt with a few tablespoons of water and add to the pan.
10. Add salt, curry leaves and cook.
11. Adjust seasoning and add the vegetable water to get desired consistency.
12. Add a few drops of coconut oil. Serve hot.

BLACK CHICKPEA TIKKIS (Serves 4)

- Black chickpeas: 80 gm
- Potato: 1 large boiled
- Onion: 1 small chopped
- Coriander leaves: few sprigs, finely chopped
- Mint leaves: a few finely chopped
- Green chilli: 1 finely chopped
- Dried mango powder: ½ tsp
- Red chilli powder: ½ tsp
- Salt: ¾ tsp
- Refined oil: 2–3 tbsp

1. Soak chickpeas in water overnight. Strain.
2. Boil chickpeas with salt till soft. Strain and mash.
3. Mash the potato and add to the chickpeas.
4. Add all the other ingredients and mix.
5. Divide into 8 equal portions and shape into tikkis.
6. Heat oil in a non-stick pan gently fry the tikkis.
7. Serve hot.

KARI PATTA CHUTNEY

- Curry leaves: 8 sprigs
- Peanuts: 4 tbsp
- Cumin seeds: 1 tsp
- Green chillies: 2
- Garlic: 3 cloves
- Ginger: ½ inch
- Tamarind paste: 1 tbsp
- Salt: ½ tsp
- Refined oil: 1 tsp

1. Heat oil in a pan.
2. Add cumin seeds, green chillies, garlic and ginger.
3. Add curry leaves without the sprigs, and roast with peanuts until brown.
4. Add tamarind paste and cook further.
5. Add salt.
6. Grind with a little water to make a chutney and serve.

SAGO VERMICELLI PAYASAM (Serves 4)

(Measuring cup size: 250 ml)

- Vermicelli: 100 gm
- Sago: 25 gm
- Coconut milk: 3 cups
- Milk: ½ cup
- Cashew nuts: ¼ cup
- Raisins: ¼ cup
- Ghee: 3 tbsp
- Jaggery: 200 gm
- Water: 1½ cups

1. Crush jaggery and place in a saucepan with ½ cup water. Stir and cook for 2–3 minutes.
2. Remove from flame and strain to remove impurities.
3. Heat 2–3 tsp ghee in a non-stick pan. Add vermicelli and fry until golden. Remove and keep aside.
4. Add remaining ghee to the pan and lightly fry cashew nuts and raisins.
5. In a deep pot, boil 1 cup water and milk, add sago and stir.
6. Cook for 10–15 minutes ensuring sago does not stick to the bottom of the pan.

7. Add 1½ cups coconut milk to the sago and continue stirring. When it starts to boil, add vermicelli and cook further.
8. Add jaggery syrup and boil for 2–3 minutes, then lower the flame and add remaining coconut milk. Add cashew nuts and raisins. Simmer for 5–7 minutes. Serve warm.

Palaharam

Unniyapam is a traditional Kerala dessert with everything truly representing the agricultural produce of the state. Rice, banana, coconut and jaggery are mixed together, placed in a traditional appe pan and the end result is sweet warm bombs. On the other hand, tres leches literally means three milks. This is a dessert which originated in Sinaloa, Mexico, and is a mix of evaporated milk, condensed milk and cream, poured over a whole milk cake. However, we are 'vocal for local', the cream is replaced with cashew nut cream and is served with our rice cake!

UNNIYAPAM WITH INDIAN TRES LECHE (Serves 8)
(Measuring cup size: 250 ml)

Unniyapam

- Sona masuri rice: 300 gm soaked for 3–4 hours
- Coconut milk: 75 ml
- Bananas: 1½ ripe
- Jaggery powder: ½–¾ cup
- Coconut pieces: 4 tbsp
- Green cardamoms powder: ¾ tsp powder
- Fennel powder: ¾ tsp
- Dried ginger powder: ¾ tsp
- Baking soda: ½ tsp
- Black sesame seeds: 1½ tsp
- Salt: to taste
- Ghee: 2 tbsp

1. Soak rice in water for 2–3 hours and strain.
2. Grind rice with a little water in a mixer.

3. Add coconut milk, bananas, jaggery powder, green cardamom powder and grind further. Batter should be a little coarse.
4. Heat ghee in a pan and fry coconut pieces and keep aside.
5. Mix coconut pieces with fennel powder, dried gringer powder, black sesame seeds and salt to taste.
6. Ferment batter at room temperature for 2–3 hours.
7. Add baking soda and mix well just before using the batter.
8. Grease paniyaram pan with ghee and place on a low flame.
9. Fill each mould with batter until three-fourths full.
10. Cover and cook for 2–3 minutes, until golden, flip, cover and cook for another 2 minutes.
11. Remove cover and toss the unniyapams till dark brown. Remove and keep aside.
12. Serve the unniyapams warm accompanied with cold tres leches.

Indian Tres Leche

- Milk: 400 ml
- Cashew nuts: 50 gm
- Water: 50 ml
- Condensed milk: 150 ml
- Cinnamon powder: ½ tsp
- Salt: a pinch
- Cardamom essence: ½ tsp

1. Soak cashew nuts in water for 20 minutes, strain and keep aside.
2. Grind cashew nuts in a mixer while gradually adding water, strain and keep aside.
3. In a thick-bottom pan boil milk and let it reduce to 300 ml.
4. Add cashew nut extract and condensed milk. Continue boiling and let the milk thicken.
5. Add cinnamon powder, salt and cardamom essence. Chill and serve.

To reheat put the unniyapam on the flame and toss.

Photo on p. 262 (Clockwise): Mama's Avial, Black chickpea tikki, Kadi patta chutney, Sago vermicelli payasam, Mushroom pepper fry and Anju's prawn with green mango curry; Photo on pg 265: Unniyappam with Indian tres leche.

For the Love of Food
(Suggested Menu Plan)

LET'S PARTY

Starters

Mutton Paniyarams	p. 21
Hurida Koli	p. 98
Chaitra's Goli Bajje	p. 81
Black Chickpea Tikkis with Kari Patta Chutney	pp. 261, 263

Mains

Anju's Prawn Green Mango Curry	p. 259
Egg Roast	p. 79
Mangala Aunty's Onion Sambhar	p. 28
Vegetable Korma	p. 19
Mushroom Pepper Fry	p. 260
Steamed Rice	
Papad	

Dessert

Sago Vermicelli Payasam	p. 263

FAMILY TIME

Mama's Appams	p. 255
Mama's Vegetable Stew	p. 256
Mangala Aunty's Green Mutton Curry	p. 229

Dessert

Fresh Cut Fruit with a Topping of Indian Tres Leches	p. 266

Parsi & Sindhi Flavours

PARSI & SINDHI FLAVOURS

Sain and Dikra at Your Table

The Sindhi and Parsi diaspora have made a huge contribution to the India we see today. Distinctly diligent people who came in with less but worked hard to build and establish themselves as an integral part of this land. Both of these communities predominantly made Mumbai their home.

The Sindhis belong to the Sindh region of Pakistan and came to India upon partition. They were primarily traders who went on to establish many businesses and flourished as a community, some moving to other cities in India. The Sindhi Hindu cuisine is largely wheat or rice based, with curries. Their proximity to Rajasthan and Gujarat has also influenced their cuisine. The journey of learning from the older generation continues here as well. Mothers of friends have always lovingly taught me the right ways of cooking and given me tips that make a difference. For instance, Hinduja Aunty fed us and packed the most scrumptious kokis for us to freeze and devour, sometimes ensuring that Uncle came to the airport in Chennai to hand them over. If that's not love, I don't know what is! Similarly, a friend, Mansi's mother-in-law, someone I have never met, has parted with her tips for making sai bhaji.

On the other hand, the Parsis migrated from Persia to settle down in Gujarat, during the Muslim conquest of Persia in 636–651 CE. Parsi literally means Persian. Meat, pav and rice dominate their cuisines and the use of eggs in many dishes is unique. Parsis are foodies by nature, and are extremely warm and pleasant as can see that in the *The Time and Talents Club Cookbook*, printed by the Parsi community since 1935. Proceeds from the sale of which are used for charitable work. I have a treasured fifth edition hand-me-down of the cookbook, given to me by my mother. Most of my learning of the cuisine dates back to college.

There is a synergy in these cuisines especially in the ingredients, many of which are local. I think when a country adopts you, you adapt to it too, and that gets carried forward to what goes on to your plate.

HINDUJA AUNTY'S SINDHI KADHI (Serves 4)

- Refined oil: 1½ tbsp
- Fenugreek seeds: ¼ tsp
- Asafoetida powder: ½ tsp
- Cumin seeds: ½ tsp
- Mustard seeds: ¼ tsp
- Kashmiri chilli powder: ¼ tsp
- Red chilli powder: ¼ tsp
- Salt: 1 tsp
- Turmeric powder: ½ tsp
- Kokum: 2 pieces soaked or tamarind paste: 1½ tsp
- Gram flour: 3–4 tsp
- Ginger: ½ inch grated
- Tomatoes: 2–3 medium boiled and puréed
- Cluster beans: 8–10 trimmed and halved
- Drumsticks: 2 cut and boiled
- Okra: 6–8 trimmed and halved
- Green chillies: 1–2 slit
- Water: 1½–2 cups
- Curry leaves: 1 sprig
- Ghee: 1 tsp

1. Heat oil in a wok/kadai. Stir fry okra with a little salt. Remove okra and keep side.
2. Add fenugreek seeds, cumin seeds and mustard seeds to the wok/kadai. Let them crackle.
3. Add gram flour and cook until light brown. Add turmeric powder, asafoetida powder and ginger.
4. Add both chilli powders, stir and add ½ cup water to smoothen the mixture, ensuring it does not burn.
5. Add puréed tomatoes and salt and cook for 3–4 minutes.
6. Add green chillies. Add tamarind paste/kokum water and cook for 2–3 minutes.
7. Add all vegetables including okra, cook a little and add more water. Add remaining salt and boil to the desired consistency.
8. To temper heat ghee in a pan and add curry leaves. Let them crackle.
9. Pour temper over kadhi and serve hot.

TULU KHUDI'S ARBI TUK (Serves 4)

- Taro (arbi): ½ kg
- Garlic paste: 1½ tsp
- Asafoetida powder: ½ tsp
- Chana masala: 1 tsp
- Red chilli powder: ½ tsp
- Caraway seeds: 1 tsp
- Salt: ½ tsp
- Refined oil: 1 tsp + extra for deep frying

1. Peel taro. Boil in salt water till cooked but not mushy.
2. Strain in a colander. Cut taro length-wise into 2 pieces
3. In a wok/kadai heat oil on a medium flame and deep fry taro.
4. Remove from oil and cool, press each piece between your palms and flatten.
5. Heat 1 tsp oil in a non-stick pan.
6. Sauté garlic paste and add asafoetida powder, chana masala, red chilli powder and caraway seeds.
7. Add taro, toss well until golden and well coated.
8. Check seasoning. Serve hot.

SALLI BOTI (Serves 4)

Salli

- Potatoes: 2–3 large grated into thin long strands.
- Salt: 1 tsp
- Refined oil: to deep fry

1. Soak the grated potatoes in salt water.
2. Strain in a colander and dry on a paper towel for 15 minutes.
3. Heat oil in a wok/kadai on a medium flame, deep fry grated potatoes until crisp.
4. Add salt, mix well and store after cooling.

Boti

- Mutton: 1 kg rib and pieces
- Onions: 3 large chopped
- Tomatoes: 4 medium blanched and peeled
- Green chillies: 3–4 chopped
- Refined oil: 3 tbsp
- Garlic paste: 1¼ tsp
- Ginger paste: 1¼ tsp
- Turmeric powder: 1¼ tsp
- Red chilli powder: 3–4 tsp
- Jaggery powder: 1 tbsp
- Vinegar: 2 tbsp (Goan vinegar preferred)
- Salt: 2–2½ tsp
- Water: 150–200 ml

1. Heat oil in a pan. Sauté onions until golden with ½ tsp salt.
2. Add mutton, ginger and garlic paste, green chillies, turmeric powder and red chilli powder.
3. Cook the meat for 10–15 minutes until brown.
4. Add tomatoes and cook further.
5. Add 1 tsp salt and water, boil, then cover and cook for 45 minutes stirring occasionally until the mutton softens.
6. Add jaggery powder, vinegar and cook for 5 minutes.
7. Check seasoning. Serve hot, topped with salli.

SAI BHAJI (Serves 4)
(Measuring cup size: 250 ml)

- Refined oil: 2–3 tbsp
- Garlic: 6 cloves chopped roughly
- Ginger: 1 tbsp chopped
- Green chillies: 1–2 chopped
- Onion: 1 medium chopped
- Tomatoes: 2 large chopped
- Spinach: 3 cups chopped
- Carrot: 1 peeled and chopped
- Potato: 1 large chopped
- Ash gourd: ½ cup chopped
- Pumpkin: ½ cup chopped
- Brinjal: ½ cup chopped
- Chana dal: ¼ cup washed and soaked in water for 1 hour
- Tamarind paste: 2 tsp
- Dill leaves: ½ cup chopped (optional)
- Fenugreek leaves: ½ cup chopped

- Coriander leaves: ¼ cup chopped
- Salt: 1–1½ tsp
- Turmeric powder: ½ tsp
- Roasted cumin powder: 1 tsp
- Coriander powder: 1 tbsp
- Red chilli powder: 1 tsp
- Kashmiri chilli powder: 1 tsp

Tempering

- Garlic: 6 cloves chopped roughly
- Ginger: 1 tbsp roughly chopped
- Red chilli powder: 1 tsp
- Kashmiri chilli powder: 1 tsp
- Green chillies: 2 chopped
- Cumin seeds: 2 tsp
- Ghee: 1 tbsp

1. Heat oil in a pressure cooker and add garlic, ginger, onion, green chillies and ½ tsp salt. Sauté until light brown.
2. Add chopped tomatoes and continue to sauté.
3. Add chopped carrots, potato, brinjal and cook.
4. Add ash gourd, pumpkin, turmeric powder, roasted cumin powder, coriander powder and both chilli powders. Mix well.
5. Then add strained chana dal, spinach, ½ tsp salt and sauté.
6. Add just enough water to cover the vegetables and then pressure cook for 3–4 whistles on a medium flame.
7. Once cool, open the cooker. Mix well and crush with a ghotna or potato masher.
8. Add fenugreek leaves and dill leaves, if using.
9. Add tamarind paste and cook for another whistle or two.
10. The dal and vegetables should be mashed coarsely and thick. There should be no liquid in the mixture.
11. If required, cook without covering until the mixture comes together.
12. Check seasoning.
13. To temper, heat ghee in a pan and sauté garlic and ginger until light brown.
14. Add green chillies, cumin seeds, red chilli powder and stir. Pour over the bhaji.
15. Mix and serve garnished with chopped coriander.

Photo on p. 274 (Clockwise): Hinduja aunty's sindhi kadhi, Sai bhaji, Parsi sali boti and Tulu Khudi's arbi tuk.

Pudding

Caramel custard, or pudding as it is called in many homes, is a dessert most of us grew up on ... wholesome and satisfying. Popularized by European restaurants in the 1900s, versions of this flan can be seen in Latin America, while the crisp crust version, called crème brûlée, comes from France. The Parsis have a version called laganu custard with the added flavour of spices like cardamom.

Milk, egg, sugar and cream are the basic ingredients of this recipe, adding the apples for tartness only gives it a fresh edge. Combine this with any meal and it works. This dessert is a great way of ensuring children have their eggs and milk, the ever-anxious mother in me dominates once again! This is certainly better than milk in the white-striped brown mug and the quarter-boiled egg in the blue bowl that I was force-fed before the six-year-old me left for school. At least here the offering is a dessert, with apple to boot!

APPLE CRÈME CARAMEL (Serves 6)

Caramel

- Granulated sugar: 110 gm
- Apple: ⅔ grated

Custard

- Cream: 200 ml
- Milk: 225 ml
- Brown sugar: 40 gm
- Eggs: 3
- Vanilla extract: 1 tsp
- Apple: ⅓ puréed

1. Peel and deseed the apple. Grate two-thirds of it and purée one-third of it.
2. Preheat the oven to 175 °C for 10–12 minutes.
3. In a non-stick pan on a medium flame add granulated sugar and let it caramelize until a little more than golden brown.

4. Add grated apples to the caramel, lower the flame and keep stirring for 10–12 minutes as apples have a high water content.
5. Pour caramel into ramekins or a 6–7 inch round baking pan and swirl.
6. Mix milk and cream together in a heavy-bottom saucepan.
7. Place the saucepan on a medium flame. Let the mixture cook for 12–14 minutes until creamy. Do not let it boil. Let the milk and cream mixture cool.
8. Whisk eggs and brown sugar until light and fluffy. Add vanilla extract.
9. Combine this with the cooled milk mixture, mixing well, and add the apple purée.
10. Pour mixture into ramekins or baking pan, ensuring that not too many bubbles form.
11. Place ramekins or baking pan in a tray filled with hot water.
12. Bake in the water bath for 40 minutes or until a toothpick inserted comes out clean.
13. Remove from the oven and cool for an hour at room temperature.
14. Then chill in the refrigerator for 8 hours or overnight.
15. Tap the sides of the pan to release suction or use a sharp knife along the edges of the pan before flipping the caramel custard onto a serving platter.

Photo on p. 277: Apple crème caramel.

For the Love of Food
(Suggested Menu Plan)

LET'S PARTY
Starters

Russian Pattice	p. 370
Chaitan's Beer Batter Fish Fingers Served with Mayonnaise	p. 436
Sindhi Tuk Chaat	p. 401
Fruity Cheese Board	p. 69

Mains

Salli Boti	p. 272
Saffron Apricot Pilaf	p. 319
Wafer Par Eda	p. 369
Spinach and Cottage Cheese Casserole	p. 117
Bhaji	p. 366
Ladi Pav	p. 365

Desserts

Apple Crème Caramel	p. 276
Chocolate Tarts	p. 58

FAMILY TIME

Pudina Keema	p. 84
Hinduja Aunty's Sindhi Kadhi	p. 271
Tulu Khudi's Arbi Tuk	p. 272
Arshi's Kabuli Pulao	p. 424

Dessert

'No Mawa' Cake	p. 374

'AYO GORKHALI'

Set Your Mouth on Fire

Nepal, a small kingdom in the foothills of the Himalayas, is home to the courageous Gorkhas. Momos and thukpa are what come to mind when we think of Nepal, little realizing that the origin of both lies in Tibet and these have been adapted in Northeast India. Nepalese cuisine has much more to offer though; there is a unique rustic appeal to every dish. It is primarily a meat-eating region, but certain communities do not eat pork; some others like the Rais do not eat goat but eat sheep. Uniquely, most dry preparations are called 'achaar', often leaving one confused, expecting pickle on the table.

Shared borders has led to a Chinese influence in the use of ingredients like soy sauce and MSG, literally white magic, until it became a sinful addition and made only an occasional appearance in our larders. Dehydrating meat and vegetables to store them for long periods is common, because of the harsh winters and the somewhat barren terrain of the country. Chillies are used in abundance and blaze the tongue as sharply as the Gorkha war cry.

Over the years, I have started loving Nepalese food. I have learned to make all of it from the people working with us, often stealing a little of their special chutney or their spicy curries. On the few days they want to give me a special treat, those dishes are on the lunch table. The help at home are our lifeline, and mutual respect and trust go a long way in ensuring domestic bliss, for me they are truly family. All the recipes here are contributions from them.

CHOILA PORK (Spice Grilled Pork) (Serves 4)

- Pork belly: 500 gm
- Turmeric powder: ½ tsp
- Salt: ½ tsp

1. Boil pork belly in turmeric powder and salt water for 20–25 minutes or until soft.

Marinade

- Turmeric powder: ½ tsp
- Home-made Chinese chilli paste: 1 tsp
- Coriander powder: ¾ tsp
- Cumin powder: 1 tsp
- Salt: ½ tsp
- Black pepper powder: ½ tsp
- Ginger paste: 1 tsp
- Garlic paste: 1 tsp
- Nutmeg: ⅛ tsp
- Asafoetida powder: ⅛ tsp
- Mustard oil: ¾ tbsp
- Lemon zest: 1 tsp
- Lemon juice: 1 tbsp

1. Make a marinade with all the ingredients.
2. Marinate boiled pork for 6–8 hours after scoring the belly.
3. Cut pork belly into thick slices and place in a non-stick pan on a low flame.
4. Cover pork slices and grill on the pan, occasionally turning sides until dark reddish brown.
5. Remove pork slices from pan and cool on a chopping board.
6. Cut pork slices into cubes.

Masala

- Tomato: 1 large (roasted on a pan with skin)
- Ginger: ½ inch
- Garlic: 2 cloves
- Dalle khursani chillies: 1 / Thai chillies: 2
- Turmeric powder: ¼ tsp
- Asafoetida powder: ⅛ tsp
- Cumin seeds: ½ tbsp roasted
- Salt: ¼–½ tsp
- Black pepper powder: ¼ tsp
- Refined oil: 1½ tbsp

SERVINGS

1. On a pan roast tomatoes with the skin till charred.
2. Grind the tomatoes with all other masala ingredients except for oil into a paste.
3. Add cubed pork and oil. Toss well.
4. Heat a wok/kadai and add the pork mixture to it.
5. Cover and cook pork on a low flame stirring occasionally till done. Check seasoning.

This recipe can be made with both boneless chicken and mutton. Cooking time and seasoning will have to be adjusted.

Tempering and Garnish

- Mustard oil: 1 tsp
- Fenugreek seeds: ¼ tsp
- Garlic: 2 cloves minced
- Spring onion: ½ cup chopped (leaves only)
- Coriander leaves: 2 tbsp chopped

1. Heat oil in a pan.
2. Add fenugreek seeds and let them crackle.
3. Add garlic.
4. Pour the mixture over hot pork.
5. Add spring onions and coriander leaves as garnish.

RAJU'S BHINDI KO BHUTUWA (Okra Stir fry) (Serves 4)

- Okra: 15–20 slit
- Small potatoes: 10 halved with skin on and soaked in salt water
- Turmeric powder: 1 tsp
- Kashmiri chilli powder: ¾ tsp
- Cumin seeds: 1 tsp
- Fenugreek seeds: ¾ tsp
- Garlic: 1 tbsp crushed
- Ginger: 1 tbsp crushed
- Yoghurt: 150 ml
- Dalle khursani chillies: 1–2 crushed / Thai chillies: 2–3
- Light soy sauce: 1½ tbsp
- Honey soy sauce: 1 tbsp
- Salt: 1–1½ tsp
- Spring onions: 1 cup chopped
- Coriander leaves: 1 cup chopped
- Tomatoes: 2 medium quartered
- Sesame oil: 1 tbsp
- Mustard oil: 1 tbsp

1. Prick the potatoes with a fork.
2. Heat both the oils together in a flat wide pan.
3. Add fenugreek seeds and cumin seeds. Let them crackle.
4. Add turmeric powder and Kashmiri chilli powder.
5. Add potatoes, ½ tsp salt and sauté.
6. On a low flame, add crushed garlic, ginger and chillies.
7. Let potatoes cook until half done.
8. Add okra, ½ tsp salt and toss.
9. Add whipped yoghurt, honey soy sauce and light soy sauce.
10. Simmer for 3–5 minutes.
11. Add quartered tomatoes, coriander leaves and spring onions, saving a few coriander leaves and spring onions for garnish.
12. Toss potatoes, okra and tomatoes till they soften. Check seasoning.
13. Serve hot, garnished with spring onions and coriander leaves.

FURMEET'S GUNDRUK (Serves 4)
(Measuring cup size: 150 ml)

Gundruk is a preparation of fermented and dried mustard leaves. The leaves are picked and put out to dry until they turn yellow. After which they are wrapped in a moist cloth and hung for three days. The bundle is then opened and the leaves are dried in the sun for another 2–3 days.

- Gundruk: 1 cup
- Onion: 1 large sliced
- Ginger: 1 inch
- Garlic: 4–5 cloves
- Green chillies: 4
- Tomato: 1 large chopped
- Coriander leaves: ½ cup chopped
- Ghee: 1 tbsp
- Water: 600 ml
- Salt: 1–1½ tsp
- Turmeric powder: ½ tsp

1. Soak gundruk in water till it doubles in size, strain and keep aside.
2. Pound ginger, garlic and 2 green chillies together.
3. Heat ghee in a wok/kadai.
4. Sauté onions with a little salt until light golden.
5. Add the ginger–garlic–chilli mixture and turmeric powder.
6. Stir fry until cooked.
7. Add tomatoes and let them soften. Add gundruk.
8. Cook well. Add 600 ml water and boil to a soup-like consistency.
9. Add salt to taste and garnish with coriander leaves. Serve hot.

RAJU'S GOLBEDHA KO ACHAAR (Tomato Chutney)

- Tomatoes: 4
- Garlic: 5–6 cloves
- Sesame: 1 tsp roasted
- Dried red chillies: 4
- Mustard oil: 1 tsp
- Green chillies: 3 slit
- Salt: 1½ tsp

1. Roast tomatoes on a tawa (iron pan). Mash with skin in a mortar and pestle.
2. Roast dried chillies and sesame in a pan and pound together with garlic.
3. Add pounded mixture to the tomatoes and add salt.
4. To temper the mixture, heat oil, add slit green chillies and pour over it.
5. To make it milder, reduce the number of both chillies by one.

Photo on p. 286 (Clockwise): Furmeet's Gundruk, Raju's golbedha ko achaar, Isskus ko tarkari, Salina's karela sadeko, Choila pork; Photo on p. 290: Yogoberry – Sikarni.

SERVINGS

SALINA'S KARELA SADEKO (Bitter Gourd Salad)
(Serves 4)

- Bitter gourd: 500 gm
- Onions: 1½ large sliced thin
- Roasted sesame seeds: 30 gm
- Salt: 1 tsp + ½ tsp
- Refined oil: to deep fry
- Green chillies: 4 halved
- Mustard oil: 1 tbsp

1. Scrape bitter gourd lightly, deseed and slice thin.
2. Apply 1 tsp salt and keep aside for 1½ hours.
3. Lightly squeeze the bitter gourd and discard excess water.
4. Heat oil in a wok/kadai and deep fry bitter gourd till crisp. Remove and keep aside.
5. In another pan heat mustard oil and fry green chillies.
6. Grind the roasted sesame seeds.
7. Mix fried bitter gourd with sliced onions, ground sesame seeds, ½ tsp salt and mustard oil with the green chillies. Serve at room temperature.

ISSKUS KO TARKARI (Chayote Squash Curry) (Serves 4)

- Chayote squash (Isskus): 800 gm
- Mustard oil: 2 tbsp
- Panch phoran: 1 tsp
- Turmeric powder: ¼ tsp
- Kashmiri chilli powder: ¼ tsp
- Red chilli powder: ¼ tsp
- Salt: ¾–1 tsp
- Ginger paste: ½ tsp
- Garlic paste: 1 tsp

1. Peel chayote and slice at a slant, thinly along with the core.
2. Heat mustard oil in a non-stick pan, add panch phoran and let it crackle.
3. Add turmeric powder and chayote. Toss well and add Kashmiri chilli powder.
4. Add salt and cook for 5–7 minutes.
5. Add garlic and ginger paste.
6. Add red chilli powder, cover and cook for 3–4 minutes.
7. Remove cover and stir until dry. Serve hot.

Yogoberry

Sikarni is a traditional spiced sweet yoghurt dessert in Nepal and Tibet. This dessert existed long before we were introduced to the cool and hip frozen yoghurt, queuing up at stores selling it with the tagline '100 percent sin, zero percent guilt'. Traditionally topped with pistachios, the addition of berries makes it interesting. If one can source the golden berries which are native to Nepal, that would be the ultimate addition. As always, we make do with what we have … a 'berry' sweet compromise!

SIKARNI (Serves 4)

- Greek yoghurt: 350 ml
- Cream: 100 ml
- Honey: 1 tbsp
- Icing/Castor sugar: 3–3½ tbsp
- Cinnamon powder: ½ tsp
- Black pepper powder: ¼ tsp
- Nutmeg powder: ¼ tsp
- Green cardamom powder: ½ tsp
- Pistachios: ¼ cup shelled and sliced thick
- Raspberries: 6
- Strawberries: 2–3 sliced
- Saffron: 6–8 strands soaked in warm milk
- Rose petals: a few

1. Mix yoghurt and cream together. Place a strainer over a bowl and layer it with a muslin cloth.
2. Transfer yoghurt–cream mix onto the muslin cloth and strain. Keep in a cool place for 3 hours and then refrigerate for 9 hours.
3. Take out from the refrigerator and transfer the thickened mixture to a bowl.
4. Whisk the mixture for 3–4 minutes with honey and sugar.
5. Add all the spices, soaked saffron and mix.
6. Add three-fourths of the quantity of pistachios, saving a few to top. Chill for 6–8 hours.
7. Scoop dollops of sikarni onto a plate, top with remaining pistachios and rose petals, berries and serve.

For the Love of Food
(Suggested Menu Plan)

LET'S PARTY
Starters
Chicken Momos with Spicy Chutney	pp. 222, 216
Sweet Chilli Prawns	p. 462
Potato Stuffed Shaphalay	p. 219
Spinach Momos with Spicy Chutney	pp. 221, 216

Mains
Kulia Bhai's Junglee Mutton	p. 182
Choila Pork	p. 283
Laal Masoor Dal	p. 141
Raju's Bhindi ko Bhutuwa	p. 284
Baingan ka Bharta	p. 102
Raju's Golbheda ko Achaar	p. 287
Steamed Rice	

Dessert
Bhapa Carrot Cake and Doi Medley	p. 147

FAMILY TIME
Mutton Chop	p. 73
Furmeet's Gundruk	p. 285
Lamba Begun Bhaja	p. 145
Salina's Karela Sadeko	p. 288
Raju's Golbedha ko Achaar	p. 287
Steamed Rice	

Dessert
Cinnamon Ice Cream	p. 43

High on Thai

HIGH ON THAI

'Sawadee'

Thailand is my go-to destination for a holiday – great hospitality, amazing food, wonderful sights and the best massages! Leave me at a spa and I can happily spend the day there, beginning with herb-infused oil hair rituals and ending with sea salt foot cleanses. All this in my endeavour to attain nirvana and stay as close to the kitchen as possible.

One of these holidays was with a very large group of friends in Koh Samui. Mama Moon, a local, taught us to cook at the villa where we were staying. A real 'Mama', her heart was in the food she laid out on the table. Her question was always, 'What you want to eat?'. She conducted a fantastic cooking class where there were no measurements involved. It was cooking purely by instinct and experience. She also packed her Thai curry pastes for us to carry back home. Who doesn't like return gifts!

Thai food is liberal in its use of spices, roots, nuts and lime with doses of coconut sugar. A big takeaway is to use your main ingredients raw, instead of cooking them the Indian way. Vegetables are never stir-fried in the pastes. Instead, they are added once the pastes are cooked and the liquid, whether it is coconut milk or stock, has been added, this helps ensure their real flavour and bite is retained.

Some of these recipes are Mama Moon's and some are from my understanding of what the cuisine is about.

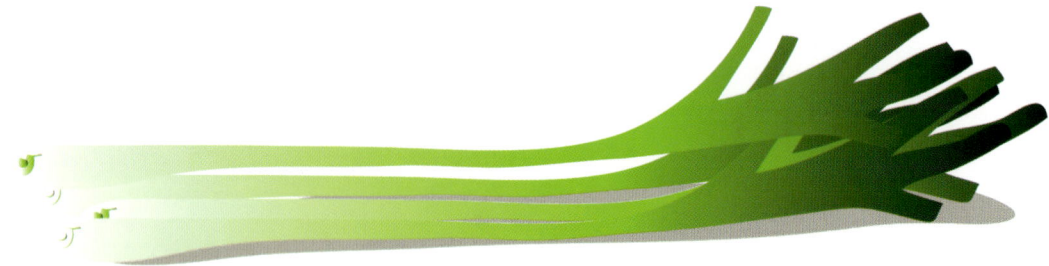

THAI GREEN CURRY PEANUT BUTTER TRAY BAKE

(Serves 2)

Garnish

- Coriander leaves: 35 gm chopped
- Peanuts: a handful crushed
- Lime wedges: 2–3 to squeeze over

Chicken Version

- Boneless chicken thighs: 2–3 sliced thin
- Onions: 1½ cut into wedges
- Broccoli: 1 small head, florets segmented
- Red bell pepper: ¼ diced
- Thai red chillies: 2 chopped thick
- Thai green curry paste: 2½–3 tbsp
- Salt: 1 tsp
- Fresh peanut butter: 3½ tbsp
- Honey: 1½ tbsp
- Coconut milk: 150 ml
- Flat rice noodles: 60 gm
- Oyster sauce: 2 tsp
- Refined oil: 1tbsp + 2 tbsp

1. Boil flat rice noodles in hot water till cooked. Strain in a colander and keep aside.
2. Heat 1 tbsp of oil in a pan, add green curry paste and cook till oil separates.
3. Put all ingredients, except for coconut milk, in a bowl and mix well with your fingers. Check seasoning.
4. Transfer the mixture to a greased baking dish.
5. Cover the dish with aluminium foil.
6. Preheat oven for 7–8 minutes to 200 °C.
7. Bake for 20 minutes and then take out of the oven. Toss the ingredients and add coconut milk. Cover and bake for another 10 minutes.
8. Bake uncovered for 10 minutes until the ingredients turn a light golden colour and appear moist.
9. Serve hot, garnished with coriander leaves, crushed peanuts and a squeeze of lime.

SERVINGS

Vegetarian Version

- Tofu: 6 cubes
- Mushrooms: 6 halved
- Broccoli: 6 florets
- Flat rice noodles: 25 gm
- Thai green curry paste: 1½–2 tbsp
- Peanut butter: 1½ tbsp
- Honey: 1 tbsp
- Oyster sauce/Hoisin sauce: 1 tsp
- Thai red chilli: 1 chopped thick
- Salt: ½ tsp
- Refined oil: 1 tbsp + 1 tbsp
- Coconut milk: 50 ml
- Salt: a pinch

1. Boil flat rice noodles in hot water till done. Strain in a colander and keep aside.
2. Heat 1 tbsp of oil in a pan, add green curry paste and cook till oil separates.
3. Let tofu cubes dehydrate on a paper towel for 30 minutes.
4. In a non-stick pan heat 1 tbsp oil. Add tofu and sauté, add mushrooms and toss.
5. Transfer to a bowl and add all other ingredients except coconut milk and mix.
6. Transfer the mixture to a greased baking dish.
7. Cover the dish with aluminium foil.
8. Preheat oven for 7–8 minutes to 200 °C.
9. Bake for 20 minutes and then take out of the oven. Toss the ingredients and add coconut milk.
10. Bake uncovered for another 10 minutes until the ingredients turn a light golden colour and appear moist.
11. Serve immediately, garnished with coriander, crushed peanuts and a squeeze of lime.

Photo on p. 297: Thai green curry peanut butter tray bake; Photo on p. 298: Thai steamed fish with lime and chilli; Photo on p. 299: The process of preparing the fish.

THAI STEAMED FISH WITH LIME AND CHILLI

(Serves 4)

Sauce

- Lime juice: 2 tbsp
- Thai red chillies: 2–4
- Green chillies: 2–4
- Chicken stock: 250 ml
- Coconut sugar: 3 tbsp
- Fish sauce: 75 ml
- Coriander stalks: 50 gm
- Garlic cloves: 6

1. Chop Thai red chillies, green chillies, coriander stalks and garlic cloves finely.
2. Mix coconut sugar in a little hot water and add all the other ingredients.
3. Mix well and leave for 10 minutes. Check seasoning.

Assembling

- Indian sea bass: 750 gm
- Pink salt: 1½ tsp
- Black peppercorns: 10 crushed
- Celery leaves: 6 stems
- Coriander leaves: 50 gm chopped
- Lemongrass stalks: 6 crushed

1. Clean whole fish, remove gills and intestines, the belly pocket should be clean. Trim tail if required.
2. Diagonally cut three slits on both sides of the fish.
3. Rub pink salt and crushed black peppercorns in the slits and in the belly opening.
4. Stuff 3 crushed lemongrass stalks in the stomach opening.
5. Line the base of a perforated compartment of a steamer with two layers of aluminium foil. Place remaining crushed lemongrass stalks on it.
6. Place the fish over the lemongrass stalks.
7. Pour three-fourths of the sauce over it and let the fish rest for 10 minutes.
8. Now heat water in the bottom layer of the steamer.

9. Place the perforated layer on it. Steam the fish for 7–9 minutes.
10. Insert a toothpick into the fish to check if cooked.
11. Heat a large non-stick pan and place the steamed fish on it. Remove all lemongrass stalks including those in the belly.
12. Add remaining sauce and boil for 2–3 minutes.
13. Make a bed of celery leaves on a serving platter. Transfer fish onto it.
14. Pour some sauce from the pan over the fish and keep the extra sauce in a bowl.
15. Garnish with coriander leaves.
16. Serve with rice and the extra sauce.

> Use fresh chicken stock, not cubes. If you do not have coconut sugar, replace with 2 tbsp of brown sugar.

MAMA MOON'S SOM TAM SALAD (Serves 2)

(Measuring cup size: 150 ml)

- Peeled raw papaya: 200 gm
- Garlic: 2 cloves large peeled
- Tomato: 1
- String bean: 1
- Lemon juice: 2 tbsp
- Palm jaggery: 1 tbsp
- Salt: ½ tsp
- Peanuts: ½ cup
- Thai red chilli: 1

1. Ensure raw papaya is firm. Using a julienne peeler peel papaya into long strips.
2. Place papaya strips in a bowl filled with ice and refrigerate.
3. Thinly slice the string bean at a slant.
4. Cut the tomato into quarters and deseed.
5. In a mortar and pestle, pound garlic cloves, tomato quarters, string bean, Thai red chilli, and ¼ cup peanuts.
6. Add lemon juice, palm jaggery and salt to the above and mix to make the salad dressing.
7. Remove papaya strips from the ice, shake well and add to the dressing.
8. Toss well, garnish with remaining peanuts and serve.

MAMA MOON'S THAI RED CURRY (Serves 4)

Red Curry Paste

- Thai red chillies: 50 gm
- Dried red chillies: 4–5
- Galangal ginger: 50 gm
- Kaffir lime zest: ½ tsp
- Shallots/Madras onions: 50 gm
- Garlic: 50 gm
- Coriander seeds: 1 tsp
- Cumin seeds: 1 tsp
- Refined oil: 75 ml

1. Grind all the ingredients except oil in a mixer.
2. Transfer to a jar, top with oil and use directly or refrigerate and store.

Curry

- Refined oil: 1½ tbsp
- Red curry paste: 5 tbsp
- Salt: ¾ tsp
- Brown sugar: 1 tbsp
- Coconut milk: 300 ml
- Coconut cream: 100 ml
- Water: 150–250 ml
- Brinjals: 2 small halved
- Broccoli: 6 florets
- Button mushrooms: 6 halved
- Baby corn: 6 halved
- Basil leaves: 8
- Kaffir lime leaves: 2
- Thai red chilli: 1
- Lemongrass stalk: 1 chopped

1. Heat oil in a wok, add brinjals and let the skin blister. Remove and keep aside.
2. Add red curry paste and cook for 5 minutes until darkish red.
3. Add coconut milk and cook for 5–7 minutes.
4. Add salt and brown sugar followed by Thai red chilli, basil leaves, lemongrass stalk and lime leaves.
5. Add coconut cream and cook for 5 minutes.
6. Add vegetables and cook for 3–4 minutes.
7. Add water gradually and cook to desired consistency.
8. Adjust seasoning and sweetness if required.
9. Serve hot.

BASIL AND LEMONGRASS SLICED GOAT MEAT STIR FRY (Serves 4)

Marination

- Boneless goat meat: 500 gm thinly sliced
- Raw papaya paste: 2 tbsp
- Garlic paste: 1 tbsp
- Fish sauce: 1 tbsp
- Light soy sauce: 1 tbsp
- Lemongrass: 1 stick chopped
- Basil leaves: 6
- Mint leaves: 6
- Thai red chilli: 2 halved
- Coconut sugar: 1 tbsp

1. Marinate meat with all ingredients for 8 hours or overnight in the refrigerator.

Stir Fry

- Refined oil: 1½ tbsp
- Sesame oil: 1 tbsp + 1 tsp
- Coriander stem: 1½ tbsp chopped
- Kaffir lime leaves: 2–3
- Basil leaves: 6
- Thai red chilli: 1 whole
- Thai yellow curry paste: 1 tbsp
- Garlic: 6 cloves halved
- Shallots: 6 halved
- Salt: to taste

1. Take out meat from the refrigerator and let it rest for an hour at room temperature.
2. In a pan heat refined oil and 1 tbsp sesame oil.
3. Add garlic, coriander stem and shallots, stir fry.
4. Add meat, marinade and stir fry for 10 minutes. Add yellow curry paste and cook.
5. Add kaffir lime leaves, Thai red chilli and basil leaves. Cover and leave on a low flame until the meat cooks.
6. Increase the flame to high and add 1 tsp sesame oil and give a quick stir fry.
7. Check seasoning and serve hot.

SESAME GARLIC BOK CHOY (Serves 4)

- Bok choy: 4 small
- Garlic: 3 tsp minced

SERVINGS

- Ginger: 1 tsp minced
- Roasted sesame seeds: 1 tsp
- Sesame oil: 2 tsp
- Light soy sauce: 1½ tbsp
- Honey: 1 tsp

1. Blanch bok choy in hot water for 45 seconds, strain and place in a bowl filled with ice.
2. Heat sesame oil and stir fry garlic.
3. Shake off excess water from the bok choy and toss it in.
4. Add sesame seeds. mix soy sauce, ginger and honey together and add.
5. Toss well on a high flame for the flavours to mix.
6. Remove and serve hot.

'Nuts About You'

Thai food uses ginger, coconut and lime in most dishes. This dessert has all these ingredients and results in a decadent baked cheesecake. Ginger nut biscuits have always been a favourite, thanks to my mother who used to make a layered dessert with ginger nut biscuits in chocolate cream. Using this as an alternative base for the cheesecake creates just the right sensory explosion. End your meal with this all-time classic dessert and guarantee yourself the pleasure of blissful slumber – a food coma is the ultimate route to attaining nirvana! All for a good cause.

GINGER NUT, COCONUT AND LIME CHEESECAKE
(Serves 6)
(Measuring cup size: 250 ml)

Base

- Ginger nut biscuits: 250 gm
- Butter: 100 gm

1. Preheat oven to 175 °C for 10 minutes.
2. Line a 9 inch diameter spring form pan with parchment.
3. Cover the outside of the tin with a double layer of aluminium foil, to ensure no leakage.
4. Crush the biscuits in a mixer or in a ziploc bag with a rolling pin.
5. Melt butter in a non-stick pan and add crushed biscuits. Mix and remove from flame. Press the mixture on to the base of the pan, using the back of a ladle.
6. Bake the base for 7–8 minutes.
7. Remove pan from the oven and let it cool.

Cheesecake Batter

- Philadelphia cream cheese: 675 gm
- Eggs: 3
- Castor sugar: 1 cup
- Coconut cream: ¾ cup
- Sour cream: 1 cup
- Lemon juice: 2 tsp
- Lemon essence: 1 tsp
- Salted caramel: 2 tbsp (recipe on p. 52)

1. All ingredients should be at room temperature. Preheat oven to 180 °C for 10 minutes.
2. Place a deep tray with hot water in the oven for a water bath.
3. Whisk cream cheese for 2 minutes in a stand mixer or using an electric whisk.
4. Add castor sugar to the cream cheese and whisk further for a minute.
5. Add sour cream followed by coconut cream and whisk for another minute.
6. Add eggs one at a time, followed by lemon juice and essence. Do not over-whip.
7. Lightly fold the mixture and keep aside.
8. Ladle salted caramel on the baked biscuit base and spread with a rubber spatula.
9. Pour the cheesecake batter into the pan. Tap the pan lightly on the counter to remove air pockets.
10. Recheck that the foil around the pan is secure, and place the pan in the water bath.
11. Bake for 65–70 minutes.
12. At the 40-minute mark, cover the top of the pan with aluminium foil to prevent browning.
13. After baking, leave the oven door partially open and allow the cheesecake to cool for an hour.
14. Remove pan from the oven. Chill for 12 hours in the refrigerator and transfer to a serving platter.

SERVINGS

Topping: Candied Lemon Peel

- Lemon: 1 large
- Castor sugar: 50 gm
- Water: 60 ml

1. Peel lemon and cut the peel into thin juliennes.
2. Boil water, sugar and lemon peel in a saucepan on a low flame for 25 minutes.
3. Top chilled cheesecake with candied lemon peel and some spoons of syrup and serve.

Photo on p. 303 (Clockwise): Sesame garlic bok choy, Mama Moon's Thai red curry, Basil and lemongrass sliced goat meat stir fry, Mama Moon's som tam salad; Photo on p. 306: Ginger nut, coconut and lime cheesecake.

For the Love of Food
(Suggested Menu Plan)

LET'S PARTY

Starters

Prawn Spring Rolls	pp. 66
Bbq Chicken Bao	p. 465
Water Chestnut, Corn and Asparagus Spring Rolls	p. 66
Twice-Fried Lotus Stem	p. 420
Wasabi Litchis	p. 69

Mains

Thai Steamed Fish with lime and chilli	p. 299
Steamed Asian Chicken with Chilli Oil	p. 444
Cottage Cheese En Papillote	p. 412
Sesame Garlic Bok Choy	p. 302
Mama Moon's Som Tam Salad	p. 300
Steamed Rice	

Desserts

Upside-Down Pineapple Yoghurt Cake	p. 396
Chocolate Tarts	p. 58

FAMILY TIME

Tom Yum Khao Soi	p. 460

Dessert

Ginger Nut, Coconut and Lime Cheesecake	p. 304

MOROCCAN MAZZAH

'Besseha' - Feasting. No Fasting!

In my mind, Marrakech always conjures up the image of bustling souks, tagine pots in myriad colours, mounds of dry and preserved fruit arranged in stalls, golden olive oil and green olives and rugs made with natural vegetable dyes used by the Berber tribes. The narrow alleys and streets of the city are a feast for the senses, with the smell of spices hanging in the air, and medinas and mosaics presenting a colourful visual treat for the eyes. Many a riad offer visitors a sumptuous meal and an equally fabulous stay.

When I come to think of it, there is an element of food in every aspect of Moroccan life, even in the hamam, a sauna and scrub hub. The scrub used by the masseurs is a combination of sea salt and almonds with other additions. They scrub you literally like you are a cow, but ensure that by the time you leave, your skin is actually as soft as that of a calf! The climax is buckets of orange infused water thrown over your skin to cleanse you. Argan oil, the magic elixir for hair, is also sourced from this land.

The influence of the Middle East can be seen in dishes from falafel to moussaka, though tagine cooking is the focus of every Moroccan meal. This is a method of slow cooking in a clay pot with a conical lid and uses a simple combination of spices like turmeric, paprika and cumin. Interestingly, community cooking still exists, as I saw in the blue city of Chefchouhen. Here, every small community has a bakery in the vicinity where inhabitants carry their dough, which they hand over to the baker, who then bakes their bread for them. Sunday is 'couscous day', where every family sits together and eats the couscous that is served alongside a tagine dish. No meal is complete without mint tea, brewed in its own distinctive pot, and then poured into a unique glass filled with mint leaves. Not for the Moroccans the usual cup and saucer story! 'Besseha' is their way of saying bon appétit. The recipes in this section are easy to make and hearty, inspired by the meals I ate on the trip.

SHAKSHOUKA (Serves 4)

(Measuring cup size: 250 ml)

- Eggs: 4
- Tomatoes: 500 gm
- Black chickpeas: ¼ cup soaked overnight
- Sausages: 150 gm, Chorizo or any other
- Red and yellow peppers: ½ each diced
- Onion: 1 large finely chopped
- Garlic: 3 cloves finely chopped
- Spinach: a small bunch roughly chopped in half
- Ready-made pasta sauce: 1–2 tbsp
- Sun-dried tomatoes: 3 pieces pounded to a paste
- Harissa powder: 1 tbsp
- Coriander powder: 1 tbsp
- Paprika powder: ½ tsp
- Stock cube: 1
- Salt: 1½ tsp
- Olive oil: 1 tbsp

1. Soak chickpeas overnight in water. Strain, parboil and partially mash them.
2. Roast tomatoes on a pan till charred, remove skin and chop.
3. Heat olive oil in a skillet (or any pan which has a lid).
4. Add chopped onion, a little salt and sauté till pink.
5. Add chopped garlic, followed by chopped or crushed sausages.
6. Add bell peppers, harissa powder, coriander powder, paprika powder and sun-dried tomatoes.
7. Add chickpeas, followed by a stock cube dissolved in water.
8. Add chopped roasted tomatoes and pasta sauce.
9. Cover and cook for 5 minutes.
10. Add spinach leaves, cover and continue cooking on a low flame till the tomatoes soften.
11. Make wide gaps in the mixture and crack an egg into each gap. Run the yolk slightly with a fork. Sprinkle a little salt and paprika powder on each yolk.
12. Cover and cook further for 8–10 minutes, until the whites of the eggs are set.
13. Serve hot in the skillet or pan with naan and yoghurt garlic sauce (recipe on p. 314).

Harissa Powder

- Dried red chillies: 5
- Cumin seeds: 1 tbsp
- Coriander seeds: 1tbsp
- Fennel seeds: 1 tbsp
- Paprika powder: 1 tbsp
- Sea salt: 1 tbsp
- Garlic powder: 1 tbsp

1. Dry roast dried red chillies, cumin seeds, coriander seeds and fennel seeds.
2. Cool and grind in a mixer.
3. Add paprika powder, sea salt and garlic powder.
4. Mix well and store in an airtight jar.

ULTA TAWA NAAN (Serves 4)

- All-purpose flour: 250 gm
- Milk: 175 ml
- Yoghurt: 2 tbsp
- Sugar: ½ tsp
- Salt: to taste
- Refined oil: 2 tbsp
- Active dry yeast: 1 tsp
- Ghee/Butter: 2 tbsp

1. Bloom yeast in a little lukewarm milk with sugar for 8–10 minutes.
2. Mix yeast mixture with flour and add salt.
3. Add oil and yoghurt.
4. Knead the dough with remaining milk and leave it to rise in a warm place for 2 hours.
5. Divide into 8 equal balls. Roll out into elongated naans.
6. Place on a very hot tawa.
7. Once the dough sticks and rises a little, turn the tawa. The naan will still be stuck to it. Keep it above the flame and cook further to attain desired colour.
8. Remove from tawa.
9. Apply ghee/butter if desired

Flour can a 50:50 mix of All-purpose flour and whole wheat flour.

Photo on p. 313: Shakshouka, Ulta tawa naan, Yoghurt–garlic sauce.

YOGHURT– GARLIC SAUCE

- Hung yoghurt: 3 tbsp
- Garlic: 2 cloves crushed
- Mint leaves: 4 finely chopped
- Salt: to taste

1. Mix all the ingredients together and serve.

MINT CHICKEN (Serves 4)

- Whole chicken: 950 gm without skin
- Olive oil: 3 tbsp
- Shallots: 6
- Garlic: 6–8 cloves
- Baby potatoes: 8 peeled, halved and poked
- Black pepper powder: ½ tsp
- Paprika powder: 1 tbsp
- Turmeric powder: ¼ tsp
- Brown sugar: ½ tsp
- Lemon juice: 2 tbsp
- Pink salt: 1½ tsp
- Apricots: 4 pitted and halved
- Mint leaves: 3–4 tbsp chopped

1. Clean the insides of the chicken and then make slits on it.
2. Cut along the breast bone of the chicken to butterfly it, this is optional.
3. Marinate chicken overnight with ½ tbsp paprika powder, ¼ tsp turmeric powder, 1 tsp pink salt, lemon juice and 3 cloves of crushed garlic.
4. Heat 2 tbsp oil in a non-stick deep pan/pot, with a tight lid or a tagine pot.
5. Pan sear the chicken, pressing down till brown. Cook for 10–12 minutes, flipping the chicken at intervals.
6. Sprinkle ½ tbsp paprika powder, brown sugar, ¼ tsp pink salt and ½ tsp black pepper powder on both sides of the chicken. Cover and cook for 5 minutes.
7. Add shallots and apricots. Cover and cook for 15 minutes, flipping once or twice.
8. Add 50 ml of boiling water along the sides of the pot. Cook covered for 15 minutes.
9. Meanwhile, in another pan, heat 1 tbsp oil. Stir fry remaining whole garlic cloves and potatoes for 8–10 minutes with ¼ tsp pink salt.

10. Transfer chicken onto a plate and place the potatoes, garlic, mint leaves and shallots in the centre of the same pot.
11. Place chicken back on top of the potatoes. This ensures that the potatoes absorb all the flavours.
12. Cover and cook further for 10–15 minutes until the chicken is ready to fall off the bone.
13. Allow the liquid to thicken on a high flame for 5 minutes, if needed.
14. Transfer potatoes, apricots, shallots and garlic on to a serving plate and place the chicken on top.
15. Serve hot with pita bread.

FALAFEL PANCAKES (Serves 4)
(Measuring cup size: 150 ml)

- Chickpeas: 1 cup
- Parsley leaves: ½ cup chopped
- Dill leaves: ¼ cup chopped
- Coriander leaves: ¼ cup chopped
- Shallots: 3 chopped
- Garlic: 2 large cloves chopped
- Black pepper powder: ½ tsp
- Paprika powder: ½ tsp
- Roasted sesame seeds: 1 tbsp
- Roasted cumin powder: 1 tsp
- Water: ¾ cup + ¼ cup
- Pink salt: 1 tsp
- Olive oil: 4–5 tsp

1. Soak chickpeas in water overnight. Strain and grind with ¾ cup water.
2. Mix all the other ingredients with the chickpeas and add ¼ cup water to make a batter.
3. In a non-stick pan, add ½ tsp olive oil and heat on a low flame.
4. Take 1 ladle of the chickpea batter and spread it on the pan in a circular motion.
5. Cook each side for 4–5 minutes. Pancakes will have a soft texture.
6. Repeat process for rest of the batter.
7. Serve hot with labneh (recipe on p. 316).

LABNEH MYRIAD (Serves 4)

- Greek yoghurt: 400 ml
- Pink salt: ½ tsp
- Olive oil: as required

Coating for Labneh

- Pistachios: 5 shelled and chopped
- Saffron: a few strands soaked in milk
- Roasted seasame seeds: 1 tbsp
- Chilli flakes: 1 tbsp
- Roasted cumin: 1 tsp
- Olives: 3 chopped
- Sun-dried tomatoes: 1–2 pieces chopped

1. Line a strainer with a muslin cloth.
2. Place the strainer over a bowl.
3. Mix pink salt and Greek yoghurt. Transfer mixture to the cloth-lined strainer.
4. Let the water drain from the yoghurt at room temperature for 6 hours and then in the refrigerator for 24–28 hours.
5. Place all coating ingredients separately on a large flat plate.
6. Transfer hung yoghurt into a bowl greased with olive oil and divide into 7–8 portions.
7. Rub 1 tsp olive oil between your palms.
8. Take a portion of the yoghurt and shape it into a ball.
9. Roll ball over one of the coating ingredients and place in a serving bowl filled with some olive oil.
10. Repeat the process of oiling palms, shaping and rolling the labneh in different coating ingredients.
11. Pour a little oil over the prepared labneh.
12. Serve chilled.

VEGETARIAN MOUSSAKA CASSEROLE (Serves 4)

- Round large aubergines: 400–500 gm
- Mushrooms: 200 gm sliced
- Onions: 2 medium halved
- Red bell pepper: 1 large halved
- Tomatoes: 2 large
- Coriander leaves: 2 tbsp chopped
- Turmeric powder: ½ tsp
- Garlic powder: 1 tsp
- Paprika powder: 1½ tsp
- Pink salt: 1½ tsp
- Olive oil: 2 tbsp
- Canned mushroom soup: 400 ml
- Almond milk: 125 ml
- Cornflour: 1 tsp

1. In a pan, dry roast tomatoes, bell pepper and onions on a low flame till charred.
2. Peel tomatoes.
3. Chop roasted tomatoes, onions and bell peppers.
4. Heat 1 tbsp oil in a pan.
5. Add sliced mushrooms, ½ tsp pink salt, garlic powder and paprika powder. Cook for 8 minutes.
6. Add all other chopped roasted vegetables and coriander leaves and cook for 2–3 minutes. Remove from flame and keep aside.
7. Slice aubergines into ¾ cm thick roundels.
8. Rub with 1 tsp turmeric powder and 1 tsp pink salt.
9. Heat 1 tbsp olive oil in another large non-stick flat pan.
10. Place the aubergine slices and cook gently on both sides for 3–4 minutes each.
11. Remove and keep aside on a plate.
12. Mix the mushroom soup and almond milk in a saucepan and boil on a low flame.
13. Mix cornflour with 2 tbsp water and add to the mixture.
14. Allow it to thicken to a sauce-like consistency.

Assembling the Moussaka

1. Preheat oven to 180°C for 10 minutes.
2. In a baking dish, spread a thin layer of the sauce.
3. Place a layer of aubergine slices and top with a layer of the mushroom mixture.

4. Repeat the same process for another layer.
5. Bake for 30–35 minutes till a skin forms and then grill for 5 minutes till golden. Serve hot.

HONEY GLAZED CUMIN CARROTS (Serves 4)

- Baby carrots: 250 gm
- Olive oil: 1½ tsp
- Pink salt: ½ tsp
- Roasted cumin seeds: 1 tsp
- Honey: ½ tbsp
- Parsley leaves: 2 tbsp chopped

1. Heat olive oil in a non-stick pan.
2. Add carrots, pink salt and toss. Cook on a medium flame for 10–12 minutes.
3. Add roasted cumin seeds and a drizzle of honey and toss.
4. Remove from flame and add chopped parsley leaves.
5. Serve immediately.

SAFFRON APRICOT PILAF (Serves 4)

- Basmati rice: 220 gm
- Vegetable stock: 500 ml
- Saffron: 12–15 strands
- Pink salt: ½ tsp
- Apricots: 50 gm chopped
- Onion: 1 large chopped
- Garlic: 3 cloves chopped
- Olive oil: 1½ tbsp

Photo on p. 318 (Clockwise): Saffron apricot pilaf, Honey glazed cumin carrots, Vegetarian moussaka casserole, Falafel pancakes, Labneh myriad, Mint chicken.

1. Rinse and soak basmati rice in water for 30 minutes. Strain.
2. Heat vegetable stock with saffron and pink salt for 2–3 minutes and reserve.
3. Heat oil in a thick-bottom deep pot.
4. Sauté onions and garlic till translucent.
5. Add strained rice and fry for a minute.
6. Add reserved stock and let it simmer.
7. Stir in apricots, cover and cook for 25–30 minutes or till the rice is cooked.
8. Serve hot.

Qatayef Deconstructed

Qatayef is a half-moon-shaped deep-fried dumpling, filled with lots of nuts and cream, flavoured with cinnamon and rose and served with honey, often sold by street vendors during Ramadan. This is a deconstructed version, made with figs poached in orange juice and cinnamon, and served with almond crepes. A perfect dessert for a Middle Eastern meal.

ALMOND CREPES WITH FIGS POACHED IN ORANGE SYRUP (Serves 6)

(Measuring cup size: 250 ml)

Almond Crepes

- Almond flour: ½ cup
- All-purpose flour: ½ cup
- Almond milk: 1½ cups
- Eggs: 2 at room temperature
- Butter: 2 tbsp
- Salt: ½ tsp

1. Sieve almond flour and all-purpose flour together with salt.
2. Whisk eggs and add to flour.
3. Add melted butter and almond milk.
4. Leave batter at room temperature for an hour.
5. Then refrigerate batter for 6 hours.

Crepes can be made in advance and heated before serving.

6. Heat a 7 inch non-stick pan with ¼ tsp butter on a low flame.
7. Add ⅙ cup batter to the pan and spread evenly by swirling the pan.
8. Cook for 30 seconds to 1 minute, flip and cook for another 30 seconds.
9. Remove and keep aside on a plate covered.
10. Repeat this process for the entire quantity of batter.
11. Fold crepes before serving with poached figs in orange syrup and a scoop of vanilla ice cream.

Figs Poached in Orange Syrup

- Dried figs: 18
- Pistachios: 18
- Oranges: 3 large
- Honey: ½ cup
- Butter: 2 tbsp
- Cinnamon: 1 inch stick

1. Soak dried figs in warm water for an hour.
2. Take out juice from the oranges and keep aside.
3. Discard water from the figs and insert a pistachio into the centre of each dried fig.
4. Mix together orange juice and honey.
5. Place butter in a non-stick saucepan and heat.
6. Pour in the juice mixture, add cinnamon stick and boil for 4–5 minutes.
7. Add figs to the pan, cover and cook on low heat for 15 minutes, until the figs are softened and the syrup has thickened to pouring consistency.
8. Serve warm with crepes.

Photo on p. 321: Almond crepes served with figs poached in orange syrup.

For the Love of Food
(Suggested Menu Plan)

LET'S PARTY
Starters

Mini Falafel Pancakes with Labneh Myriad	pp. 315, 316
Kulia Bhai's Junglee Mutton	p. 182
Mushroom Burger Patties	p. 481
Fruity Cheese Board	p. 69

Mains

Mint Chicken	p. 314
Shrimp in Garlic and Parsley	p. 327
Vegetarian Moussaka Casserole	p. 317
Arshi's Kabuli Pulao	p. 424
Beetroot and Goat Cheese Salad	p. 352
Apple Hummus	p. 484
Pita Bread	p. 484

Dessert

Pistachio Cake Accompanied with	p. 135
Rose Muhallabelia Cream	p. 137

FAMILY TIME

Hara Bhara Cheesy Kebab	p. 64
Shakshouka with Ulta Tawa Naan	pp. 311, 312

Dessert

Orange Almond Cake	p. 378

ITALIAN SOJOURN

Eat, Pray, Love

Venice is the city that never ceases to amaze me. Each visit offers something new to experience. The thought that all this may disappear one day leaves one wishing to capture every visual. The large canals and bridges, cobbled streets, the flirtatious gondoliers, the surging crowds, art stores, antique book stores, cafes at Piazza San Marco, and the spectacular night rides on the water taxis leave one mesmerized. This meal is an obeisance to that beautiful city I love. It takes me back to something enjoyed after a lazy walk along those lanes and eaten at leisure in the sun, with a silent prayer that future generations get to experience this love in the air.

Italian food is all about ingredients. Use the best EVOO (extra virgin olive oil), balsamic vinegar and Parmesan, throw in some garlic and the best meals worth the Italian chef's kiss or al bacio happen in minutes. A few years ago another trip to the country that is home to these ingredients was an eye-opener.

Pasta always brings back memories of 19-year-old me, toiling to make batches and batches of it by hand. One kilo of flour, with 12 eggs, kneaded together and put through a manual pasta maker to turn out the most amazing fresh fettuccine. However, the lazier 46-year-old me uses the packaged variety. The multitude of their shapes and colours adds another dimension to a plate. These fun-loving Italians, with a glint in their eyes, even have 'naughty' shapes of pasta in packets on sale!

Come summer and mangoes in the brightest hues, flavours and textures are in abundance, whether in Italy or in India. Using it in every form becomes a part of my cooking agenda. The firmer varieties like safeda and hamam work well in salads.

TAGLIATELLE AGLIO OLIO (Serves 2)
(Measuring cup size: 250 ml)

- Tagliatelle: 120 gm
- Button mushrooms: 8 large halved
- Spinach: 1 cup
- Bell pepper: ½ cored and cut diagonal
- Extra virgin olive oil: 2 tbsp
- Garlic: 6 large cloves
- Chilli flakes: 1 tsp
- Mixed herbs: 1½ tsp
- Parmesan cheese: 2–3 tsp grated
- Salt: ¾ tsp

1. Boil water in a pot. Add tagliatelle to the boiling water.
2. Cook till al dente. Strain and reserve some of the water. Give the colander a shake and keep aside. Do not run cold water over pasta.
3. Heat olive oil in a pan over a medium flame and add garlic. Let it sizzle, then add mushrooms and bell peppers.
4. Once the mushrooms and bell peppers are partially cooked, add spinach, chilli flakes, mixed herbs and salt.
5. Once the spinach wilts, add in the pasta and toss well.
6. Add a little pasta water for additional moisture.
7. Add Parmesan cheese, toss and adjust seasoning.
8. Serve with some extra virgin olive oil and Parmesan cheese on the side.

SHRIMP IN GARLIC AND PARSLEY (Serves 2)
(Measuring cup size: 150 ml)

- Shrimp: 8–10 large with tail
- Lemon juice : 2 tbsp
- Lemon zest : 1 tbsp
- Parsley leaves: 1 cup chopped
- Garlic: 8 cloves sliced fine
- Onion: 1 small chopped
- Extra virgin olive oil: 2 tbsp
- Chilli flakes: ¾ tsp
- Salt: ¾ tsp

1. Marinate shrimp in lemon juice and zest for an hour.
2. Heat oil in a pan on medium flame.

1. Add garlic and let it sizzle.
2. Add onions with a little salt. Cook till translucent.
3. Add parsley leaves.
4. Add shrimps and spread all around the pan.
5. Flip the shrimps when one side turns pink.
6. Add chilli flakes and remaining salt.
7. Remove from flame and serve.

SUMMER HUES ROCKET AND MANGO SALAD

(Serves 2)

- Rocket leaves: 100 gm
- Mango: 1 large (firm) sliced
- Onion: 1 medium (sliced and soaked in water)
- Balsamic vinegar: 3 tsp
- Extra virgin olive oil: 4 tsp
- Black pepper powder: ¼ tsp
- Salt: ½ tsp
- Walnuts: 6

1. Place rocket leaves in an ice bath for 30 minutes.
2. Mix balsamic vinegar, olive oil, black pepper powder and salt to make a dressing.
3. Strain rocket leaves and oinions and place in a bowl with mango slices.
4. Add dressing and toss salad. Serve topped with walnuts.

TIGELLE BREAD (Serves 6)

Tigelle is a rustic bread from the mountain region of Modena. Originally cooked between two round clay tiles lined with chestnut leaves and placed by the fireplace, until special skillets called tigellers came into use. This bread is usually slit open and stuffed with local cheeses, cured meats and pickled vegetables. Considered to be a poor man's food in the past,

now there are specialized carts selling this popular street food. Also, it has found a place on restaurant menus.

The original version uses lard; however, this is a lighter version with olive oil and a little sugar and the end product is like a soft pillowy pita, perfect for breakfast even with jam.

- All-purpose flour: 500 gm
- Lukewarm water: 150 ml
- Lukewarm milk: 150 ml
- Active dry yeast: 5 gm
- Sugar: 1 tsp
- Olive oil: 25 ml
- Salt: 5 gm

1. Bloom yeast in a mix of lukewarm milk and water with sugar.
2. Mix flour with salt and knead along with bloomed yeast adding oil gradually.
3. The dough will be sticky at first and then becomes stretchy after 5 minutes of kneading.
4. Place the dough in a greased bowl and let it rest in a warm place for an hour.
5. Knock the dough back and roll into a ½ mm thick sheet and cut into 5–6 cm discs with a cookie cutter.
6. Place each disc on a greased parchment-lined baking tray and cover with a moist cloth. Let it proof for an hour.
7. Remove from proof, leave it out for 7–10 minutes so that it comes off the parchment easily. Cook on a non-stick pan for 4 minutes on each side till it puffs.
8. Slit and stuff with any cured meat, fried egg or spinach and mushroom stir fried with onions, garlic and mixed herbs. Serve warm.

When Life Gives You Lemons

Southern Italy's Campania region produces large volumes of lemons. So many lemons, in fact, that limoncello is this region's popular aperitif, with Sorrento being its home. This is a quaint town with sun-drenched piazzas and winding streets in the old town that ooze charm. Drive up the 50 km Amalfi coast and the views are breathtaking.

An espresso in the sun accompanied by a slice of cake with the lemons off the surrounding trees – that's the thought behind this pound cake. Take me back!

LEMON POUND CAKE (Serves 6)

- All-purpose flour: 225 gm
- Sugar: 225 gm
- Butter: 225 gm
- Eggs: 4
- Baking powder: ¾ tsp
- Lemon essence: 1 tsp
- Lemon juice: 4 tsp
- Lemon zest: 1½ tsp
- Milk: 50 ml

1. Ensure eggs and butter are at room temperature.
2. Preheat oven to 170°C for 10 minutes.
3. Grease and line an 8–9 inch baking pan with parchment.
4. Sieve flour with baking powder.
5. Whisk sugar and butter until creamy.
6. Add eggs and continue whisking.
7. Gradually add the flour mixture.
8. Add lemon zest, lemon juice and lemon essence.
9. Add milk and fold the batter.
10. Pour the batter into the baking pan and tap the pan on the counter gently.
11. Bake for 30–35 minutes.
12. Let the cake cool in the pan. Transfer to a wire rack and remove the parchment.
13. Dust with sugar, slice and serve.

The quantities of the ingredients can be halved and the cake baked in a 6 inch pan as well. The baking time will reduce marginally.

Photo on p. 329 (Clockwise): Summer hues rocket and mango salad, Shrimp in garlic and parsley, Tagiatelle aglio olio; Photo on p. 330: Tigelle bread; Photo on pg 333: Lemon pound cake.

SERVINGS

'Under the Tuscan Sun'

Reading 'Under the Tuscan Sun' by Frances Mayes, an American travel writer and poet, in my early twenties left me with a heady feeling and a deep desire to visit Tuscany. Mayes description of the small town of 'Cortona' – where she impulsively gets off a bus on a road trip and buys an old villa named 'Bramasole'. Her journey through the renovation of the villa to find love, interspersed with chapters like Summer Kitchen Notes with local recipes, was a wonderful read.

The food in this region is rural, rustic and hearty. The people here were historically poor, hence the meals were simple and easy to make in large quantities. There are no complicated methods. The seasoning used is largely rosemary and basil, with truffles and mushrooms picked in the wild. Crusty bread, eaten with garlic and olive oil, is an integral part of their food, as are tomatoes. Though, of course, when one sets out to buy truffles by the gram today, they certainly don't seem *cucinapovera* (poor cooking).

The popular 'farm to table' would be an appropriate description of what to expect from this meal. Warm buttery cheesy bread, soaked in tomato cream and a bite of meat with a crunch of salad hits the right spot! Mansi, a friend and ex-colleague, shared her recipe for garlic bread. A trained chocolatier and a close friend for over two decades, I have spent time with her over the years discussing recipes. There is no better person, with whom to talk about food than someone who loves to cook and bake as much as I do!

MANSI'S CHEESE FILLED GARLIC PARSLEY BRAIDED WREATH BREAD (Serves 6)

(Measuring cup size: 250 ml)

- All-purpose flour: 2½ cups
- Sugar: ¾ tsp
- Active dry yeast: 2¼ tsp
- Lukewarm milk: 1¼ cups
- Salt: 1 tsp
- Butter: 75 gm
- Garlic: 10 cloves
- Parsley leaves: 4 tbsp chopped
- Mozzarella cheese: 90 gm
- Olive oil: 35 ml + 20 ml for brushing
- Oregano: 1 tsp
- Chilli flakes: 1 tsp

- Black peppercorns: 4–6 crushed
- Olives: 8–10 whole

1. Bloom yeast in lukewarm milk in a bowl with sugar.
2. Leave the mixture for 8–10 minutes until frothy.
3. Gradually mix in the flour and salt and knead to a soft dough. Dough may be sticky.
4. Place the dough in an oiled bowl covered with a moist cloth and leave in a warm place to rise for 1½ hours.
5. While dough is rising, blitz garlic, parsley leaves and add softened butter and olive oil.
6. Add crushed black peppercorns, oregano and chilli flakes. Mix well and keep aside.
7. Once the dough has doubled in volume, knock it back on a lightly floured surface and roll into a 14 x 8 inch rectangle.
8. Spread the garlic–butter mixture on the rolled out dough leaving an inch on all sides creating a border.
9. Sprinkle with grated cheese.
10. Now gently start rolling up from one side to make a tight vertical log.
11. Slit the roll through the centre with a knife, leaving an inch from the top.
12. Start braiding the two parts by taking one part over the other.
13. Tuck the ends in.
14. Place braid in a 10 inch oiled bundt pan and secure the two ends.
15. Wrap in moist cloth and proof for another 45 minutes in a warm place.
16. Top with olives.
17. Preheat oven to 190 °C for 10 minutes.
18. Bake for 35 minutes. At the 25-minute mark, brush with olive oil.
19. Remove from oven. Cool on a wire rack for about an hour.
20. Unmould and serve warm.

The quantities of the ingredients can be halved and the bread cane be baked in a 5–6 inch bundt pan as well. The baking time will reduce marginally.

CREAMY MUSHROOMS AND SPINACH (Serves 4)

- Button mushrooms: 250 gm large (remove the stems and poke with a fork)
- Spinach: 50 gm
- Garlic: 6 cloves chopped
- Scallions: 6 (white portion)
- Cherry tomatoes: 12
- Tomatoes: 2 medium

- Red bell pepper: ½,
- Cherry tomatoes: 10
- Sun-dried tomatoes: 2–3
- Basil leaves: 6–8
- Cream: 75 ml
- Milk: 175–190 ml
- Salt: 1½ tsp
- Black pepper powder: ¾ tsp
- Paprika powder: 1½ tsp
- Mixed herbs: 1 tsp
- Olive oil: 2 tbsp
- Olives: 6–8

1. Roast tomatoes and red bell pepper on a pan till charred and chop.
2. Heat oil in a pan. Add scallions and sauté with ½ tsp salt till translucent and pink.
3. Add garlic and sauté, then add roasted tomatoes and cook for 5–7 minutes.
4. Add mixed herbs.
5. Add roasted bell peppers and cherry tomatoes. Cover with a lid.
6. Cook for 5 minutes. Add mushrooms and sauté. Then add paprika powder, remaining salt and black pepper powder. Cover again with a lid.
7. After 5 minutes, add spinach. Let it soften, then add basil leaves and simmer for 2–3 minutes.
8. Add sun-dried tomatoes and olives.
9. Mix cream and milk together until smooth. Add to the pan and simmer till sauce-like consistency.
10. Check seasoning and remove from flame.
11. Serve hot.

BALSAMIC CHICKEN SALAD WITH YOGHURT MUSTARD DRESSING (Serves 2)

- Boneless chicken breast: 250 gm

Marinade

- Olive oil: 1 tbsp
- Lemon juice : 1 tbsp
- Chilli flakes: ½ tsp

- Oregano: ½ tsp
- Garlic: 2 cloves
- Dijon mustard: ½ tsp
- Salt: ½ tsp
- Black pepper powder: ½ tsp
- Parsley leaves: 1 tbsp chopped
- Brown sugar: ½ tbsp

1. Marinate chicken with all the ingredients for 4–6 hours.

Grill

- Balsamic vinegar: 30 ml
- Dried rosemary: ½ tbsp
- Honey: 1 tsp
- Salt: a pinch
- Refined oil: 1 tbsp

1. Mix all the ingredients to make a grill mix.
2. Heat a non-stick grill pan brushed with oil and place the marinated chicken breast.
3. Cook the chicken breast on each side for 4 minutes.
4. Pour the grill mix on the chicken breast, ensuring both sides are coated.
5. Cover and cook for 10 minutes, flipping the chicken at intervals.
6. Cool and slice chicken breast.

Yoghurt Mustard Dressing

- Hung curd: 150 ml
- Honey: 1 tbsp
- Salt: ½ tsp
- Black pepper powder: ¼ tsp
- Mustard: 1½ tsp heaped

1. Mix all the ingredients to make a smooth dressing.
2. Check seasoning.

Assembling the Salad

- Boiled eggs: 2 sliced and sprinkled with salt and black pepper powder
- Lettuce leaves: 6
- Onion: 1 sliced soaked in water
- Cherry tomatoes: 8–10 halved
- Balsamic chicken: sliced

1. Assemble the salad ingredients in a bowl.
2. Pour the dressing over it.
3. Toss well before serving.

Don't Put Me Down!

Tiramisu literally means 'pick me up', either because the combination of coffee and brandy gives you a burst of energy or because after eating it you go boozy and need to be picked up yourself! Whatever be the reason – one look at this dessert and I want to pick up my fork and dig in! It's probably why this is the most famous dessert from Italy.

The history of its origin strikes up the debate of who made it first. There is a version that dates back to 1960, to the restaurant La Becherrie in Treviso, close to Venice. Another starts in Udine, where this dessert made its first appearance, at a hotel restaurant named Restaurant Roma. The certification of origin has been granted to the latter but the former hasn't given up its claim either!

After reading a book written originally in Italian by an author of Indian origin, leisurely prose describing the solitude of a town in Italy, all I craved was this pick-me-up! I tweaked this dessert for a third time and made a desi–firang version, with an Indian instant coffee having a high chicory content and adding the best cognac.

TIRAMISU (Serves 8)

- Boudoir sponge fingers: 24
- Eggs: 2
- Mascarpone cheese: 250 gm chilled
- Cream: 50 ml chilled
- Water: 500 ml
- Instant coffee: 7 tbsp
- Castor sugar: 3½ tbsp
- Brown sugar: 5 tbsp
- Vanilla essence: 1 tsp
- Cognac: 2 tbsp
- Cinnamon powder: ¼ tsp

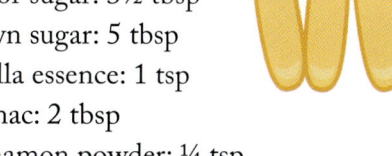

Topping

- Chocolate shavings or unsweetened cocoa powder

1. Separate egg yolks and whites. Refrigerate whites.
2. In a thick-bottom non-stick saucepan add yolks, 3 tbsp of brown sugar and whisk.
3. Place saucepan on a double boiler and continue whisking for 3–4 minutes, until the sabayon is double in volume. Do not overcook as it will get very sticky. Cool to room temperature.
4. In another bowl, whisk mascarpone cheese till light and fluffy, add cream and whisk further with cinnamon powder. Be careful as overmixing can lead to curdling.
5. Add cognac and vanilla essence to the cheese mixture. Keep this refrigerated.
6. In a stand mixer or bowl, whisk egg whites with 1½ tbsp castor sugar until peaks form.
7. Fold cooled sabayon with mascarpone cheese and further fold in whisked egg whites. Divide this into 2–3 equal portions depending on the number of layers you require and the size of your dish. Keep refrigerated.
8. Boil 500 ml water with 7 tbsp coffee, 2 tbsp brown sugar and 2 tbsp castor sugar until it thickens and reduces to 400 ml. Cool to room temperature.
9. Soak each sponge finger in coffee one at a time and line the base of the serving dish.
10. Top with a portion of the cheese-egg-cream mixture.
11. Repeat the process of layering by alternating the sponge fingers and the cheese-egg-cream mixture. The topmost layer will be the latter.
12. Chill tiramisu in the refrigerator for 12 hours. Do not cover.
13. Dust with unsweetened cocoa powder and serve.

Regular sponge cake layers can be used instead of boudoir sponge fingers.

Photo on p. 337 (Clockwise): Mansi's cheese filled garlic parsley wreath braid, Creamy mushroom and spinach, Balsamic chicken salad with yoghurt and mustard dressing; Photo on p. 339: Tiramisu.

For the Love of Food
(Suggested Menu Plan)

LET'S PARTY
Starters

Chicken Burger Patties	p. 482
Keema Scotch Eggs	p. 119
Spiced Hasselback Potatoes	p. 415
Fruity Cheese Board	p. 69

Mains

Chicken Baked with Mascarpone and Lime	p. 446
Shrimp in Garlic and Parsley	p. 327
Creamy Mushrooms and Spinach	p. 335
Spaghetti Aglio Olio	p. 327
Swati's Rocket and Strawberry Salad	p. 427
Tigelle Bread	p. 328

Desserts

Tiramisu	p. 339
Lemon Tarts Topped with Blueberries	p. 383

FAMILY TIME

Pumpkin Mozzarella Balls	p. 90
Sole en Papillote with Compound Basil Butter	p. 433
Green Apple Salad in Vinaigrette	p. 40
Tagliatelle Aglio Olio	p. 327

Dessert

Mansi's 'Coco' Cake	p. 488

LONDON DIARIES

From Market to Market

London comes close to being my favourite city in the world. Every trip only creates memories that make me smile. I don't know whether it's the familiarity or the ease of commuting or just the fact that the city has lots to offer. There are lovely parks, fabulous museums, entertainment, theatre, restaurants, nightlife and of course, amazing retail therapy, it certainly brings out the Shopoholic Rebecca Bloomwood in me. Yes! The mannequins in the store windows do call me in.

The Borough Market was introduced to us by a friend and is now a must-do on every trip. Located next to London Bridge, it has existed for over a thousand years and boasts of being the birthplace of the British Street food movement as well as being a place committed to dishing out traditional food – meats, cheeses, artisanal cakes, spreads, chocolates, breads and pastries, vegan stalls are all under one roof.

The film-lover in me has watched Hugh Grant in *Notting Hill* and that stirred my heart. So the next stop after Borough Market was Portobello Road Market with over a thousand shops filled with antiques and collectibles. Some say that the origin of the name of the popular large mushroom variety is courtesy this market. An ode to the lazy touristy afternoon spent there lies in the pages of this section or maybe it's a star-struck ode to the man in the movie –'I am also just a girl, standing in front of a boy, asking him to love her'!

Multiple visits to these markets have led us to further explore markets and areas like Camden Town and Brick Lane – each unique in the cuisines they offer and remarkably different from the rest of the city.

Most recipes in this section are inspired from the produce at these markets. Their traditions are mirrored in my versions using a few basics from all the learning at my alma mater.

MIXED FLOUR SPICED SODA BREAD (Serves 4)

- Whole wheat flour: 1 cup
- All-purpose flour: 1 cup+2 tbsp if required
- Oats: 1–2 tsp
- Milk: 1 cup + 1 tbsp
- Lemon juice: 1½ tsp
- Brown sugar: 1 tsp
- Butter: 25 gm
- Parsley leaves: 2 tbsp chopped
- Garlic: 2–3 cloves
- Cheddar cheese: 30 gm
- Chilli flakes: 1 tsp
- Salt: ½ tsp
- Baking soda: ¾ tsp
- Olive oil: 1 tbsp

1. Preheat oven to 200 °C for 15 minutes.
2. In a pan, sauté garlic in olive oil lightly, remove and pound in a mortar and pestle.
3. Mix lemon juice and milk and leave it aside for 10 minutes to make buttermilk.
4. Sieve both flours with baking soda thrice.
5. Cream butter and brown sugar, add parsley leaves, Cheddar cheese, chilli flakes, sautéd garlic and salt.
6. Add flour, make a well in the centre and pour in buttermilk.
7. Knead into a dough, adding another 2 tbsp flour if required for it to come together.
8. Place the dough in a greased 5x9 inch loaf pan.
9. Brush with 1 tbsp milk and top with oats.
10. Bake for 25–30 minutes. At the 20-minute mark, apply melted butter.
11. Insert a toothpick in the centre to check if baked – it should come out clean.
12. Cool in the pan and transfer to a wire rack.

Soda bread is best eaten toasted. Instead of a pan, the dough ball can be baked on a parchment-lined baking tray and the top of the dough marked with a cross.

Photo on p. 346: The process of making the bacon wrapped meat loaf; Photo on p. 347: Bacon wrapped meat loaf; Photo on p. 348 (Clockwise): Pork chops in parsley demi glaze, Cheesy bubble and squeak, Beetroot goat cheese salad.

SERVINGS

BACON WRAPPED MEAT LOAF (Serves 4)

- Chicken mince: 300 gm
- Bacon: 6 rashers
- Onion: 1 small chopped
- Garlic: 3 cloves chopped
- Olive oil: 1 tsp
- Capsicum: 1 tbsp diced
- Red bell pepper: 1 tbsp diced
- Leek: 2 tbsp chopped
- Paprika powder: ½ tsp
- Salt: ¾ tsp
- Egg: 1 beaten
- Parsley leaves: 1 tbsp chopped
- Mustard sauce: 1 tsp
- Breadcrumbs: 1 tbsp

Sauce Mix

- Tomato ketchup: 2 tsp
- Sriracha sauce: 2 tsp
- Dijon mustard: 2 tsp
- Worcestershire sauce: 2 tsp

 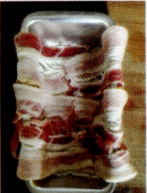 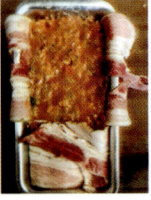 

1. Fill a deep tray with hot water and place in the oven at 200 °C for 15 minutes.
2. Mix all the sauces together and keep aside.
3. Line the base of a 2½ x 5 inch loaf pan with parchment.
4. Heat oil in a pan and stir fry onions, garlic, red bell pepper, capsicum and leek with ½ tsp salt for a few minutes.
5. Place bacon rashers, ensuring they overlap each other at the bottom of the loaf pan. The rashers should hang over the sides of the pan (Shown in the image above).
6. Soften the chicken mince by giving it a short grind in a mixer.
7. In a bowl, add chicken mince, sautéed vegetables, beaten egg, paprika powder, parsley leaves and breadcrumbs.
8. Season with ¼ tsp salt and add mustard sauce.
9. Give all the ingredients a good mix.
10. Transfer mix into the loaf pan lined with bacon.
11. Apply a layer of the sauce mix, saving the rest for later.
12. Fold the extended pieces of rashers over the mince and tuck into the side of the pan.

13. Bake for 1 hour 10 minutes.
14. At the 40-minute mark, brush the meat loaf with the sauce again and move to the top rack.
15. At the 50-minute mark, take the loaf pan out of the oven and remove the water bath. Gently drain the liquid from the loaf pan into a bowl and reserve juices.
16. With the help of a piece of parchment, invert the loaf pan on to a baking tray.
17. Apply the remaining sauce on all sides of the meat loaf and place the baking tray back in the oven on the top rack.
18. Bake to a reddish brown colour.
19. Remove from the oven. Let it cool down before slicing.
20. Serve slices warm or with the pouring sauce as explained below.

Pouring Sauce

Heat 1 tsp all-purpose flour with 1 tsp butter in a pan till dark brown, add ¼ cup chicken stock to the reserved juice and boil. Check seasoning.

Meat loaf on Sticks

A great way of enjoying meat loaf is as an appetizer. Cut into squares, skewer onto a toothpick. Add some cheese, a piece of fresh, dried or preserved fruit and some green olives.

PORK CHOPS IN PARSLEY DEMI-GLACE (Serves 4)
(Measuring cup size: 250 ml)

- Pork chops: 750–800 gm with bone

Brining

- Water: 2 cups + ½ cup
- Salt: 1½ tbsp
- Brown sugar: ¾ tbsp

SERVINGS

1. Boil water with salt and sugar, let it simmer till salt and sugar dissolve.
2. Cool the solution and add an additional ½ cup water.
3. Spread pork chops in a deep dish and pour the solution over.
4. Let it rest in a cool place for 2–3 hours.

Marinade

- Tomato ketchup: 1½ tbsp
- Worcestershire sauce: 3 tbsp
- Brown sugar: 1 tbsp
- Garlic paste: 1½ tbsp
- Garlic powder: 1½ tbsp
- Onion powder: 1½ tbsp
- Black pepper powder: 1½ tsp
- Salt: ½ tsp
- Mustard powder: 1½ tbsp
- Paprika powder: 1½ tsp
- Chilli flakes: 1½ tsp

1. Make a marinade with all the ingredients.
2. Trim the pork chops a little, but ensure that there is still enough fat on them.
3. Run a knife along the rind making cuts at 1 inch gaps.
4. Make slits in the chops and marinate for 2–3 hours outside and then for 12 hours in the refrigerator.

Searing

- Olive oil: 1–2 tbsp

1. Remove the pork chops and leave at room temperature for an hour.
2. Heat olive oil in a non-stick pan.
3. Place pork chops and sear for 3–4 minutes on each side.
4. Place in an ovenproof dish and cover with foil.
5. Preheat oven to 170 °C for 15 minutes. Place a baking tray filled with water.
6. Place the dish in the water bath and bake for 1 hour.
7. Reduce temperature to 150 °C and bake for another 15–25 minutes or till soft.
8. Take out from the oven, reserve juices in a bowl and let the pork chops rest covered.

Demi-glace

- Parsley leaves: 2 tbsp chopped
- Butter: ½ tbsp
- All-purpose flour: ¾ tbsp
- Balsamic vinegar: 1 tbsp
- Pork juice: Entire quantity

1. Heat butter in a non-stick pan. Add flour and stir to make a dark brown roux.
2. Add reserve pork juice and stir till smooth.
3. Add balsamic vinegar and parsley leaves.
4. Place the cooked chops in the pan and coat evenly with the demi-glace.
5. Let it rest for 1 minute and serve.

CHEESY BUBBLE AND SQUEAK (Serves 4)
(Measuring cup size: 250 ml)

- All-purpose flour: 1½ tbsp
- Butter: 1¼ tbsp
- Milk: ½ cup
- Cheddar cheese: 60 gm
- Onion powder: ½ tsp
- Cabbage: 1 cup cut into thick squares
- Salt: ¼ tsp + ½ tsp
- Mustard powder: 1 tsp
- Black pepper powder: ½ tsp
- Onion: 1 medium sliced
- Garlic: 2 cloves
- Potatoes: 350 gm boiled and peeled

1. Mash potatoes until smooth and lump-free.
2. Heat ¼ tbsp butter in a pan. Add the cabbage and let it soften.
3. Add ¼ tsp salt followed by onion and garlic.
4. Cook well until the mixture is soft.
5. Heat 1 tbsp butter in a pan. Add flour and stir to make a blonde roux.
6. Remove from flame, add milk and stir. Place back on the flame.
7. Now add cheddar cheese and mix well.
8. Add the cooked cabbage mixture to it and cool.
9. Add remaining salt, black pepper powder, mustard powder and onion powder.

10. Add potatoes and mix well.
11. Grease a small non-stick pan on a high flame. Transfer the cabbage–potato mixture on to the pan and pat down.
12. Lower the flame to medium and let the mixture cook for 7–8 minutes.
13. Heat a flat pan and flip bubble and squeak on to it and cook for 5–7 minutes.
14. Flip it back to the small pan and let it brown for another 4–5 minutes.
15. The mixture will be firm. Flip on to a serving plate. Serve hot.

BEETROOT AND GOAT CHEESE SALAD (Serves 4)
(Measuring cup size: 250 ml)

- Beetroot: 1 medium
- Olive oil: 1 tbsp + ¼ cup
- Ginger: 1 inch shredded
- Onion: 1 medium
- Orange: 1 peeled, 3 segments removed and the rest juiced
- Goat cheese: 3 tsp
- Lettuce: 1–2 leaves
- Walnuts: 6 tossed in ¼ tbsp butter and 1 tsp brown sugar
- Balsamic vinegar: 2–3 tbsp
- Mint leaves: 8–10
- Salt: ½ tsp + a pinch
- Black pepper powder: ½ tsp

1. Parboil beetroot, peel and slice thinly. Slice onion and soak in water.
2. Mix balsamic vinegar, ¼ cup olive oil, ½ tsp salt, black pepper powder and orange juice together to make a dressing.
3. Heat oil in a pan. Add beetroot slices, ginger and a pinch of salt. Cook till three-fourths done. Let beetroot cool.
4. Strain onion and add along with mint leaves to the dressing.
5. Add beetroot and lettuce.
6. Remove all ingredients from dressing and place on a plate.
7. Top with goat cheese, walnuts, orange segments and serve.
8. Remaining dressing can be served separately.

RED PESTO, CORIANDER GARLIC BUTTER BRAID

(Serves 4)

- All-purpose flour: 160 gm
- Sugar: ½ tsp
- Active dry yeast: 1¼ tsp
- Lukewarm milk: 115 ml
- Salt: ½ tsp
- Butter: 30 gm
- Garlic: 5 cloves
- Coriander leaves: 1 tbsp chopped
- Mozzarella cheese: 35 gm
- Olive oil: 20 ml + 10 ml
- Oregano: ½ tsp
- Chilli flakes: ½ tsp
- Black pepper corns: 4 crushed
- Red pesto: 3 tsp
- Olives: 3 chopped (optional)

1. In a bowl bloom yeast in lukewarm milk with sugar.
2. Leave mixture for 8–10 minutes till it turns frothy.
3. Gradually mix in the flour, salt and knead to a soft dough. The dough may be a little sticky.
4. Place the dough in an oiled bowl and cover with a moist cloth. Leave in a warm place to rise for 1½ hours.
5. While the dough is rising, blitz garlic and coriander and add softened butter and 20 ml olive oil.
6. Add crushed black peppercorns, oregano and chilli flakes. Mix well and keep aside.
7. Once the dough has doubled in volume, knock it back on a lightly floured surface and roll into a rectangle, approximately 10 x 6 inches.
8. Apply a layer of red pesto on the rolled-out dough, leaving a border of an inch all around.
9. Spread the coriander mixture over the red pesto layer.
10. Sprinkle grated mozzarella cheese.
11. Now gently start rolling up from one side to make a tight vertical log.
12. Slit the rolled log through the centre with a knife after leaving an inch from the top.
13. Start braiding the two parts by taking one part over the other.
14. Tuck the ends in.
15. Place the braid in an oiled loaf pan.
16. Wrap in a moist cloth and proof for another 45 minutes in a warm place.
17. Preheat oven to 190 °C for 10 minutes.

18. Bake for 35 minutes. At the 25-minute mark, brush with olive oil.
19. Once baked, remove the bread the from oven. Cool on a wire rack for about an hour and then unmould and serve warm.

> The quickest way to warm bread is to wrap it in a moistened kitchen towel and place it in the microwave for 30 seconds.

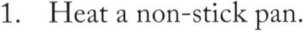

CHICKEN ESCALOPE WITH CREAMY VEGETABLES

(Serves 2)

Chicken Escalope

- Boneless chicken thighs: 2
- Garlic paste: 1 tsp
- Black pepper powder: ½ tsp
- Salt: ½ tsp
- Chilli flakes: ½ tsp
- Olive oil: 1 tbsp

1. For the escalopes, place the boneless chicken thighs on the cling film, and using a mallet flatten them to a 1 cm thickness.
2. Marinate with garlic paste, black pepper powder, salt and chilli flakes for 2–3 hours.
3. In a non-stick pan heat olive oil.
4. Place the escalopes in the pan and cook, flipping midway.
5. Serve accompanied with creamy vegetables.

Creamy Vegetables

- Mushrooms: 50 gm
- Carrots: 50 gm
- Beans: 50 gm
- Broccoli: 50 gm
- Sun-dried tomatoes: 2–3 pieces
- Corn: 1 tbsp
- Oregano: ¼ tsp
- Chilli flakes: ½ tsp
- All-purpose flour: 1 tsp
- Butter: 1 tsp
- Milk: 75 ml
- Olive oil: 1 tsp
- Salt: ¼ tsp

1. Heat a non-stick pan.
2. Add flour and sauté till golden, then add butter, stir and add milk.
3. Cook for 4–5 minutes and keep aside.

4. Heat olive oil in a pan, add mushrooms and toss, add chopped vegetables, sun-dried tomatoes, oregano, chilli flakes and salt.
5. Cook till three-fourths done.
6. Add the sauce made earlier and simmer till the vegetables are cooked.
7. Serve as an accompaniment to chicken.

QUATTRO FORMAGGI PORTOBELLO MUSHROOMS (Serves 4)

- Portobello mushrooms: 4
- Onion: 1 medium chopped
- Sun-dried tomatoes: 2 large quarters chopped
- Cream cheese: 2 tbsp
- Ricotta cheese: 3 tbsp
- Goat cheese: 2 tbsp
- Mozzarella cheese: 3–4 tbsp grated
- Baby spinach: 8 leaves washed and dried
- Ready-made marinara sauce: 7–8 tbsps
- Panko: 4 tbsp
- Butter: 75 gm softened

1. Remove stem and clean insides of portobello mushrooms with a sharp spoon.
2. Preheat oven to 180 °C for 10 minutes.
3. In a bowl, mix chopped onions with sun-dried tomatoes.
4. Add ricotta cheese, cream cheese, goat cheese and mix well.
5. Rub each mushroom with softened butter.
6. Cover a wire rack with foil and place the mushrooms.
7. Make slits in the foil and place the wire rack on a baking tray. All the excess moisture from the mushrooms will collect in the tray and the oven stays clean.
8. Fill the inside of each mushroom with 1½ tbsp of marinara sauce.
9. Add the cheese mix.
10. Top with spinach leaves and grated mozzarella cheese.
11. Cover with a layer panko crumbs.
12. Melt remaining butter and pour over the mushrooms.

13. Bake for 20–25 minutes and then broil for 5 minutes till golden.
14. Serve hot with a side of salad or buttered asparagus and some roasted potatoes.

'Mon Cheri' – My Love for Cherries!

Come summer and one can see the best of fruit in the London markets. The imported cherry is an expensive treat but in the month of June one can get a fair share of the local variety in our country too. Red, plump and juicy with dollops of sweetness, one can't deny its health benefits – but also, sugar is an important food group for me!

FRESH CHERRY COMPOTE CAKE WITH MASCARPONE CHEESE FROSTING (Serves 6)

Cherry Compote

- Cherries: 100 gm pitted
- Sugar: 50 gm
- Orange juice: 50 ml

1. Chop cherries and cook with sugar in a saucepan till thick.
2. Add orange juice and cook to a chunky jam-like consistency.
3. Cool and keep aside.

Cake

- All-purpose flour: 120 gm
- Sugar: 100 gm
- Butter: 100 gm
- Eggs: 2
- Baking powder: 4 gm
- Milk: 50 ml
- Compote: 75 gm
- Vanilla essence: ½ tsp

1. Ensure butter, eggs and compote are at room temperature. Preheat oven to 170 °C for 10 minutes.
2. Grease and line a loaf pan with parchment.
3. Sieve flour and baking powder. Cream butter and sugar.
4. Add eggs one at a time. Add cherry compote, vanilla essence and milk.
5. Gradually fold sieved flour into the mixture.
6. Pour batter into the loaf pan and tap the pan on the counter.
7. Bake for 35–40 minutes until a toothpick inserted into the centre comes out clean.
8. Let the cake cool in the pan, transfer to a wire rack and remove parchment.

Mascarpone Cheese Frosting

- Unsalted Butter: 50 gm
- Powder sugar: 35 gm
- Cornflour: ½ tsp
- Mascarpone cheese: 90 gm

1. Ensure butter and Mascarpone cheese are at room temperature.
2. Place all of the above ingredients in a bowl and whisk till creamy and light.
3. Place in a piping bag.

Assembling the Cake

1. Pipe the frosting on to the cooled cake or just slather it on. Top with cherries.
2. Refrigerate for 1 hour before slicing and serving.

Alcoholiday!

No Bailey's but the urge to bake with it. In a bid to make my own version of Bailey's using Irish whisky as a base I added condensed milk, cream and coffee to it. The result? A crusty, crunchy, yet moist cake. Using whatever is available sometimes works just as well ... and alcohol always helps the cause!

IRISH CREAM CINNAMON CRUMBLE CAKE (Serves 6)

Coffee Cinnamon Crumble

- Butter: 30 gm chilled
- Granulated sugar: 80 gm
- Coffee: 1 tsp
- Cinnamon powder: 1 tsp
- All-purpose flour: 30 gm
- Baking powder: ¼ tsp

1. Chop butter, add all the other ingredients and crumble with a fork. Refrigerate.

Cake

- All-purpose flour: 125 gm
- Baking powder: ¾ tsp
- Brown sugar: 85 gm
- Butter: 75 gm
- Egg: 1
- Irish whisky: 35 ml
- Condensed milk: 35 ml
- Cream: 35 ml
- Milk: 60 ml
- Instant coffee: 3 tsp

1. Ensure butter, eggs and milk are at room temperature.
2. Preheat oven to 180°C for 10 minutes and line a 6–7 inch cake pan with parchment.
3. Sieve flour and baking powder together.
4. Mix lukewarm milk and coffee together, and let it cool to room temperature.
5. Mix whisky, condensed milk and cream together.
6. Whisk together butter and brown sugar.
7. Add egg and whisk, then add the whisky mixture and coffee mixture. Whisk further.
8. Fold in the flour. Pour the batter into a cake pan and top with coffee cinnamon crumble evenly. Tap pan on the counter to remove air pockets.
9. Bake for 45–50 minutes.
10. Remove pan and let it cool.
11. Run a knife along the edges and transfer the cake to a wire rack.
12. Remove parchment. Allow the cake to cool and serve sliced.

Photo on p. 355 (Clockwise): Quattro fromaggi portobello mushrooms, Red pesto coriander garlic butter braid, Chicken escalope with creamy vegetables; Photo on p. 358: Fresh cherry compote cake, Mascarpone cheese frosting; Photo on p. 361: 'No Baileys' Cinnamon crumble cake.

For the Love of Food
(Suggested Menu Plan)

LET'S PARTY
Starters

Cornmeal Sausage Galette	p. 89
Pumpkin Mozzarella Balls	p. 90
Asparagus Cottage Cheese Tartlets	p. 383
Keema Scotch Eggs	p. 119

Mains

Pork in Parsley Demi-Glace	p. 349
Creamy Mustard Chicken with Sun-dried tomatoes	p. 115
Baked Spicy Yoghurt Cauliflower Steaks	p. 116
Quattro Formaggi Portobello Mushrooms	p. 356
Beetroot and Goat Cheese Salad	p. 352
Red Pesto, Coriander Garlic Butter Braid	p. 353

Desserts

Irish Cream Cinnamon Crumble Cake	p. 360
Lemon Tarts Topped with Blueberries	p. 383

FAMILY TIME

Pumpkin Mozzarella Balls	p. 90
Bacon Wrapped Meat Loaf	p. 346
Spinach and Cottage Cheese Casserole	p. 117
Vegetarian Bread Rolls	p. 120

Dessert

Fresh Cherry Compote Cake	p. 357

CHAI TIME

Afternoon in Colaba

Colaba in Mumbai is literally where my life began. The Naval Hospital in this neighbourhood is my birthplace. I went to kindergarten in nearby Cuffe Parade. My major stepping stone to complete independence is here too, at the Taj Mahal Hotel. There is certainly a karmic connection to the place.

The area is all about quaint lanes, shops and many eateries. Irani cafes are very popular hangouts. In the nineteenth century, Zoroastrian Irani immigrants to British India opened these little cafes which began as provision stores, shelves stacked with soaps and canned food like Polson and Dippy's. Some functioned as tea shops, selling 'bun maska', cakes and biscuits. Chai was drunk from a saucer, with a 'sarrappo' slurping sound! The cafes had a standard appearance, with high ceilings, marble-top tables, classic black furniture, large mirrors, glass jars filled with dry snacks, cakes and the classic red-and-white checked tablecloths. The number of these cafes has dwindled.

Over time, these cafes altered their menus to include many Parsi delicacies. The Russian pattice is one such delicacy – a soft cutlet, and since it is a white or 'gora' cutlet as against the darker meat ones, it became known as the Russian pattice. 'Eeda' or eggs are put over anything edible from okra to keema as well as over 'salli' potato sticks or wafers and this is eaten with pav. It took me four attempts to create a foolproof pav. If the colour was right, the texture was wrong, and if the texture was right, the colour was wrong. Phew!

Pav bhaji had humble beginnings outside the textile mills in Mumbai. A mix of vegetables was put together and spiced up, served with pav, thus ensuring a quick and cheap meal. To have this in a butter-laden puff is heavenly. Making puff pastry is tedious, but the beautiful layers and crunch make the job well worth it. This was a midnight task for me since it needed a super chilled kitchen and no other activity around.

The only thing left to put on the table are the golgappas from Kailash Parvat.

LADI PAV (Serves 4)
(Measuring cup size: 250 ml)

Yeast Mix

- Active dry yeast: 2¼ tsp
- Sugar: 2½ tbsp
- Milk: 3 tsp
- Water: 3 tbsp

Pav Mix

- All-purpose flour: 3 cups
- Baking powder: 1 tsp
- Salt: 1 tsp
- Butter: 3 tbsp + 1 tbsp for basting
- Refined oil: 2 tbsp
- Milk: 250 ml + 2–3 tbsp for brushing

1. Bloom yeast in lukewarm milk, mixed with sugar and water, for 8 minutes.
2. Sieve flour along with baking powder.
3. In a stand mixer, with a dough hook, or in a bowl, place the flour and salt.
4. Make a well in the flour and add bloomed yeast in the centre. Cover with flour and leave for 5 minutes.
5. Stir and then move to speed 2 and then speed 4 if using a mixer or gently knead together by hand adding milk gradually.
6. Add butter and oil gradually and knead for 15 minutes by hand or 7–8 minutes in the mixer.
7. Transfer the dough to a greased bowl and cover with a moist cloth. Proof in a warm place for 1½ hours till the dough doubles.
8. Place dough on a kitchen counter and knock it down and knead for 5 minutes.
9. Grease an 8 inch square baking pan.
10. Divide the dough into 9 equal portions, approximately 90 gm each, and roll into balls.
11. Place the balls in the pan, with a little distance between them, giving them space to rise.
12. Cover with a moist cloth and further proof for 45 minutes.
13. Preheat oven to 200°C for 20 minutes.
14. Brush the proofed pav with milk.
15. Bake pav for 12–13 minutes in the middle rack. Do not open the oven door.
16. Broil for 2 minutes on the top rack.
17. Remove from oven and brush the top of the pav with butter immediately.
18. The top of the pav may be hard but will soften on cooling.

19. Wrap the bottom of the pan with a moist cloth to allow it to cool quickly and immediately remove from the pan to prevent condensation.
20. Wrap pav in a paper towel and place in an airtight container. This can be stored for 2–3 days at room temperature.

BHAJI PUFF PATTIES (Serves 6)

Bhaji

- Cauliflower: 3 big florets
- Capsicum: 1 small
- Beans: 50 gm
- Carrot: 50 gm
- Peas: 50 gm
- Potatoes: 250 gm peeled
- Onions: 275 gm chopped
- Salt: 1 tsp
- Lemon wedges: 2
- Tomatoes: 350 gm chopped
- Tomato purée: 15 ml
- Cumin powder: 1½ tsp
- Turmeric powder: 1 tsp
- Pav bhaji masala: 3 tsp
- Kashmiri chilli powder: 1¼ tsp
- Refined oil: 2 tbsp
- Butter: 50 gm
- Water: 185–225 ml
- Coriander leaves: 2 tbsp chopped

1. Chop all the vegetables.
2. Boil all the vegetables except onions and tomatoes in 300 ml water strain and mash.
3. Heat oil in a pan. Add 250 gm chopped onions with ½ tsp salt and sauté for 10–12 minutes till golden and translucent.
4. Add chopped tomatoes, tomato purée and cook. Add mashed vegetables.
5. Add cumin powder, turmeric powder, Kashmiri chilli powder, pav bhaji masala and ½ tsp salt.
6. Add butter and cook.
7. Add water in small quantities and cook for at least 20 minutes on a low flame.
8. Keep the bhaji moist for regular pav bhaji.
9. Serve hot with remaining chopped onions, lemon wedges and coriander leaves.

Puff Patties

- Cooked bhaji: 6 heaped tsp
- Cheddar cheese: 30 gm grated

1. Mix bhaji with Cheddar cheese and keep refrigerated.

Puff Pastry

- All-purpose flour: 150 gm
- Salted butter: 150 gm chilled
- Lime juice: ¼ tsp
- Chilled water: 90 ml

The kitchen should be cold. Use a stone kitchen counter to knead and roll. Cream each of the six portions of butter one at a time, keeping the rest frozen. Dust the surface with flour while rolling.

1. Sieve flour and make a dough with 15 gm of the chilled butter and lime.
2. Add chilled water gradually and knead to a ball.
3. Divide remaining butter into 6 portions and keep chilled.
4. Cream one portion of butter at a time.
5. Roll out the dough to a rectangle approximately 12 x 8 inches.
6. Apply a portion of the creamed butter to two-thirds of the rectangle, leaving a ¼ inch edge on all sides.
7. Fold the rectangle into three folds along its length.
8. Fold the non-buttered portion of the rectangle into the buttered portion and then fold it again.
9. Let the pastry rest for 15 minutes, then wrap in a moist cloth and refrigerate for 15 minutes.
10. Turn the rectangle 90 degrees, such that the shorter side is towards you.
11. Repeat steps 5, 6, 7, 8, 9 and 10 four more times.
12. The final fold and roll will be without butter.
13. After the final fold, wrap the pastry and freeze between parchment and cling film.
14. Rest for 3 hours in the refrigerator before using.

SERVINGS

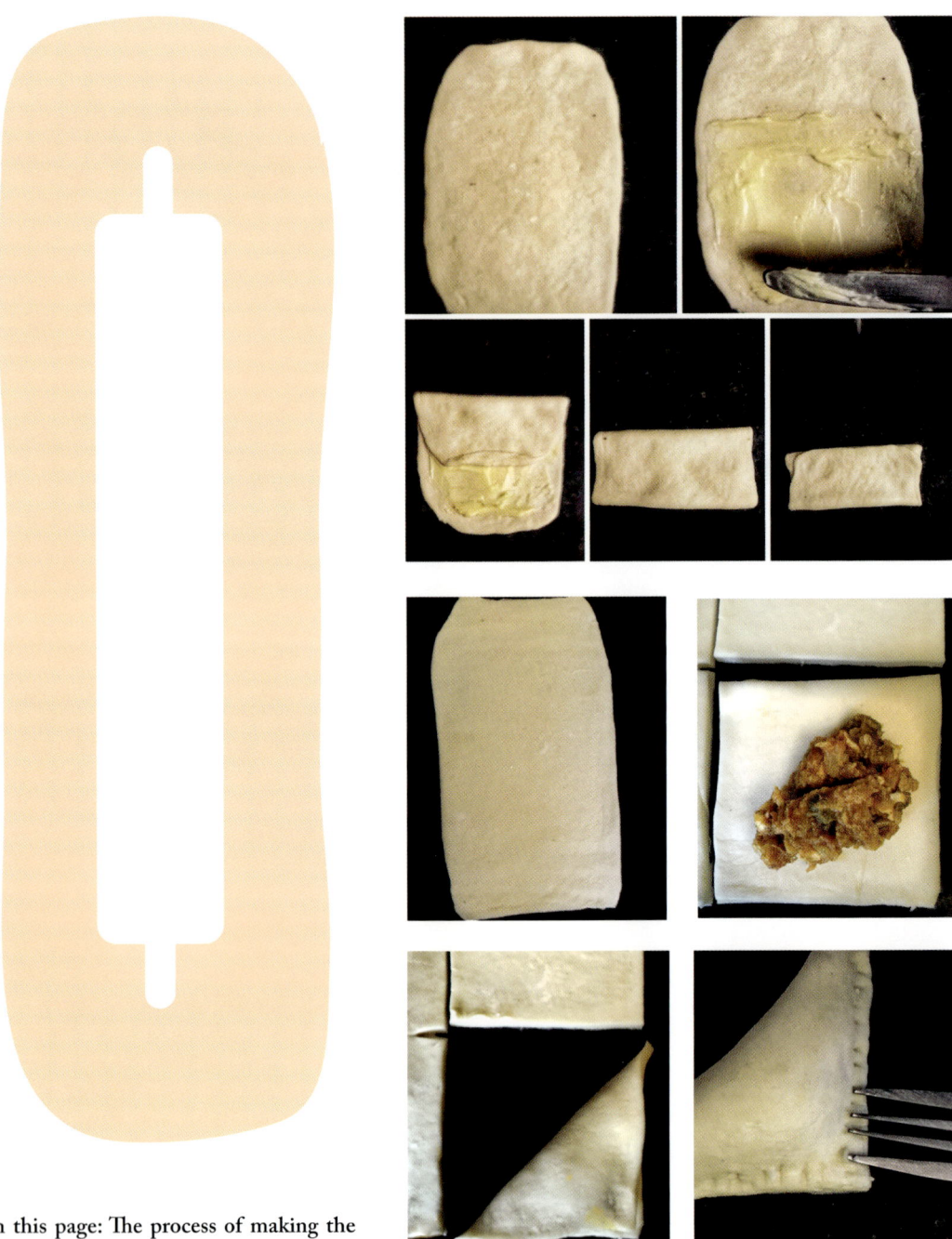

On this page: The process of making the puff pastry and the Bhaji patties.

* 368

Assembling Puff Patties

1. Roll out the puff pastry on a flour-dusted cold surface to approximately 11x 7 inches.
2. Cut the puff pastry into six, 3½ inch squares.
3. Place 1 tsp of the bhaji mix in the centre of the square. Fold the dough to make a triangle. Seal the edges with water. With a fork, lightly press the edges.
4. Place on a parchment-lined tray. Brush with melted butter or egg wash.
5. Preheat oven to 200 °C for 10–12 minutes. Bake puff patties for 20–22 minutes.
6. Broil on upper rack for 2 minutes or until golden.
7. Remove and cool on a wire rack. Serve warm.

KHARI TWIST (Each rectangle makes 1)

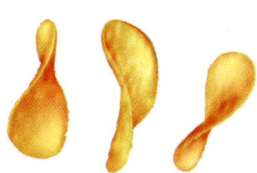

1. Cut rectangular strips of puff pastry to approximately 3 x 1 inches each.
2. Twist twice in the centre to make a bow.
3. Apply melted butter and sprinkle with carom seeds.
4. Place on a parchment-lined baking tray.
5. Preheat oven to 200 °C for 10 minutes. Bake the khari for 18–20 minutes.
6. Remove from oven, let cool and store in an airtight container.

WAFER PAR EEDA (Serves 2)

(Measuring cup size: 250 ml)

- Spiced potato wafers: 1 cup
- Ginger paste: 1 tsp
- Garlic paste: 1 tsp
- Tomatoes: 2 medium chopped
- Eggs: 2
- Red chilli powder: ½ tsp
- Turmeric powder: ¼ tsp
- Green chilli: 1 chopped
- Coriander leaves: 4 tsp chopped
- Salt: ½ tsp
- Refined oil: 1 tbsp

SERVINGS

1. Whisk eggs with ¼ tsp salt.
2. Heat oil in a 7–8 inch non-stick pan or skillet.
3. Add ginger and garlic paste and sauté.
4. Add chopped tomatoes, green chilli, coriander leaves, ¼ tsp salt and cook till soft.
5. Add turmeric powder, red chilli powder and mix well. Add 1 cup lightly crushed spiced wafers, saving a few and spread evenly across the pan.
6. Add whisked eggs in the centre and give the pan a swirl to spread the eggs.
7. Add the saved spicy wafers on top.
8. Cook on a low flame till the eggs set. Serve hot with pav.

RUSSIAN PATTICE (Gora Chicken Cutlet)

(Serves 6)

- Whole chicken leg: 2
- Ginger–garlic paste: ¼ tbsp
- Salt: 1½ tsp
- All-purpose flour: 1 tbsp
- Ghee: 1 tsp
- Green chillies: 2–3 chopped fine
- Milk: 1 tbsp
- Cheddar cheese: 50 gm grated
- Black pepper powder: ¼ tsp
- Potato boiled: 1 medium
- Egg: 1 whisked
- Breadcrumbs: 1 cup
- Refined oil: to pan fry

1. Boil chicken in 350 ml water, add ginger–garlic paste and ½ tsp salt.
2. Remove chicken legs and cool.
3. Debone, shred chicken and chop finely.
4. Heat ghee, add all-purpose flour and stir fry till light brown. Add milk and make a paste.
5. Add chopped chicken, green chillies, Cheddar cheese and mix.
6. Add remaining salt and black pepper powder.
7. Remove from flame and add the boiled potato. Check seasoning.
8. Refrigerate the mixture for 3–4 hours.

9. Divide the mixture into 10 equal balls and flatten a little.
10. Refrigerate on an open plate for 45 minutes.
11. Whisk an egg, dip the pattice in it and then coat with breadcrumbs. Let pattice rest for 15 minutes. Heat oil in a pan and fry the pattice to a light golden colour.
12. Serve hot with ketchup.

JEERA BISKUT (Serves 6)

- All-purpose flour: 100 gm
- Powdered sugar: 20 gm
- Salt: ½ tsp
- Baking powder: 1 tsp
- Milk: 1½ tbsp
- Roasted cumin seeds: 1½ tsp
- Salted butter: 50 gm

1. Using a whisk cream together butter and powdered sugar until light.
2. Add all-purpose flour, baking powder, salt and 1 tsp roasted cumin seeds.
3. Mix well and then add milk to bind the mixture. Roll into a single cylinder about 3 cm in diameter and wrap in cling film.
4. Refrigerate for 30 minutes.
5. Preheat oven to 200 °C for 8 minutes.
6. Remove cling film and cut the cylinder into discs.
7. Place the discs on a baking tray, and brush lightly with milk and drizzle the remaining roasted cumin seeds.
8. Bake for 15–18 minutes.
9. Transfer to a wire rack.
10. Store in an airtight container, once cooled.

In case making a cylinder is difficult, roll the dough into a 4 mm sheet and cut into discs with a cookie cutter.

Photo on p. 371 (Clockwise): Ladi Pav, Wafer par Eeda, Russian Patties, Bhaji Patties, Bhaji, Khari Twist. Photo on p. 372: Jeera Biskut; Photo on p. 376: 'No Mawa' Cake.

SERVINGS

'Malai Marke'

Malai, cheeni on bread has been a childhood favourite. The crunch and sweetness of the granules of sugar with smooth cream on toasted white bread is unmatched. This brings to mind a bowl of malai in the refrigerator and the thought of making mawa cake.

In the absence of mawa I made a cheat version – 'No mawa'. The end result was so like the mawa cake one can find in the Irani Cafes, with an old-world, desi, rustic warmth. Eat it alongside Phetela Coffee aka Dalgona's original version.

'NO MAWA' CAKE (Serves 6)
(Measuring cup size: 250 ml)

'No Mawa' (Makes 50 gm)

- Milk powder: ¼ cup
- Butter: ½ tsp
- Milk: 30 ml

1. Heat butter in a non-stick pan and let it melt.
2. Add milk.
3. Add milk powder and cook, till the mixture thickens. Do not let it brown.
4. Stir continuously to get a smooth thick mixture.
5. Remove from flame and let it cool before using.

Cake

- All-purpose flour: 60 gm
- Semolina: 40 gm
- Powdered sugar: 75 gm
- Fresh cream: 60 gm
- Baking powder: ¾ tsp
- Vanilla essence: 1 tsp
- Butter: 30 gm
- No mawa: 50 gm
- Eggs: 1
- Milk: 1–2 tbsp
- Almonds: a handful sliced

1. Ensure that the eggs, butter, milk and cream are at room temperature.
2. Grease a 6–7 inch round cake pan or 6 muffin cups and line with parchment or dust with flour on the insides.
3. Preheat oven to 170 °C for 8–10 minutes.
4. Sieve flour, semolina and baking powder.
5. Whisk butter and powdered sugar, add 'no mawa' and then add fresh cream.
6. Add egg and vanilla essence and continue whisking.
7. Mix gradually and fold the mixture.
8. Add milk to give the batter the right consistency.
9. Pour the batter into the cake pan or muffin cups. Spread evenly and top with chopped nuts.
10. Tap the pan or muffin cups on the counter to remove any air pockets.
11. Bake for 25–30 minutes, till a toothpick inserted in the centre comes out clean.
12. Remove the cake pan or muffin cups from the oven and cool.
13. Transfer cake or muffins to a wire rack to cool further.

Photo on p. 371 (Clockwise): Ladi Pav, Wafer par Eeda, Russian Patties, Bhaji Patties, Bhaji, Khari Twist. Photo on p. 372: Jeera Biskut; Photo on p. 376: 'No Mawa' Cake.

'Cuppa Tea, Love'

There is something charming about the tea traditions of the English. I don't know if it is from my favourite Enid Blytons or whether it has to do with *Pride and Prejudice*. Warm scones, jam, finger sandwiches and cake always sounded good even without Mr. Darcy walking in!

The British tradition of drinking tea originated from our land, just much fancier in its service. At age 40, it was an experience to get dressed and sit down for tea at the Ritz Tea Room. Hey, it was my Barbara Cartland moment – right down to the Chantilly lace blouse and billowing skirt! The Ritz owes its modernized kitchen to Chef Augusta Escoffier, the chef de cuisine who created some of the most elevated yet original dishes and codified French cuisine for the ages in his *Le Guide Culinaire*, still in print today. The *Larousse Gastronomique*, which is treated as 'the' kitchen Bible, also owes its basis to Chef Escoffier.

Just as tea transported itself to foreign lands, so did the Madras curry powder, straight from Fort St George in today's Chennai to a store named Barrie's, in London's Leicester Square. A blend of many spices that are used in our kitchens regularly were used by the English to make their version of curry which originated from the Tamil word 'kari' for sauce or relish. I have used it as an interesting element in the egg sandwich.

I once entered our kitchen on my midnight prowl and saw a pot with orange segments steeped in hot water. It smelt fresh, and my first thought was that this would find its way to the girls for their beauty regimen. Two days later, I saw, sitting on our kitchen counter a beautiful jar of delicious orange marmalade made by our house help. This was made by someone whom we all assumed didn't know anything about cooking. The cake is a tribute to his jar of marmalade.

SERVINGS

PRADEEP'S ORANGE MARMALADE   (Makes 250 gm)

- Oranges: 4
- Orange zest: 1 orange
- Water: 3 litres
- Sugar: 150 gm

1. Peel oranges, remove skin for each orange segment, discard seeds and keep only the pulp aside.
2. Boil orange zest and orange pulp in 3 litres of water for about 20 minutes.
3. Leave to cool overnight.
4. Place back on a low flame, and reduce to one-third the volume.
5. Add sugar and continue to boil, till it thickens.
6. Remove from flame and let it cool to room temperature. Bottle in an airtight glass jar.

ORANGE ALMOND CAKE   (Serves 6)
(Measuring cup size: 250 ml)

- All-purpose flour: 115 gm + 1 tsp
- Castor sugar: 60 gm
- Granulated sugar: 55 gm
- Butter: 100 gm + 2 tbsp
- Olive oil: 2 tbsp
- Eggs: 2
- Baking powder: ½ tsp
- Almonds slivers: 2 tbsp
- Fresh orange juice: 45 ml
- Orange zest: 1 tbsp
- Orange essence: ½ tsp
- Orange marmalade: 2–3 tbsp

1. Ensure eggs, butter and orange juice are at room temperature.
2. Preheat oven to 170°C for 10 minutes.
3. Grease a 6–7 inch round pan and line with parchment.
4. Sieve all-purpose flour and baking powder.
5. Whisk together butter, oil and both sugars.

6. Add eggs and whisk further. Add flour gradually and fold.
7. Add orange juice and zest. Coat almond slivers in 1 tsp of flour and fold.
8. Transfer batter to the baking pan. Tap the pan on the counter and place in the oven.
9. Bake for 50–55 minutes. Insert a toothpick in the centre, it should come out clean.
10. Cool in the pan, transfer to a wire rack and remove parchment.
11. Cut the cake into two layers with a thread or a knife and sandwich with softened orange marmalade. Press down gently to ensure that the layers stick.

Frosting

- Powdered sugar: ½ cup
- Orange juice: 2 tbsp
- Cream: 1 tbsp
- Milk: 1–2 tbsp
- Orange essence: ½ tsp
- Roasted almonds: 6 sliced
- Orange zest: 1 tbsp

1. Whisk powdered sugar, cream, orange juice and orange essence together. Add milk as needed.
2. Ladle frosting over the cake. Top with sliced almonds and orange zest.

BACON, HONEY, SPICED BUTTERMILK SCONES
(Makes 9)

- Bacon rashers: 125 gm diced
- All-purpose flour: 200 gm
- Butter: 90 gm chilled and cubed
- Baking powder: 1 tsp
- Baking soda: ½ tsp
- Spiced buttermilk: 85 ml
- Honey: 60 ml + 10 ml for drizzling
- Brown sugar: 2½ tsp
- Egg: 1 small whisked
- Dried rosemary: 1 tsp

1. Line a baking tray with butter paper.
2. Fry diced bacon till it is crisp. Remove from pan and cool.
3. Sieve all-purpose flour with baking soda and baking powder.
4. Add brown sugar and rosemary.

SERVINGS

5. Place flour in a bowl and whisk. Gradually add butter and whisk till crumbly.
6. Add bacon, followed by buttermilk and honey. Whisk for 1 minute.
7. Using an ice cream scoop, transfer a scoop of batter on to a parchment-lined baking tray. Ensure there is distance between each scoop of batter. Brush with egg wash.
8. Preheat the oven to 170 °C for 5 minutes.
9. Bake the scones for 12 minutes. Drizzle honey and bake further for 8 minutes.
10. Take out from the oven and serve warm with cream cheese.

> The bottom of the scones should be soft to the touch. This scone has a deep golden appearance, because of the honey drizzle.

TARTLETS (Makes 40 mini tartlets)

- All-purpose flour: 220 gm
- Butter: 100 gm
- Chilled water: 4 tbsp

1. Rub all-purpose flour and butter together with your hands until crumbly.
2. Add water and knead to a dough.
3. Wrap in cling film and rest refrigerate for 30 minutes.
4. Take out and roll to ½ cm thick between two layers of cling film sheets.
5. Remove the upper layer of the cling film and carefully transfer the dough to a 10 inch tart pan or cut into discs and place into mini tart shells.
6. Press the edges with your fingers. Prick the base with a fork.
7. Preheat oven to 180 °C for 8 minutes.
8. Place baking beans on the tart/mini tart shells and bake blind for 15 minutes. Remove baking beans.
9. Let them rest before filling.
10. Tart shells can also be frozen at this stage for later use.

Photo on p. 381 (Clockwise): Pradeep's orange marmalade, Bacon honey buttermilk scones, Orange almond cake, Chicken mince tarts, Asparagus cottage cheese tartlets.

CHICKEN MINCE TARTLETS (Serves 6)

- Tart shells: 15
- Chicken mince: 100 gm
- Onion: ¼ large
- Tomato ketchup: ¼ tsp
- Tabasco sauce: 2–3 drops
- Paprika powder: ¼ tsp
- Cream: 40 ml
- Milk: 10 ml
- Cornflour: ½ tsp
- Mozzarella cheese: 20 gm
- Sun-dried tomato: 1 large piece chopped
- Basil leaves: 3–4 chopped + few for topping
- Butter: 1 tsp
- Salt: ½ tsp

1. Heat butter in a non-stick pan.
2. Add onion with a little salt and cook until translucent.
3. Add basil leaves and chicken mince.
4. Add sun-dried tomatoes and tomato ketchup.
5. Add tabasco sauce, paprika powder and remaining salt. Cook till done.
6. Remove from flame and let it cool.
7. Add cream, cornflour dissolved in milk, and mozzarella cheese. Mix well.
8. Fill partially pre-baked tartlets with the chicken mixture and top with a basil leaf.
9. Preheat oven to 175 °C for 8 minutes.
10. Bake the tartlets for 12–15 minutes.
11. Serve warm.

ASPARAGUS COTTAGE CHEESE TARTLETS
(Serves 6)

- Tart shells: 15
- Cottage cheese: 100 gm
- Asparagus: 3 stems chopped
- Cherry tomatoes: 7–8 halved
- Onion: ½ large chopped
- Tomato ketchup: ¾ tsp
- Tabasco sauce: 3–4 drops
- Paprika powder: ¼ tsp
- Salt: ½ tsp
- Cream: 30 ml
- Milk: 20 ml
- Butter: ½ tsp
- Mozzarella cheese: 20 gm
- Parmesan cheese shavings: 2 tbsp

1. Heat butter in a non-stick pan.
2. Add onions with a little salt and cook until translucent.
3. Add asparagus and sauté.
4. Add tomato ketchup, tabasco sauce and paprika powder.
5. Remove from flame and allow it to cool down.
6. Add mozzarella cheese, cream, milk and cottage cheese. Mix well.
7. Fill asparagus mixture into partially pre-baked tartlets and top with cherry tomatoes.
8. Preheat oven to 175 °C for 8 minutes.
9. Bake tartlets for 12–15 minutes.
10. Serve warm, topped with Parmesan cheese.

LEMON TARTS TOPPED WITH BLUEBERRIES
(Serves 6)

Tart shells (Makes 8, 5 cm tarts)

- All-purpose flour: 100 gm
- Butter: 50 gm
- Egg: ½, beaten
- Icing sugar: ½ tbsp

1. Rub all-purpose flour, icing sugar and butter together until crumbly.
2. Add egg and knead to a dough.
3. Wrap in cling film and refrigerate for 30 minutes.
4. Take out and roll out to ½ cm thickness between two cling film sheets.
5. Remove the upper layer of cling film. Cut 6 cm discs and transfer the dough to tart moulds. Press the edges with your fingers and prick the base with a fork.
6. Preheat oven to 180 °C for 8 minutes.
7. Place baking beans on the tart shells and bake blind for 15 minutes.
8. Remove baking beans and bake further at 170 °C for 6–8 minutes.
9. Take out from the oven and let the tart shells cool.

Lemon Curd (Makes 300 gm)

- Egg yolks: 4
- Granulated sugar: 120–130 gm
- Butter: 100 gm
- Salt: a pinch
- Lemon juice: 40 ml
- Yellow food colour: a pinch

1. Whisk egg yolks, granulated sugar and lemon juice together in a saucepan.
2. Place the saucepan on a double boiler and whisk for 10–12 minutes till the mixture thickens to coating consistency.
3. Remove from flame and add cold butter. Whisk until the butter melts and blends.
4. Add a pinch of yellow food colouring and a pinch of salt.
5. Place saucepan back on the double boiler and whisk mixture for another 5 minutes.
6. Let lemon curd cool and then refrigerate for 24 hours before using.

Assembling Lemon Tarts

Lemon curd can be frozen for a few weeks. It can be brought down to the refrigerator to defrost for 24 hours.

- Tart shells: 8 small
- Blueberries: 10 halved
- Lemon curd: 150 gm
- Icing sugar: 1–2 tsp to dust

1. Pipe chilled lemon curd into tart shells and top with blueberries and a dusting of icing sugar.

SERVINGS

MADRAS CURRY POWDER EGG FINGER SANDWICHES (Serves 4)

- White bread: 4 slices
- Eggs: 2 hard-boiled
- Mayonnaise: 4 tbsp
- Madras curry powder: ½ tsp
- Celery leaves: 1½ tbsp chopped

1. Peel and chop boiled eggs.
2. In a bowl mix together mayonnaise, madras curry powder and celery leaves.
3. Add boiled eggs and mix gently.
4. Spread the mixture equally on 2 slices of bread and top each with the other 2 slices.
5. Gently press each sandwich, cut and remove crust.
6. Diagonally cut the sandwich to make four triangles.
7. Keep the sandwiches wrapped in a moist cloth if not being served immediately.

Photo on p. 386 (Clockwise): Madras curry powder egg finger sandwiches, Lemon tart topped with blueberries.

And Some More ...

The story of the humble cake rusk or russ begins in Persia, with the baking of bread a day or two old again to make a crisper version, like a biscuit with a longer shelf life. In the lanes of Chandni Chowk, there are bakers who create trays of this by the dozen in a shift. It is a favourite snack, eaten in North India with milk tea. The concept of double baking ensures a dry and crisp product, and is used in many parts of the world like the Italian biscotti or the German zwieback. The aroma from this version transports you to a biscuit factory.

RUSS (Makes 3 loaves)

- All-purpose flour: 250 gm
- Whole wheat flour: 100 gm
- Baking powder: 2 tsp
- Butter: 180 gm
- Powdered sugar: 350 gm
- Eggs: 5 medium
- Dried cranberries: ½ cup
- Trail mix: ½ cup
- Milk: 180 ml
- Orange or any other fruit essence: 1 tsp
- Vanilla essence: 1½ tsp

1. Eggs and butter should be at room temperature.
2. Preheat oven to 180°C for 10 minutes.
3. Sieve together all-purpose flour, whole wheat flour and baking powder.
4. Chop trail mix and dried cranberries. Whisk butter and sugar together.
5. Add eggs one at a time and continue whisking. Add both essences.
6. Add flour mixture and milk, alternating between the two. Whisk at a low speed.
7. Fold in trail mix and dried cranberries.
8. Bake for 30–35 minutes, till a toothpick inserted in the centre comes out clean.
9. Let the loaves cool in the pan and then turn onto a wire rack.
10. Slice when cool. Place again in a cold oven at 160°C and bake for 25 minutes.
11. At the 15-minute mark, flip the slices once.
12. Remove from oven.
13. The slices will crisp further on cooling.
14. Store in an airtight jar.

For a crisper version, bake for 35 minutes, flipping sides at the 20-minute mark or do a third bake the following day of the stored russ for 8 minutes.

NANKHATAI (Makes 16 large)

The literal Persian meaning of nan is dough, and khatai is biscuit. Also popularly called 'biskut' in North India and Pakistan. It is a nice addition to an evening tea and a part of iftar during Ramadan. Try it with a little jam and it's spot on.

For me, it brings back memories of 'Needs', a little bakery in the defence area of Wellington. As kids, trudging up to this sweet haven was a treat. The elderly gentleman who owned the place would give us hard-boiled sweets as a bonus. Before the storm of packaged biscuits and cookies, these were the closest option in our lives.

Mama, of course, made them at home, and her version had semolina in them. There are versions which have eggs in them too.

This version of nankhatai has been made using a recipe that I noted down in my Hotel Management School Patisserie journal. I still have that journal and it tells me that I made these for the first time on 23 September 1993! Gosh, I am ancient! In those days, ammonium bicarbonate (I have forgotten that we used this leavening agent!) was an addition which I have swapped for basic baking soda.

- All-purpose flour: 150 gm
- Ghee: 50 gm
- Butter: 50 gm
- Powdered sugar: 110 gm
- Baking powder: 1 tsp
- Baking soda: 1 tsp
- Sour curd: 1 tsp
- Green cardamom powder: ½ tsp
- Cardamom/Vanilla essence: ½ tsp
- Almonds: for each biscuit

1. Sieve all-purpose flour and baking powder.
2. Whisk together ghee, butter and powdered sugar till creamy.
3. Add baking soda, cardamom powder, sour curd and cardamom/vanilla essence. Whisk further.
4. Gradually add in the flour and knead to a soft dough.
5. Divide into 16/20/24 portions, depending on the size you prefer.
6. Make into balls, flatten the top and firmly press an almond on each.

7. Place on a parchment-lined baking tray.
8. Preheat oven to 170 °C for 5 minutes.
9. Place cookie tray in the oven and bake for 20–25 minutes.
10. Nankhatais harden on cooling.

CANTUCCI (Coffee Almond Biscotti) (Makes 40–45)
(Measuring cup size: 250 ml)

'Cantucci de Prato' is the traditional name for the popular biscotti. Originating in the Tuscan region of Italy, 'bis' literally means twice and 'cotto' refers to baked. The cantucci is essentially a twice-baked, long, dry, thin, wafer-like cookie. Every region in Italy has its own version with a change in nuts and other additives.

The tradition of double baking dates back to the Romans. This ensured a long shelf life and a convenient food for travel. The cantucci is best had dunked in wine or coffee – the mild sweetness of the cantucci helps in not overpowering the flavour of the drink accompanying it.

Changing the rule, this is a thrice-baked version, ensuring absolute crispness and crunch. If in the mood, dip one-third of the wafer in molten chocolate for that extra kick.

- All-purpose flour: 2½ cups + a few tbsp for shaping
- Roasted almonds: ¾ cup
- Butter: 56 gm
- Brown sugar: ¾–1 cup
- Baking powder: 1½ tsp
- Cinnamon powder: ¼ tsp
- Instant coffee powder: 2½ tsp dissolved in a few drops of water
- Eggs: 2½
- Almond essence: ½ tsp
- Vanilla essence: 1 tsp

1. Soak almonds in water for an hour.
2. Peel and chop the almonds and dry on a paper towel.

3. Preheat oven to 175 °C for 8 minutes.
4. Sieve all-purpose flour with baking powder.
5. Whisk brown sugar and butter till creamy. Add cinnamon powder.
6. Add eggs, one at a time, followed by almond essence, vanilla essence and coffee powder.
7. Add flour mixture gradually and mix well.
8. Add chopped almonds and mix.
9. Transfer dough on to a counter and divide into two. Shape into 2 logs of 3 x 11 inches. Add extra flour if needed.
10. Transfer the logs on to a parchment-lined baking tray.
11. Bake for 20–22 minutes. Ensure the logs are firm.
12. Remove the logs and let them cool for 20 minutes.
13. Slice at an angle into biscottis about ⅙ inch thick.
14. Preheat oven to 175 °C for 5 minutes. Place the biscottis on the parchment-lined tray and bake again for 10–12 minutes.
15. Take out the tray from the oven, transfer the biscottis to a wire rack and cool.
16. Bake again in the oven at 175 °C for 5–7 minutes without preheating the oven.
17. Cool the biscottis completely and then store.

CARROT CAKE – SIMPLICITY (Serves 6)
(Measuring cup size: 250 ml)

Every cook I have come across has taught me something new and wonderful to carry forward. Raju 'bhaia' completely wooed me with this one – it is light, has the perfect amount of sugar and, of course, is as healthy as a dessert can be. 'Simplicity' is the best description for this cake.

It tastes lovely eaten plain, warm or cold, with your evening tea, especially in the winters when carrots are at their best. If in the mood for more, top it with a cream cheese glaze.

SERVINGS

- Grated carrots: 1½ cups
- Powdered sugar: 1 cup
- All-purpose flour: 1 cup
- Raisins and walnuts: ½ cup dusted with flour
- Refined oil: ¼ cup
- Cinnamon powder: ½ tsp
- Baking powder: ½ tsp
- Baking soda: ½ tsp
- Salt: ¼ tsp
- Vanilla essence: 1 tsp
- Eggs: 2

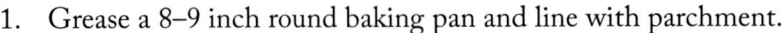

1. Grease a 8–9 inch round baking pan and line with parchment.
2. Preheat oven to 150 °C for 10 minutes.
3. Sieve all-purpose flour with baking powder, baking soda and salt.
4. Whisk together powdered sugar and oil.
5. Add eggs one at a time.
6. Add grated carrot and whisk further.
7. Add cinnamon powder and vanilla essence.
8. Add sieved flour gradually.
9. Fold in raisins and walnuts.
10. Pour batter into the baking pan and tap it on the counter to remove air pockets.
11. Bake for 40–45 minutes until a toothpick inserted in the centre comes out clean.
12. Let the cake cool in the pan, transfer to a wire rack and remove parchment.
13. If using the glaze, refrigerate for 2–3 hours before serving.

> While grating carrots, use the outer part and discard the hard centre. The quanty of the ingredients can be halved and the cake can be baked in a 6 inch pan. Baking time will reduce marginally.

Cream Cheese Glaze

- Cream cheese: 150 gm
- Powdered sugar: 50 gm
- Milk: 4 tbsp
- Vanilla essence: ½

1. Soften cream cheese.
2. Add powdered sugar, milk, vanilla essence and mix.
3. Gently heat mixture in a microwave for 30 seconds or on a low flame in a thick-bottom pan for a few minutes. Transfer to a jug or milk pot.
4. Pour the glaze over the cake starting from one end at the top, allowing it to drip down on the sides.
5. Smoothen the top with a spatula.
6. Refrigerate for 2–3 hours and serve.

UPSIDE-DOWN PINEAPPLE YOGHURT CAKE
(Serves 6)

Often baked in a cast iron skillet, this timeless cake from the late 1800s has an American origin. The batter is placed over sugar and fruit and once baked, the cake is flipped to show the gorgeous macerated fruit and the juices run right through the cake. But considering many of us are complete vegetarians in our part of the world or are vegetarians on certain days of the week, we want our cakes without eggs, hence an eggless version.

Pineapple is a widely used fruit in Asian desserts, adding coconut sugar gives it the sticky topping with a caramelized flavour and yoghurt gives it lightness. Enjoy with your cup of tea or end a Thai meal with it.

- All-purpose flour: 250 gm
- Baking powder: 2 tsp
- Baking soda: 1 tsp
- Lemon zest: 1½ tbsp
- Sugar: 150 gm
- Butter: 115 gm
- Yoghurt: 250 ml
- Milk: 75 ml
- Vanilla essence: 1 tsp

Upside-dowm Layer

- Coconut sugar: 2–3 tbsp
- Brown sugar: 2–3 tbsp
- Canned pineapple slices: 6–7

Coconut sugar can be replaced with regular brown sugar. The quantity of all ingredients can be halved and the cake can be baked in a 7 inch diameter pan. Baking time may reduce marginally.

1. Preheat oven to 180 °C for 10 minutes.
2. Grease a 9 inch diameter cake pan and line with parchment.
3. Spread a mix of brown sugar and coconut sugar evenly at the bottom of the pan.
4. Place pineapple slices over the sugar layer ensuring there are no gaps.
5. Sieve flour with baking powder and baking soda.
6. Whisk butter and sugar. Add yoghurt, vanilla essence and whisk with lemon zest.
7. Add flour gradually and whisk for a minute, add milk and fold the batter.
8. Gently pour the batter into the pan. Tap the pan lightly on the counter so that the batter settles at the bottom of the pan.

9. Bake for 35 minutes till a toothpick inserted in the centre comes out clean.
10. Let the cake cool in the pan for 20 minutes.
11. Run a knife carefully along the sides of the pan.
12. Flip the cake onto the serving platter and cool further.
13. The serving platter should be of the right size to support the cake while flipping.

TUTTI FRUTTI POUND CAKE – MY LUNCH BOX TREAT (Serves 6)

Another childhood favourite, this was a constant in my lunch box at school. Making the tutti frutti also was an interesting process and that too from watermelon rind, as recommended by a friend, with a desi video on how to make it. However a store-bought version will work well too.

A great teatime add-on, with a buttery, melt-in-the-mouth texture and sugar granules. It's time to take out the convent embroidery tea napkins and get back to being that 8-year-old.

- All-purpose flour: 100 gm
- Tutti frutti: 50 gm
- Milk: 50 ml
- Eggs: 2
- Butter: 115 gm
- Sugar: 115 gm
- Baking powder: ¾ tsp
- Lemon essence: ¾ tsp

1. Eggs and butter should be at room temperature.
2. Grease and line a 3 x 9 inch loaf pan with parchment.
3. Preheat oven to 160 °C for 7–8 minutes.
4. Sieve flour and baking powder together.
5. Whisk butter and sugar until creamy.
6. Add eggs, essence and whisk. Gradually fold in the flour.

7. Coat tutti frutti with the last 3 tbsp of flour, to ensure uniform mixing of tutti frutti in the cake.
8. Add milk and fold the batter gradually.
9. Fold in the floured tutti frutti and pour the batter into the loaf pan.
10. Tap the pan on the counter to remove air pockets.
11. Place the loaf pan in the oven and bake for 35 minutes on the middle rack.
12. Remove and let the cake cool in the pan, then transfer to a wire rack and remove parchment. Slice cake and serve.

Photo on p. 388: Russ; Photo on p. 390: Nankhatai; Photo on p. 392: Cantucci; Photo on p. 395: Carrot cake; Photo on p. 397: Upside-down pineapple yoghurt cake; Photo on p. 400: Tutti frutti pound cake.

SOMETHING SWEET AND SOMETHING SOUR – CHAAT AND HALWA

Most of us just love the taste of all the sweet, sour and spicy versions of chaat available at street corners and markets. We all have a favourite vendor too and every state in India has its own version. Originally chaat was made with papdi, a fried starchy biscuit mixed with boiled potatoes, yoghurt and various chutneys, but now chaat has taken on many avatars. This one is special, it uses the classic tuk – a Sindhi fried version of vegetables – and is topped with everything delightful.

Halwa is a dense, sweet desert made in India and the Middle East. Again, there are many versions of it and it can be made with different grains, pulses and vegetables. Cooked in clarified butter on a low flame, with additions of milk sometimes and sugar always, the end result is something to savour. This whole wheat version is made with jaggery and brown sugar, since I am trying really hard at ensuring it is less sinful!

SINDHI TUK CHAAT WITH ANARDANA CHUTNEY AND SAI CHUTNEY (Serves 6)

Batter

- Gram flour: 2 tbsp
- Salt: ¼ tsp
- Red chilli powder: ½ tsp
- Coriander powder: ½ tsp
- Cumin powder: ½ tsp

1. Mix all the ingredients with water to make a batter of coating consistency.

Chaat

- Baby potatoes: 12
- Small brinjals: 2–3
- Chickpeas: 60 gm
- Refined oil: to fry
- All-purpose flour: 2 tsp
- Cornflour: 2 tsp
- Yoghurt: 200 ml
- Tamarind chutney: 3–4 tsp
- Chaat masala: 1 tsp
- Powdered Sugar: 1 tsp

SERVINGS

- Cumin powder: 1 tsp
- Coriander powder: 1 tsp
- Red chilli powder: ½ tsp
- Dried mango powder: 1 tsp
- Kashmiri chilli powder: ¾ tsp

1. Soak chickpeas for 8 hours, boil, strain and keep aside.
2. Peel baby potatoes and soak in salt water. Slice brinjals into thin roundels and soak in water.
3. Mix together cumin powder, red chilli powder, dried mango powder and keep aside.
4. Pat baby potatoes dry. Heat oil in a thick-bottom wok/kadai and fry them.
5. Remove potatoes from wok/kadai, cool and press each between your palms, to make them into flat discs. Fry the potatoes again in oil.
6. Transfer to a paper towel and keep aside.
7. Remove brinjal slices from water, pat dry and drop in batter made earlier.
8. Deep fry batter coated brinjal slices in the wok/kadai used earlier until golden. Transfer to a paper towel to drain excess oil.
9. Mix the flour and cornflour with 4 tsp of water. Add boiled chickpeas and toss well.
10. Deep fry chickpeas and transfer to a paper towel to drain excess oil.
11. Sprinkle the spices mixed earlier on the fried potatoes, brinjals, chickpeas.
12. Toss well and arrange on a platter.
13. Whisk yoghurt with powdered sugar and pour over fried potatoes, brinjals slices and chickpeas. Add the anardana chutney, sai chutney and chaat masala.
14. Serve immediately on assembling.

Anardana Chutney

- Pomegranate seeds: ½ cup
- Coriander leaves: ¾ cup
- Mint leaves: 5–6
- Green chillies: 4
- Black salt: ½ tsp
- Roasted cumin seeds: 1 tsp
- Black peppercorns: 2–3
- Ginger: 1 inch

1. Grind all the ingredients together in a mixer.
2. Add more salt if needed.

Sai Chutney

- Coriander leaves: ½ bunch
- Mint leaves: ¼ bunch
- Garlic: 4 cloves
- Green chillies: 6
- Red chilli powder: ¼ tsp
- Lemon juice: 1½ tsp
- Ginger: 1 inch
- Onion: ½
- Peanuts: 8–10
- Sugar: ½ tsp

1. Grind all the ingredients together in a mixer.
2. Add salt to taste.

GURWALA ATTA HALWA (Serves 6)
(Measuring cup size: 250 ml)

- Whole wheat flour: 1 cup
- Ghee: 1 cup
- Brown sugar: ¾ cup
- Jaggery powder: ½ cup
- Water: 3 cups
- Almonds: 6–8 soaked, peeled and chopped

1. Boil 1 cup water in a thick-bottom deep wok/kadai. Add brown sugar and jaggery powder. Boil for another 6–7 minutes.
2. Add remaining water and boil until sugar dissolves.
3. On another flame, heat ghee in a thick-bottom wok/kadai. Do not let it smoke. Lower the flame, add flour and stir for 8–10 minutes till it turns brown.
4. Pour the sugar–jaggery syrup into the flour mixture gradually, stirring continuously. Be careful as the syrup will bubble and it might burn your hands.
5. Keep stirring the halwa until it becomes smooth, soft and glossy.
6. Serve hot, garnished with chopped almonds.

Photo on p. 403: Sindhu tuk chaat, Anardana chutney, Sai chutney, Gurwala atta halwa; Photo on p. 404: Aloo Chop.

FRY 'EM UP – ALOO CHOP AND SABUDANA VADAS

Tea with anything fried is straight out of a Hindi movie, especially if it is raining and romantic 'Bollywood' songs are playing in the background! Aloo chop is the Odiya version of the delightful aloo bonda, straight off the street vendor's cart wrapped in newspaper. This recipe is from one of them. Place it in a pav with chutney and it will become a vada pav. Now trending is a vada croissant! Sabudana vadas are another one of these yummy fried treats. Tapioca pearls are popular after a long day of fasting due to their high carbohydrate content and easy-to-digest properties. Fast or no fast, these certainly disappear rather quickly off the plate!

ALOO CHOP (Serves 6)

- Potatoes: 500 gm
- Refined oil: 2 tbsp
- Mustard seeds: 1 tsp
- Dried red chillies: 2–3 chopped
- Curry leaves: 3 sprigs (use only the leaves)
- Ginger: 1½ tsp crushed
- Garlic: 1½ tsp crushed
- Coriander leaves: 1 tbsp chopped
- Cumin powder: 1 tsp
- Coriander powder: 1 tsp
- Red chilli powder: ¾–1 tsp
- Turmeric powder: ½ tsp
- Green chilli: 1 chopped
- Salt: 1 tsp

1. Boil, peel and mash potatoes. Heat oil in a non-stick pan.
2. Add mustard seeds, dried red chillies and curry leaves. Let them crackle. and then add crushed ginger and garlic. Sauté.
3. Add cumin powder, coriander powder, red chilli powder and turmeric powder.
4. Add mashed potatoes and salt. Mix well.
5. Add chopped green chillies and coriander leaves to the potatoes and mix further.
6. Divide into 12 portions of 35 gm each and shape into balls. Keep aside.

Batter

- Gram flour: 100 gm
- Baking powder: ¼ tsp
- Turmeric powder: ¼ tsp
- Salt: ½ tsp
- Water: 175 ml

1. Mix all the ingredients to make a smooth batter. Keep aside.

Frying

- Refined oil: to deep fry

1. Heat enough oil in a deep wok/kadai on a medium flame and then lower the flame.
2. Coat each potato ball with batter and gently drop into the oil.
3. Deep fry till golden and crisp.
4. Serve hot.

SABUDANA VADA (Serves 6)
(Measuring cup size: 250 ml)

- Sabudana (tapioca pearls): ½ cup
- Potatoes: 2 medium
- Roasted peanuts: ¼ cup
- Green chillies: 2–3 chopped
- Coriander leaves: 3 tbsp chopped
- Rice flour: 1 tbsp heaped
- Lemon juice: 2 tsp
- Pink salt: ½ tsp
- Salt: ½–¾ tsp
- Roasted cumin powder: ¾ tsp
- Refined oil: to deep fry

1. Wash sabudana well and soak in water overnight. The water level should be slightly higher than the sabudana.
2. Strain sabudana and let it rest in the strainer for another hour.
3. Boil and peel potatoes and roughly crumble them with your fingers. Do make sure that the potatoes are not wet otherwise the vada will get soggy.
4. Dry roast peanuts and crush coarsely using a mortar and pestle.

Making large-sized sabudana vadas can lead to a soggy centre.

5. Mix all the ingredients, except the oil, and check seasoning.
6. Divide the mixture into 15 balls of 40 gm each and then flatten them slightly.
7. Refrigerate for an hour on an open plate.
8. Heat sufficient oil in a wok/kadai to deep fry. Fry vadas on a low flame until golden and crisp. Serve hot with chutney.

PEANUT–YOGHURT CHUTNEY

- Roasted peanut: 1½ tbsp
- Yoghurt: ¼ cup
- Red chilli powder: ½ tsp
- Cumin powder: ¼ tsp
- Turmeric powder: ⅛ tsp
- Sugar: ½ tsp
- Salt: ⅙ tsp
- Mint leaves: 8–10 chopped

1. Powder roasted peanuts and add all other ingredients.
2. Mix well and serve with hot vadas.

Photo on p. 409: Sabudana Vada, Peanut yoghurt chutney.

Being Vegetarian

On days that one goes meat-free, or if one is a flexitarian, or has a visitor who is one, the constant thought we all have is what can one cook to ensure a satisfying meal. I have seen many a host actually fret! Vegetarian food can be creative, great to taste and can satisfy even the cravings of a carnivore. All it takes is getting over the mindset. Today, the market is flooded with many fresh and frozen meat substitutes as well.

Personally, being a vegetarian has only helped in the thought process of thinking beyond the normal dal–sabzi combination or the usual pasta and noodles story. The colour on the table actually comes from all things vegetarian. Imagine eating everything that is fifty shades of brown!

Recipes in these pages are a combination of flavours that add up to a complete meal. As always, friends and family have contributed to making the spectrum more interesting, like the ratatouille which is as authentic as it can get, coming from the designer of the book who has French genes. Of course, twisting the recipe is always a part of the deal.

COTTAGE CHEESE EN PAPILLOTE (Cottage Cheese in Parchment with Asian Compound Butter) (Serves 2)

Asian Compound Butter

- Salted butter: 20 gm
- Peanut butter: 1 tsp
- Coriander leaves: 1½ tsp chopped
- Thai red chilli: ½ chopped
- Lime juice: ½ tsp

SERVINGS

1. Mix all the ingredients together until smooth. Place 2 cling film sheets one on top of each other. Place the butter mixture and roll into a cylinder, making a knot at each end.
2. Freeze for 6–8 hours.

Cottage Cheese en Papillote

- Cottage cheese: 100 gm
- Shallots: 6
- Garlic: 3 cloves crushed
- Mushrooms: 5 sliced thick
- Lemongrass: 2 stalks
- Basil leaves: 3–4
- Mirin: 1 tbsp
- Dashi powder: 1 tsp dissolved in 1 tbsp water
- Balsamic vinegar: 1 tbsp
- Olive oil: 1 tsp
- Honey soy sauce: ½ tbsp
- Thai red chilli: 1 slit
- Chilli oil: 1 tsp
- Black pepper powder: a pinch
- Soy sauce: 1 tbsp
- Thai sweet chilli sauce: ½ tbsp
- Red bell pepper: 1 small quartered

1. Cut cottage cheese into thick rectangles. Press them down between two layers of a paper towel for 30 minutes to remove excess water and make them firm.
2. Marinate cottage cheese with all the ingredients for an hour or two.
3. Take a large sheet of parchment and fold it into a square. Cut an arc from the folded side and another from the open side (as shown on p. 412).
4. Rub olive oil on the inside of the parchment. Cut compound butter into slices.
5. Arrange cottage cheese on one side of the parchment, and place compound butter slices, (saving a few for later) between the pieces. Top with marinated mushrooms, shallots, bell pepper, lemongrass stalk and basil leaves. Discard Marinade.
6. Cover with the top parchment.
7. Start sealing the parchment from one side by pleating it, one fold over the other.
8. Continue till the other end and apply pressure on the edges with a mallet. This becomes a vacuum bag for the cottage cheese and mushrooms to cook in.
9. Preheat oven to 210°C for 5 minutes.
10. Place the cottage cheese and mushroom parcel on a baking tray.
11. Bake for 18–20 minutes.
12. To open, cut through the parchment vertically with a knife.
13. Top with a few slices of compound butter and serve in parchment.

Cottage cheese can be substituted with tofu.

SPICED HASSELBACK POTATOES WITH BROCCOLI IN CHEESE CHILLI SAUCE (Serves 2)

Hasselback Potatoes

- Small potatoes: 5–6
- Butter: 2 tbsp
- Olive oil: 3 tbsp
- Garlic: 4 cloves peeled and crushed
- Thyme: 1 sprig
- Chilli flakes: 2 tsp
- Salt: 1–1¼ tsp
- Black pepper powder: ½ tsp
- Dried mixed herbs: 1½ tsp

1. Preheat oven to 200 °C for 15 minutes. Line a baking tray with parchment.
2. Cut potatoes with skin at 3 mm gaps, keeping the bottom intact to form an accordion and place on the baking tray.
3. Heat butter and olive oil in a pan. Add garlic and sauté until golden.
4. Add the thyme sprig and let it simmer and absorb the flavours for 2 minutes.
5. Remove the pan from the flame and strain the flavoured oil.
6. Brush the oil over the potatoes, and rub in the chilli flakes, salt and black pepper powder.
7. Brush some more oil on the potatoes. Bake the potatoes for 30 minutes.
8. Take the tray out of the oven and brush the remaining oil over the potatoes. Sprinkle mixed herbs and bake again for 30 minutes.
9. Serve hot accompanied with the broccoli in cheese chilli sauce.

Broccoli In Cheese Chilli Sauce

- Cheddar cheese: 90 gm grated
- Tomato ketchup: 1 tbsp
- Tabasco sauce: 1 tsp
- Chilli flakes: 1 tsp
- Milk: 100 ml
- Broccoli: 200 gm
- Spring onion bulbs: 5 sliced
- Butter: 1½ tbsp
- Salt: ¼ tsp
- Sun-dried tomatoes: 2 chopped

1. Make the cheese chilli sauce by blending Cheddar cheese, tomato ketchup, tabasco sauce and chilli flakes together, adding milk gradually.

2. Heat butter in a non-stick pan.
3. Add the spring onion bulbs and cook until translucent.
4. Toss in the broccoli and cook until three-fourths done.
5. Add the cheese chilli sauce and simmer for 10 minutes.
6. Coat broccoli well and add sun-dried tomatoes.
7. Serve hot.

SOYA NUGGET BALLS IN BARBECUE SAUCE WITH CHILLI LONG BEANS AND CRISP FRIED LOTUS STEM (Serves 2)

Soya Nugget Balls

- Soya nuggets: 40 gm
- Gram flour: 4 tbsp
- Onion: ½ large chopped
- Green chillies: 2 chopped
- Coriander leaves: 1 tbsp chopped
- Garlic paste: ½ tsp
- Ginger paste: ½ tsp
- Salt: ¾ tsp
- MSG: ¼ tsp (optional)
- Refined oil: to deep fry

1. Soak soya nuggets in hot water for 1 hour.
2. Drain and squeeze out the water.
3. Shred soya nuggets into thin pieces.
4. Add all the other ingredients and mash well to make a smooth mixture.
5. Divide into 6 equal portions and shape into balls with wet hands.
6. Heat oil in a deep wok on a medium flame.
7. Deep fry nuggets until golden brown.
8. Transfer to a paper towel to drain excess oil.

Photo on p. 413: Cottage cheese en papillote; Photos on p. 412 and 414 The process of making the cottage cheese en papillote and Asian compound butter.

Barbeque Sauce

- Tomato ketchup: 2 tbsp
- Brown sugar: 1¼ tbsp
- Mirin: 2 tbsp
- Rice vinegar: 2 tbsp
- Dark soy sauce: 1 tbsp
- Shallots: 5–6 sliced
- Garlic: 2 tsp heaped chopped
- Thai red chillies: 2 chopped
- Sesame oil: 1 tbsp + 2 tbsp
- Water: 50 ml

1. Mix together tomato ketchup, brown sugar, mirin, rice vinegar, dark soy sauce and 1 tbsp sesame oil.
2. Heat 2 tbsp sesame oil in a non-stick pan on a high flame. Add garlic, shallots and Thai red chillies and stir fry.
3. Add the sauce mix and boil.
4. Add water and simmer.
5. Add the soya nugget balls and toss on a high flame.
6. Check seasoning.
7. Serve hot with steamed rice.

Chilli Long Beans

- Long beans: 200 gm
- Chilli paste: 2 tbsp
- Oyster sauce/ Hoisin sauce: 1½ tbsp
- Sugar: 1 tsp
- Sesame oil: 2 tbsp
- Vegetable stock: 2–3 tbsp
- Garlic: 6 cloves minced
- Shallots: 2–3 sliced or chopped

1. Cut long beans into 2 inch pieces.
2. Mix together chilli paste, sugar and oyster sauce.
3. Heat sesame oil in a pan. Stir fry garlic and shallots on a high flame.
4. Add the sauce mix and continue stirring. Add beans and toss well. Add 2–3 tbsp of stock.
5. Let the beans crisp up and serve.

Photo on p. 416: Spiced hasselback potatoes with broccoli in cheese and chilli sauce; Photo on p. 419: Soya nugget balls in barbeque sauce, Chilli long beans, Crisp fried lotus stem.

Twice-Fried Lotus Stem

- Lotus stems: 100 gm peeled and sliced thin
- Vinegar: 2–3 tsp
- Boiling water: 500 ml
- Refined oil: to fry
- Pink salt: 1 tsp
- Garlic powder: ½ tsp

1. Mix vinegar in boiling water, add lotus stems and let them soak for 15 minutes.
2. Strain lotus stems, transfer to a paper towel and let them dry for 15–20 minutes.
3. Heat oil in a deep-bottom wok and fry the lotus stems for 3–4 minutes or until light brown. Transfer to a paper towel to drain excess oil.
4. Deep fry lotus stems again in hot oil, tranfer to a paper towel to drain excess oil.
5. Toss with pink salt and garlic powder. Serve hot.

AKKI ROTI WITH MADRAS KATHAL MASALA AND TALLINA'S PINEAPPLE CURRY (Serves 4)

(Measuring cup size: 150 ml)

Akki Roti

- Water: 3½ cups
- Ghee: 1 tsp + extra for cooking rotis
- Salt: ½ tsp
- Sugar: ½ tsp
- Rice flour: 1 cup
- Coriander leaves: 1 tbsp chopped
- Curry leaves: 1 tbsp chopped
- Green chillies: 1–2 chopped fine

1. In a wok/kadai boil water with ghee, sugar, salt and turn off the flame.
2. Add rice flour and gradually mix to a smooth but sticky dough.
3. Add coriander leaves, curry leaves and green chillies.
4. Divide into 8 equal portions and shape into balls.
5. Dust with flour and gently roll into 5–6 inch diameter rotis.

6. Heat a non-stick flat pan.
7. Place a roti on the pan and let it cook for 2 minutes.
8. Gently prick with a fork and apply ¼ tsp ghee. Cook for 2 minutes and then flip.
9. Apply a dab of ghee. Cook for 3–4 minutes.
10. Flip again, remove from pan and serve hot.

Madras Kathal Masala

- Raw jackfruit segments: 500 gm
- Salt: 1 tsp
- Turmeric powder: ½ tsp
- Red chilli powder: 1 tsp
- Madras curry powder: 1 tsp
- Black pepper powder: 1 tsp
- Refined oil: deep fry

1. Rub jackfruit with salt and leave it for an hour in a colander to drain out excess water.
2. Wash and then dry jackfruit segments on a paper towel for 30 minutes.
3. Mix turmeric powder, red chilli powder and black pepper powder together and coat over jackfruit segments and keep aside for 1 hour.
4. Heat oil in a wok/kadai and deep fry the jackfruit segments until golden.
5. Transfer to a paper towel to drain excess oil and keep aside.

Masala

- Onion: 1 large chopped
- Ginger: 1 inch crushed
- Garlic: 5 large cloves crushed
- Cinnamon: 1 inch stick
- Cloves: 3–4
- Green cardamoms: 2
- Salt: ½ tsp
- Curry leaves: 2 sprigs
- Red chilli powder: ½ tsp
- Madras curry powder: 1½ tsp
- Tomato: 1 large chopped
- Coconut milk: ½ cup
- Ghee: 1 tbsp
- Sugar: ¼ tsp

1. In a pan, dry roast whole spices and then coarsely grind them using a mortar and pestle.
2. Heat ghee in a non-stick pan. Add sugar and caramelize.
3. Add onions and sauté until golden along with 8–10 curry leaves.
4. Add crushed ginger and garlic. Sauté.

5. Add crushed whole spices, red chilli powder and Madras curry powder.
6. Add tomato and sauté. Add the fried jackfruit and toss.
7. Cover and cook for 8–10 minutes till tomato soften.
8. Add the remaining curry leaves and coconut milk.
9. Let the curry simmer for 8–10 minutes.
10. Check seasoning. Let it rest for some time for better flavour.
11. Reheat and serve.

Pineapple Curry

- Pineapple slices: 250 gm chopped
- Fresh grated coconut: ½ cup
- Green chillies: 2
- Ginger: 2 inches
- Refined oil: 2 tbsp
- Mustard seeds: ½ tsp
- Turmeric powder: ½ tsp
- Onion: 1 medium chopped
- Sambhar powder: 1 tbsp
- Jaggery: 15 gm
- Water: 1 cup
- Salt: ¾ tsp
- Ghee: 1 tsp
- Mustard seeds: ¼ tsp
- Dried red chillies: 2
- Curry leaves: 2 sprig

1. Grind ginger, green chillies and grated coconut together in a mixer.
2. Heat oil in a non-stick pan.
3. Add mustard seeds, a sprig of curry leaves and let them crackle.
4. Add onion and ¼ tsp salt, sauté until pink.
5. Add turmeric powder, coconut paste and fry until the oil separates.
6. Add sambhar powder followed by pineapple, remaining salt and stir.
7. Add jaggery and water.
8. Cover and simmer until the gravy thickens and pineapples are mushy.
9. To temper, heat ghee in a pan, add mustard seeds, red chillies and remaing curry leaves. Let them crackle.
10. Pour over the pineapple curry. Serve hot.

Photo on p. 422 (Clockwise): Akki roti, Tallina's pineapple curry, Madras kathal masala; Photo on p. 425: Arshi's chukandar ka saalan with kabuli pulao; Photo on p. 428: Nandini's ratatouille as a potpie, Swati's rocket and strawberry salad.

ARSHI'S KABULI PULAO ACCOMPANIED WITH CHUKANDAR KA SAALAN (Serves 2)

(Measuring cup size: 250 ml)

Kabuli Pulao

- Chickpeas: 100 gm soaked in water overnight
- Bay leaf: 1
- Black cardamom: 1
- Turmeric powder: a pinch
- Salt: ½ tsp
- Water: 300 ml

1. In a pressure cooker on a high flame cook chickpeas with whole spices, turmeric powder, salt and water. After two whistles reduce the flame and simmer for 10 minutes.
2. Open the pressure cooker once cool.
3. Strain chickpeas and keep aside, reserve the water.

Pulao

- Rice: 125 gm
- Onion: 1 medium sliced
- Ginger–garlic paste: 1 tsp
- Green chilli: 1 slit
- Ghee: 2 tbsp
- Bay leaf: 1
- Black cardamom: 1
- Cinnamon: 1 inch stick
- Cumin seeds: ½ tsp
- Kashmiri chilli powder: ½ tsp
- Red chilli powder: ½ tsp
- Salt: ½ tsp
- Chickpea water + water: 450 ml
- Cooked chickpeas: entire quantity

1. Soak rice in water for 30 minutes. In a wide-bottomed pot with a lid, heat ghee.
2. Add bay leaf, cinnamon, black cardamom and cumin seeds. Let them crackle.
3. Add sliced onions with ¼ tsp salt and cook until pink and translucent.
4. Add ginger–garlic paste and cook for 2–3 minutes, then add both chilli powders.
5. Add cooked chickpeas, reserved chickpea water and water.
6. Strain the rice and add to the pot.
7. Simmer for 3–4 minutes. Add green chilli, cover and cook. Check seasoning.
8. Serve hot with chukandar ka saalan.

Chukandar ka Saalan

- Beetroot: 250 gm peeled and cut into 6 pieces
- Onion: 100 gm grated
- Tomato: 1 large grated
- Ginger: ½ inch crushed
- Garlic: 2 cloves crushed
- Green chilli: 1 slit
- Oil: 2 tbsp
- Turmeric powder: a pinch
- Red chilli powder: ½ tsp
- Coriander powder: ¾ tsp
- Salt: ¾ tsp
- Water: 1 cup

1. Heat oil in a pressure cooker pan. Add crushed ginger and garlic. Sauté until golden.
2. Add grated onion and ¼ tsp salt. Cook until brown.
3. Add turmeric powder, grated tomato and cook.
4. Add coriander powder, red chilli powder and 3–4 tsp water.
5. Add beetroot and green chilli. Cook for 3–4 minutes.
6. Add water, remaining salt, boil and shut the lid of the pressure cooker.
7. On a high flame, wait for one whistle, reduce flame and after two whistles turn off the flame. Let the pressure cooker cool before opening. Serve hot.

NANDINI'S RATATOUILLE AS A POTPIE WITH SWATI'S ROCKET AND STRAWBERRY SALAD
(Serves 2)

Ratatouille

- Onion: 1 medium
- Tomato: 1 large
- Long brinjal: 1 small
- Zucchini: ¼ with skin
- Garlic: 3 big cloves sliced thin
- Olive oil: 50 ml

- Paprika powder: ¼ tsp
- Dried mixed herbs: ¾ tsp
- Salt: ½ tsp.
- Black pepper powder: ¼ tsp

1. Dice onion, tomato, brinjal and zucchini.
2. Heat olive oil in a non-stick pan on a medium flame and sauté garlic until golden.
3. Add onion with salt and cook for 2–3 minutes.
4. Add all other vegetables, followed by black pepper powder, paprika and mixed herbs.
5. Let the vegetables cook until soft and brown.

Assembling the Potpie

- Puff pastry: 2 squares (recipe on p. 367)
- Basil leaves: 3–4
- Parmesan cheese: 2 tsp grated (optional)
- Egg: 1 whisked or Butter: 1 tbsp

1. Preheat oven to 200 °C for 12 minutes.
2. Cut the puff pastry squares into discs larger than the ramekins.
3. Fill ramekins equally with the ratatouille until three-quarters full.
4. Top with 1 tsp grated Parmesan cheese if using and 1–2 basil leaves on each.
5. Brush egg/melted butter on the rim of the ramekins. Place puff pastry discs over the filling, securing the sides.
6. Brush the top of the puff with egg wash/melted butter.
7. Cut ½ inch slits in the centre of the puff pastry.
8. Place ramekins on a baking tray and bake for 20–25 minutes until the pastry tops are golden brown.
9. Take out from the oven, let it rest for a few minutes and serve.

Rocket and Strawberry Salad

- Rocket leaves: 50 gm
- Strawberries: 10 halved
- Cherry mozzarella: 10 pieces
- Cucumber: 1 small diced
- Sugar 1 tbsp
- Walnuts: 8–10
- Sweet onion sauce: 4 tbsp
- Pink salt: ¼ tsp
- Aglio olio oil: 2–3 tbsp

1. Heat sugar in a non-stick pan and let it caramelize.
2. Toss in the walnuts and let them coat well. Remove from flame and reserve.
3. To make the dressing, mix together sweet onion sauce, aglio olio oil and pink salt.
4. Toss rocket leaves, strawberries, cherry mozzarella, cucumber, walnuts and the dressing in a bowl. Serve immediately.

To make aglio olio oil, heat 50 ml of olive oil with 2 big cloves of crushed garlic and 1 tbsp of fresh parsley leaves. Allow it to cook for 3–4 minutes. Let the oil rest for 15–20 minutes and then strain.

Something Smells Fishy!

Fish is eaten in all regions of the world. As it is a healthy protein, many have opted to become pescatarian. In many cultures, fish is considered vegetarian; Thailand is one such place where one is asked, 'You vegetarian, you eat fish?' This leaves a vegetarian like me wondering how this moving creature is supposed to be part of my plate.

Fish has even been used as a cure for asthma at a famous clinic in Hyderabad, where a small live murrel is put down one's throat! Fish prasadam is what the locals call it. Deemed auspicious, this aquatic being also finds its place in religious practices and is an integral part of wedding ceremonies in the eastern states of India.

Most cooking techniques can be used with fish, thus making it versatile. As I do often, reaching out to a classmate who runs an Indian restaurant in Germany helped get just the right recipe for beer batter fish. Similarly Cherry, a dear friend who is Burmese, a fabulous host and cook, has given me live classes on food from her homeland. The recipes have broadened my knowledge of Burmese food far beyond just khow suey. Every time I cook, a technique I learnt in college comes to mind, like making compound butter which is an age-old method. For a student who always wanted to find an easy way out of the food production classes, I have certainly come a long way.

SERVINGS

The dishes below can be made and eaten as a main course – if you must, adding a portion of any carbohydrate is an option.

CHUTNEY POMFRET STUFFED WITH CARAMELIZED SPICY PRAWNS (Serves 2)

- Pomfret: 2 (250 gm each)

1. Clean and remove scales.
2. Cut the pomfret along the belly and remove the centre bone.
3. Cut diagonal slits on the front and back of the fish.

First Marinade

- Ginger paste: 1½ tsp
- Garlic paste: 1½ tsp
- Lemon juice: 1 tbsp
- Turmeric powder: ¾ tsp
- Red chilli powder: ¾ tsp
- Cinnamon powder: ¼ tsp
- Salt: ¾ tsp

1. Mix all the ingredients and marinate the pomfret for an hour.

Second Marinade

- Coriander leaves: 1½ cup chopped
- Mint leaves: ¾ cup chopped
- Green chillies: 5–6
- Ginger: ¾ inch
- Lemon juice: 1½ tbsp
- Salt: 1 tsp
- Peanuts: 1½ tbsp
- Tomato ketchup: 1 tbsp
- Tandoori masala: 1 tsp optional but adjust spice levels accordingly

Photo on p. 431: Chutney pomfret stuffed with Caramelised chilli prawns.

SERVINGS

1. Grind all the ingredients except lemon juice to a coarse paste in a mixer.
2. Add lemon juice.
3. Check seasoning. The marinade should be tangy and sharp.
4. Reserve 1 tbsp of marinade. Rub remaining marinade into the fish evenly and leave for 1 hour.

Stuffing

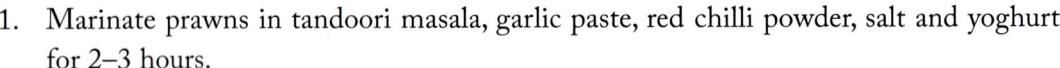

- Refined oil: 2–3 tsp
- Prawns: 12 medium
- Tandoori masala: 2 tsp
- Red chilli powder: ½ tsp
- Salt: ½ tsp
- Garlic paste: 1 tsp
- Yoghurt: 1½ tbsp
- Onion: 1 small sliced thin
- Sugar: ¾ tsp

1. Marinate prawns in tandoori masala, garlic paste, red chilli powder, salt and yoghurt for 2–3 hours.
2. Heat 2 tsp oil in a pan, add ¾ tsp sugar and onion and let it caramelize.
3. Add prawns and cook. Remove from flame and let them cool.
4. Chop 8 prawns and add the reserved second marinade to them. Heat 1 tsp oil in a pan and cook marinated prawns.
5. Divide prawn mixture into 2 portions. Skewer the remaining whole prawns.

Assembling the Pomfret

- Mustard oil: 3–4 tbsp
- Banana leaf/foil: 2 piece

1. Heat oil to smoking point and keep aside.
2. Stuff the belly of the pomfret with the chopped prawn mixture.
3. Brush oil on the banana leaf/foil, place the pomfret, pour sufficient smoked oil over it and wrap. Place on a baking tray.
4. Preheat oven to 180 °C for 10 minutes. Bake pomfret for 20–25 minutes. The pomfret will be moist when the banana leaf/foil is opened.

5. Heat a non-stick grill pan and brush with a generous layer of smoked oil.
6. Transfer the baked pomfret onto the pan. Cook the pomfret on a low flame till it dries out and attains a deep colour. Flip and grill the other side.
7. Transfer onto a plate and serve with remaining skewered prawns.

SOLE EN PAPILLOTE WITH COMPOUND BASIL BUTTER (Sole in Parchment) (Serves 1)
(Measuring cup size: 150 ml)

Sole en Papillote

- Sole: 1 fillet (150 gm)
- Salt: ½ tsp
- Black pepper powder: ¼ tsp
- Lemon juice: ½ tbsp

1. Marinate sole with salt and black pepper powder for an hour.
2. Add lemon juice 45 minutes prior to baking.

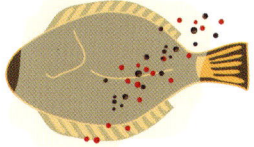

- Baby potatoes: 4 poked and parboiled in salt water
- Cherry tomatoes: 6 pricked with a fork
- Lemon slices: 1–2
- Red bell pepper: ¼ cut into squares
- Lemon juice: ½ tbsp
- Salt: 1 tsp
- Butter: 1 tsp
- Black pepper powder: ½ tsp
- Mixed herbs: ½ tsp
- Shallots: 3–4 quartered
- Green chilli: 1 chopped fine
- Garlic: 2 cloves crushed
- Spinach: 4–5 leaves
- Compound butter: 5 slices

1. Take a large sheet of parchment and fold it into a square.
2. Cut an arc from the folded side and another from the open side (refer to picture on p. 412 and 414).
3. Rub olive oil on the inside and place on a board. Prick potatoes with skin and parboil.

4. Toss potatoes in a pan with 1 tsp butter and a pinch of black pepper powder. Cool and quarter.
5. Prick cherry tomatoes with a fork and toss in a bowl with shallots, green chillies, bell pepper, spinach, garlic, lemon juice and mixed herbs.
6. Add salt and remaining black pepper powder. Check seasoning.
7. On one side of the parchment place potatoes and some of the vegetables.
8. Place the fish on top. Place spinach on the side.
9. Top with the remaining vegetables and 3 slices of compound butter.
10. Cover with the other side of the parchment.
11. Start sealing the parchment from one side by pleating it one fold over the other.
12. Continue till the other end and apply pressure on the edges with a mallet. This becomes a vacuum bag for the fish to cook in.
13. Preheat oven to 210 °C for 5 minutes. Place fish parcel on a baking tray.
14. Bake for 18–20 minutes.
15. To open the parchment cover, cut through vertically with a knife.
16. Top with a few roundels of compound butter, lemon slices and serve in the parchment.

Compound Basil Butter

- Basil leaves: ¼ cup finely chopped
- Salted butter: ¼ cup softened
- Chilli flakes: ½ tsp
- Garlic: 2 cloves minced

1. Mix together softened butter, garlic, chilli flakes and chopped basil.
2. Place on a cling film sheet and roll to form a cylinder.
3. Twist both ends of the cling film and knot (refer picture on p. 412).
4. Freeze for 3–4 hours. Remove the cling film, slice and use as desired.

Photo on p. 434: Sole en papillote with Compound basil butter; Photo on pg 437: Chetan's beer batter fish with Mustard remoulade sauce, Bratkartoffeln; Photo on p. 438: Ma Cherry's Ngaa zabaling paung, Khayamti thot; Photo on p. 442: Soy ginger salmon, Sesame garlic kale.

CHAITAN'S BEER BATTER FISH WITH MUSTARD REMOULADE SAUCE AND BRATKARTOFFELN
(Potatoes and Bacon) (Serves 2)

Beer Batter

- Sole/Cod/Bhetki: 2–3 fillets (300 gm)
- Refined oil: 1 tbsp + for deep frying
- Egg: 1
- Flour: 90 gm
- Cold beer: 100 ml
- Cold club soda: 50 ml
- Salt: ½ tsp + ¼ tsp
- Black pepper powder: ¼ tsp
- White pepper powder: ½ tsp
- Caraway seeds: ½ tsp
- Paprika powder: 1 tsp

1. Pat fish dry and place on a board to dry out for 30 minutes and cut into desired pieces.
2. Sprinkle ¼ tsp salt and black pepper powder on the fish pieces.
3. Separate egg yolk and white.
4. In a bowl mix egg yolk, flour, 1 tbsp oil, beer, club soda, ½ tsp salt, white pepper powder, caraway seeds, and paprika powder together.
5. In a separate bowl, whisk the egg white until stiff and gently fold into the mixture made earlier. Let the batter rest for 15 minutes.
6. Heat oil for deep frying in a pan, dip the fish in batter and fry until golden. The flame should not be high, as the batter will burn easily. Serve hot.

Mustard Remoulade Sauce

- Mayonnaise: 3–4 tbsp
- Egg: 1 hard-boiled chopped
- Onion: ½ small chopped
- Jalapeños/Gherkins: 2 chopped
- Dijon mustard: 1 tsp
- Parsley leaves: 1–2 tbsp
- Salt: if required

1. Mix all the ingredients together.
2. Cover and refrigerate for an hour or two before serving.

Bratkartoffeln

- Potatoes: 4
- Onion: 1 medium sliced thick
- Brown sugar: 1 tsp
- Balsamic vinegar: 2 tsp
- Olive oil: 2 tsp
- Bacon: 4 rashers chopped
- Parsley leaves: 2 tbsp chopped
- Salt: 1 tsp
- Black pepper powder: 1 tsp

1. Prick potatoes and parboil. Cut into wedges.
2. Heat olive oil in a pan, add bacon, onions and stir fry.
3. Once done, transfer on to a paper towel and keep aside.
4. In the same pan, add potatoes, balsamic vinegar, brown sugar, salt, black pepper powder and toss.
5. Transfer to a parchment-lined baking tray.
6. Preheat oven for 8 minutes at 220°C. Bake potatoes for 20–25 minutes.
7. Place the baked potatoes back in a pan and heat along with the cooked bacon and onions. Top with parsley leaves.
8. Toss and serve hot.

MA CHERRY'S NGAA ZABALING PAUNG AND KHAYAMTI THYOT (Baked Lemongrass Fish and Tomato Salad) (Serves 2)

Ngaa Zabaling Paung

- Sole: 2 fillet (300 gm)
- Ginger–garlic paste: 2 tbsp
- Green chillies: 2
- Fish sauce: 4 tbsp
- Refined oil: 2 tbsp
- Lemongrass: 3 stems crushed
- Onions: 2 large sliced thick
- Turmeric powder: ¾ tsp
- Red chilli powder: 1 tsp
- Salt: ¼ tsp + 1 tsp
- Basil leaves: 10–12
- Brown sugar: 1 tsp

1. Grind green chillies to a paste and mix with ginger–garlic paste, fish sauce and ¼ tsp salt. Marinate fish for 1 hour in this mixture.
2. Heat oil in a pan. Add onions and sauté till light brown along with lemongrass, turmeric powder, red chilli powder and brown sugar. Add 1 tsp salt gradually and cook till onions soften.
3. Line a baking dish with a banana leaf and spread half the quantity of the onion mixture on it.
4. Place the fish over this mixture. Top with remaining onion mixture and fresh basil leaves. Cover the dish with foil.
5. Preheat oven to 200 °C for 10 minutes and bake the fish for 40 minutes.
6. Remove foil grill fish for 4–5 minutes.

Khayamti Thot

- Garlic: 3 tbsp sliced and fried
- Onions: 1 tbsp fried
- Turmeric powder: ¼ tsp
- Roasted red chilli powder: ¼ tsp
- Hot refined oil: 40 ml

1. Mix all the ingredients together in a jar and top with hot oil to make a dressing.

- Tomatoes: 2 large sliced
- Cabbage: ¼ sliced (equal in weight to the tomatoes)
- Roasted gram flour: 1¼ tbsp
- Roasted red chilli powder: 1 tsp
- Onions: 2 large sliced
- Lemon: 1 large
- Green chillies: 3 chopped (remove seeds to reduce spice if desired)
- Coriander leaves: 2 tbsp chopped
- Fish sauce: 1½–2 tbsp (can be substituted with sugar and salt to taste)
- Roasted sesame seeds: 1 tbsp

1. In a bowl mix tomatoes, onion and cabbage together.
2. Add coriander leaves, green chillies and squeeze lemon juice over them.
3. Add desired quantity of dressing, roasted gram flour and red chilli powder.
4. Add fish sauce. Check seasoning.
5. Using your fingers give the ingredients a good mix, while gently crushing them.
6. Add roasted sesame seeds, transfer to a salad bowl and serve.

SOY GINGER SALMON WITH SESAME GARLIC KALE (Serves 2)

Soy Ginger Sauce

- Light soy sauce: 60 ml
- Honey: 3–4 tsp
- Brown sugar: 3 tsp
- Ginger: 2 tsp thinly shredded
- Thai bird's eye chilli: 2–3 small slit
- Paprika powder: 1½ tsp
- Sesame oil: 1 tsp
- Black pepper powder : a pinch
- Salt: a pinch

1. Mix all the ingredients for the sauce together and reserve.

Salmon

- Salmon: 2 fillets (300 gm)
- Salt: a pinch
- Black pepper powder: a pinch
- Olive oil: 2–3 tbsp

1. Dry the salmon fillets with a paper towel.
2. Heat olive oil in a non-stick pan.
3. Place the fillets in the pan, and cook both sides until golden. Also cook the edges of the fillets.
4. Sprinkle salt and black pepper powder.
5. Pour two-thirds of the reserved soy ginger sauce into the pan and transfer the salmon into it. Cook for 2 minutes.
6. Place on a bed of kale with sauce and serve with steamed rice.

Sesame Garlic Kale

- Kale: 4 stems with leaves
- Sesame seeds: 2 tsp
- Garlic: 3 tsp finely chopped
- Sesame oil: 2 tsp

1. Put the kale into boiling water for 30 seconds or up to a minute.
2. Strain in a colander and top with ice cubes.

3. Heat sesame oil in a pan.
4. Add garlic and sauté.
5. Strain the kale leaves again, shake off excess water and add to the pan. Toss
6. Add the remaining quantity of reserved soy ginger sauce and stir fry.
7. Add sesame seeds.
8. Place kale and sauce on a plate.

Chickened In!

Chicken is the ubiquitous meat in today's times. The sheer fact that the taste of the meat does not overpower the ingredients added to it helps create variety. Most cooking techniques can be used with chicken – grilling, baking, boiling, frying – they all work!

The flourishing poultry trade is an indication that families everywhere consume truckloads of chicken in their lifetime! From butter chicken to Kentucky fried chicken, this fowl has no boundaries. These recipes make for complete meals or can be added to your menu as starters, using smaller pieces of the meat.

STEAMED ASIAN CHICKEN WITH CHILLI OIL
(Serves 2)

Steamed Asian Chicken

- Boneless chicken thighs: 4
- Light soy sauce: 5–6 tbsp
- Garlic: 6 cloves juice extracted + 4 cloves sliced
- Salt: 1 tsp
- Dark soy sauce: 1 tbsp to marinate
- Ginger: 4 tbsp julienned
- Thai red chillies: 4 sliced
- Spring onions: 2 sliced
- Sesame oil: 6 tsp

1. Pierce chicken pieces with a fork and marinate in 2 tbsp light soy sauce, dark soy sauce, salt and garlic juice for 4 hours.
2. Place on a plate and top each piece of chicken with the remaining ingredients.
3. Heat water in the lower compartment of the steamer. Place the plate in the upper compartment of the steamer. Steam for 8–10 minutes.
4. Open midway and ladle the liquid from the plate on to the chicken pieces.
5. Insert a toothpick and check if chicken is cooked.
6. Take out chicken once done. Slice and serve topped with 2–3 tbsp chilli oil.
7. Serve with steamed rice.

Chilli Oil

- Chilli flakes: 3 tbsp
- Black peppercorns: 1 tbsp ground
- Salt: ½ tbsp
- Sugar: ½ tbsp
- Garlic: 3 cloves minced
- Ginger: 1 tbsp minced
- Kashmiri chilli powder: 1½ tbsp
- Scallion stem: 1 minced
- Fresh chillies: 4 minced
- Hot refined oil: 80 gm

1. Blend all ingredients except the hot oil in a bowl.
2. Add hot oil and mix again.
3. Let the mixture cool.
4. Refrigerate in an airtight jar and use as needed.

CHICKEN BAKED WITH MASCARPONE AND LIME
(Serves 2)

- Whole Chicken leg: 2
- Lime juice: 2 tbsp
- Garlic juice: 1 tbsp
- Salt: ½ + 1 tsp
- Mascarpone cheese: 2½–3 tbsp
- Fresh rosemary: 1 tbsp chopped
- Fresh thyme: 1 tbsp chopped
- Chilli flakes: 1 tsp
- Black pepper powder: 1 tsp
- Cherry tomatoes: 6–8
- Lime slices: 2–3
- Basil leaves: 6–8

1. Make 3 slits on the chicken pieces along the top and sides.
2. Marinate chicken pieces in garlic juice, lime juice and ½ tsp salt for 4 hours.
3. Mix mascarpone cheese with rosemary, thyme, chilli flakes, black pepper powder and 1 tsp salt.
4. Stuff the cheese mixture into the slits of the chicken pieces.
5. Place the chicken pieces in a pie dish and cover with foil.
6. Preheat oven to 200°C for 10 minutes and bake the chicken for 20 minutes.
7. Remove foil and add cherry tomatoes, basil leaves and lime slices. Grill for 20 minutes. If the chicken appears a little dry, add a few tablespoons of chicken stock. Serve hot.

Photo on p. 445: Steamed Asian chicken with chilli oil; Photo on p. 447: Chicken baked with mascarpone and lime; Photo on p. 449: Koyla tawa murgh.

KOYLA TAWA MURGH (Serves 4)

(Measuring cup size: 250 ml)

- Whole chicken leg: 4

Marinade

- Refined oil: 75 ml
- Yoghurt: 125 ml
- Ginger–garlic paste: 1 tbsp
- Lemon juice: 2 tbsp
- Chilli flakes: ½ tsp
- Yellow chilli powder: ¼ tsp
- Salt: 1 tsp
- Carom powder: ½ tsp
- Garam masala: 1 tsp

1. Mix all the above ingredients to make a marinade. Make slits on the chicken pieces.
2. Marinate the chicken pieces for 6 hours in the refrigerator.
3. Take out from the refrigerator 20 minutes prior to cooking.

Masala

- Refined oil: 60 ml
- Onion: 1 cup chopped
- Garlic: 2 tbsp chopped
- Tomato: ½ cup chopped
- Roasted cumin powder: 1 tsp
- Kashmiri chilli powder: 1 tbsp level
- Lemon: ½ sliced thin
- Green chillies: 2–3 chopped (deseed if you want it less spicier)
- Green cardamom powder: ½ tsp
- Mint leaves: 2 tbsp chopped
- Coriander leaves: ½ cup chopped
- Salt: ¾ tsp
- Coal: 1 piece
- Ghee: 1 tsp

1. Heat oil on a low flame in a flat non-stick pan. Make sure you have a lid that fits it.
2. Add onions, ¼ tsp salt and garlic. Sauté till translucent.
3. Add tomato and green chillies. Cook till they soften.
4. Add all the spice powders and remaining salt.
5. Add coriander leaves, mint leaves and lemon slices.
6. Cover and cook for 2–3 minutes.

7. Remove the lid and transfer the chicken along with the marinade to the pan.
8. Cover and cook for 8–10 minutes.
9. Open the lid, check seasoning and flip the chicken.
10. Cover again and cook for 8–10 minutes.
11. Meanwhile, over another flame, heat the coal until it glows red and place it in a piece of aluminium foil shaped like a small bowl.
12. Once the chicken is done, open the lid. Place the heated coal in the centre and drizzle a few drops of ghee over it. It will begin to smoke.
13. Cover with a lid tightly for 3 minutes. Remove from flame and serve.

SLOW COOKED CHICKEN LOLLIPOPS WITH TANGY DIPPING SAUCE, SWEET POTATO FRIES AND CURLY KALE FRIES (Serves 4)

Slow Cooked Chicken Lollipops

- Chicken lollipops: 12
- Garlic: 8 cloves
- Ginger: 1 tbsp chopped
- Lemon juice: 1½ tbsp
- Lemon zest: ½ tsp
- Lemongrass stalk: 3 white portion roughly chopped
- Coriander stems: 2 tbsp chopped
- Coriander leaves: 3 tbsp chopped
- Light soy sauce: 2 tbsp
- Home-made Chinese chilli paste: 1½ tsp
- Green chillies: 3 chopped (or more if you want it spicier)
- Fish sauce: 2 tbsp
- Oyster sauce: 1½ tbsp
- Turmeric powder: ½ tsp
- Palm sugar/Brown sugar: 2 tsp
- Black pepper powder: ½ tsp
- Rice flour: 5 tbsp
- Refined oil: 4 tbsp
- Salt: ½ + ½ tsp

1. In an electric chopper, add lemongrass, along with coriander stems garlic, ginger, green chillies, Chinese chilli paste, palm sugar and light soy sauce. Chop till coarse.
2. Transfer chopped mixture to a bowl and add lemon zest and juice, chopped coriander

leaves, fish sauce, black pepper powder, oyster sauce, turmeric powder and ½ tsp salt.
3. Check seasoning.
4. Add the mixture to chicken lollipops with 1 tbsp oil.
5. Marinate for 8 hours or overnight in the refrigerator.
6. Take out of the refrigerator an hour before pan frying.
7. Heat the remaining oil in a wide non-stick pan.
8. Remove chicken lollipops from the marinade.
9. Mix rice flour with ½ tsp salt and place chicken lollipops in it.
10. Dust off excess flour and pan fry.
11. Let each side sear well and cook on a low flame until slightly crisp and browned.
12. Flip and press down gently a couple of times.
13. Remove from pan and serve hot with the dipping sauce.

Tangy Dipping Sauce

- Garlic: 2 tbsp minced
- Green chillies: 2 chopped
- Thai red chillies: 2 chopped
- Coriander leaves: 2 tbsp chopped
- Onion or shallots: 2 tbsp chopped
- Palm sugar: 25–30 gm
- Lemon juice: 2 tbsp
- Fish sauce: 1½ tbsp
- Light soy sauce: 1 tbsp

1. In a saucepan, mix all the ingredients together and boil for 4–5 minutes.
2. Check seasoning.
3. Serve with chicken and fries.

Sweet Potato Fries

- Sweet potatoes: 300 gm
- Cornflour: 1½ tbsp
- Pink salt: ¾ tsp
- Garlic powder: 1 tsp
- Oil: to deep fry

1. Peel the sweet potatoes and cut into batons ¼ inch thick.
2. Add all the ingredients except the oil and mix well. Let it rest for 10 minutes.
3. Heat oil in a deep wok and fry the sweet potatoes until they are golden.
4. Transfer to a paper towel to drain excess oil.

SERVINGS

Curly Kale Fries

- Curly kale: 150 gm

1. Wash leaves and let them dry out on a paper towel.

- All-purpose flour: 4 tbsp
- Cornflour: 1 tbsp
- Club soda: ½ cup
- Salt: ½–¾ tsp
- Oil: to deep fry

1. Whisk all the ingredients to make a batter. Check seasoning.
2. Heat sufficient oil in a wok for deep frying over a medium flame.
3. Dip the leaves in batter and coat well.
4. Drop the leaves in oil and fry until light golden.
5. Transfer to a paper towel to drain excess oil. Serve hot.

Photo on p. 452: Slow cooked chicken lollipops, Sweet potato fries, Tangy dipping sauce, Sweet potato fries, Curly kale fries.

Kung Fu Panda in the House

KUNG FU PANDA IN THE HOUSE

Panda Adventures

Panda is a teenager now, with all the signs and symptoms of Generation Z. He's been the reason for many of our cooking expeditions, sometimes purely to prevent packaged food and delivery sites from taking over our lives!

There is no greater bond or love than that of a mother and child. Talking about him takes me back to my mother who still cooks and bakes a lot. Back in my childhood, there was nothing that I did not get to eat at home – from soufflés and chiffon cakes to biryanis and curries. I remember being fed by her occasionally, even at age 10! As a 14-year-old, I was encouraged by her to begin my baking journey. I remember the times when cream, straight off boiled and cooled milk, was what we used to top our Black Forest gateau!

Panda likes Indian curries, but he is largely an Asian food buff. Strongly influenced by Japanese animation, he started eating food from this region at a very young age. Bowls of rice or noodles and anything to do with chicken is what he loves to see on the table, practically anything that can be eaten with chopsticks – something his mother still can't get around to using! The recipes in this section have his Asian favourites as well as some from other cuisines.

'There is no secret ingredient. Don't have to make something special. You just have to believe it's special.' Those are the words of Mr Ping, Po's adoptive father from the animation film *Kung Fu Panda*. That's the gospel truth when it comes to food, for sure!

CREAM CHEESE PANCAKES WITH CHUNKY FRESH STRAWBERRY SAUCE AND HOME-MADE PANCAKE SYRUP (Serves 2)

(Measuring cup size: 150 ml)

The smell of pancakes is the best way to woo lazy Panda out of his bed so that he can begin his day at school. His love for pancakes, with lots of chocolate sauce and fruits (read bananas!), has been the constant go-to to turn this horizontal being vertical! This is a slightly different version, and while it's not the healthiest offering, a little indulgence once in a while certainly works in my favour.

Cream Cheese Mix

- Cream cheese: 2 tbsp
- Cream: 75 ml
- Powdered sugar: 2 tbsp

1. Whisk all the ingredients together.

Pancake

- All-purpose flour: ¾ cup
- Egg: 1
- Baking powder: ¼ tsp
- Powdered sugar: 1 tsp
- Blueberries: 8–10
- Milk: ¼ cup
- Salt: ¼ tsp
- Butter: ½ tsp per pancake
- Cream cheese mix: entire quantity

1. Sieve flour with baking powder in a bowl. Add egg, powdered sugar, salt and whisk.
2. Add the cream cheese mix and whisk well and add milk to make the pancake batter.
3. Brush butter on a 6–7 inch non-stick pan and place on a medium flame.
4. Add a ladle of batter in the centre of the pan and swirl it to spread in the pan.
5. Let it cook on a low flame. Once bubbles form, cover and cook for 2 minutes.
6. Flip the pancake and let it cook on the other side till golden brown.
7. Flip again and transfer to a plate. Repeat process for remaining batter.

Chunky Fresh Strawberry Sauce

- Strawberries: 200 gm
- Powdered sugar: 2–3 tbsp

1. Coat strawberries with powdered sugar and leave for 3–4 hours in the refrigerator.
2. Place in a non-stick pan and cook for 8–10 minutes, until it becomes a chunky sauce. Check the sweetness.
3. Let the sauce cool and transfer to a jar and refrigerate.
4. Serve with pancakes.

Home-made Pancake Syrup

- Honey: 1 tbsp
- Brown sugar: 1 cup
- Butter: 1 tsp
- Hot water: ½ cup

1. Heat brown sugar and honey in a non-stick pan on a low flame.
2. Stir until the sugar dissolves.
3. Add hot water and continue stirring.
4. Add butter and boil for 3–5 minutes.
5. Let the syrup cool, and then transfer to a jar and refrigerate.

Photo on p. 458: Cream cheese pancakes, Chunky fresh strawberry sauce, Home-made pancake syrup; Photo on p. 461: Tom yum khao soi; Photo p. 464: Kung fu panda orange chicken; Photo on p. 467: BBQ chicken bao; Photo on p. 468: Bhai's fried instant noodles; Photo on p. 471: 'Gimbap' rolls in a bowl; Photo on p. 474: Oyakadon; Photo on p. 477: 'Chindese' chopsuey.

TOM YUM KHAO SOI AND SWEET CHILLI PRAWNS

(Serves 4) *(Measuring cup size: 250 ml)*

'Khao' means rice in Thai and for us, it means 'eat'. So, here is a bowl of rice noodles topped with everything possible, ready to gobble!

While the Burmese khow suey is popular and something we all love, this version has all the flavours of Thailand. It's a lot easier than toiling on a chicken/mushroom with spices and then making an additional gravy with coconut milk and lentils.

Panda loves tom yum soup so adding this to noodles was an instant pleaser!

Tom Yum Khao Soi

- Flat rice noodles: 150 gm
- Refined oil: 1 tbsp
- Garlic: 2 tsp minced
- Ginger: 1 tsp minced
- Broccoli: 4 florets halved
- Mushrooms: 6–8 halved
- Baby corn: 6 halved
- Lemongrass: 1 stalk chopped
- Spring onions: 3 white portions sliced
- Tom yum paste: 2½ tbsp
- Home-made Chinese chilli paste: 1 tsp (more if you want it spicier)
- Bird's eye chilli: 1 chopped
- Turmeric powder: ½ tsp
- Stock cubes: 2 dissolved in hot water
- Soy sauce: ½ tsp
- Salt: to taste
- Gram flour: 1 tbsp
- Coconut milk: 800 ml
- Kaffir lime leaves: 3–4

1. Boil noodles in water till almost done, strain in a colander and keep aside.
2. Dry roast gram flour in a pan until it turns golden.
3. Remove from flame. Mix in coconut milk gradually and smoothen the mixture. Ensure there are no lumps.
4. Place the pan back on the flame and boil.
5. Add dissolved stock cubes. Boil further and add salt, if needed.
6. Add soy sauce before removing gravy from the flame.
7. In another wok, heat oil, add garlic followed by ginger. Sauté.
8. Add spring onions, turmeric powder and salt.

9. Once the onions are translucent, add tom yum paste. Cook further and add home-made Chinese chilli paste.
10. Add all the vegetables and cook for 3–4 minutes.
11. Add the coconut gravy and boil further. Ensure the vegetables retain their crunch.
12. Add lemongrass, kaffir lime leaves and bird's eye chilli.
13. Adjust spice levels and salt.

Garnish

- Boiled eggs: 4–5 whites sliced
- Fried noodles: ½ cup
- Spring onions: 4–5 leaves chopped
- Onions: 1–2 finely sliced
- Peanuts: ½ cup crushed
- Coriander leaves: ½ cup chopped
- Chilli paste in oil: ¼ cup
- Garlic: ½ cup sliced and fried
- Bird's eye chilli: ¼ cup chopped

Sweet Chilli Prawns

- Prawns: 8–10 large with tail
- Lemon juice: 4 tbsp
- Salt: 1 tsp
- Black pepper powder: 1 tsp
- Thai sweet chilli sauce: 2–3 tbsp
- Garlic: 3–4 cloves minced
- Cornflour: 1 tbsp
- Refined oil: 1–2 tbsp

1. Marinate prawns in lemon juice, salt and black pepper powder for an hour.
2. Toss in cornflour.
3. Heat oil and stir fry the garlic and prawns.
4. Add Thai sweet chilli sauce and stir fry on high heat.

Can be made with tofu. Stir fry tofu in oil with salt and pepper. Toss in cornflour. Heat oil and stir fry garlic. Add tofu and cook on each side. Toss in Thai sweet chilli sauce.

Assembling

1. Assemble the bowl with noodles at the bottom, followed by gravy and all the garnishes and top with sweet chilli prawns.

Photo p. 464: Kung fu panda orange chicken; Photo on pg 467: BBQ chicken bao.

KUNG FU PANDA ORANGE CHICKEN (Serves 2)

- Boneless chicken thighs - 250 gm cut into 1½ inch pieces

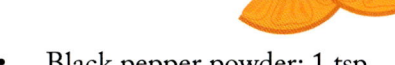

Marinade

- All purpose flour: 2 tbsp
- Corn flour: 2 tbsp
- Egg: 1
- Black pepper powder: 1 tsp
- Salt: 1 tsp
- Refined oil: to pan fry

1. Mix all the marinade ingredients together, except oil.
2. Add chicken and leave at room temperature for 1 hour.
3. Heat oil in a non-stick pan. Fry chicken in batches and transfer to a paper towel to drain excess oil.

Orange Sauce

- Refined oil: 1 tsp
- Ginger paste: 1 tsp
- Garlic paste: 1 tsp
- Chilli flakes: ½–1 tsp
- Light soy sauce: 2 tbsp
- Vinegar: 3 tbsp
- Orange: 1
- Brown sugar: 1 tbsp
- Sesame oil: 1–2 tsp
- Cornflour: 1–2 tsp
- Water: 2–3 tbsp
- Salt: ½ tsp

For a spicier version, add a finely chopped Thai chilli and reduce the brown sugar.

1. Squeeze orange to extract juice.
2. Heat oil in a non-stick pan.
3. Add ginger and garlic paste, sauté. Add brown sugar, salt and let it caramelize.
4. Add chilli flakes, soy sauce, vinegar, orange juice and cook until smooth and glossy.
5. Dissolve cornflour in 1 tbsp water, add to the sauce and cook till it thickens.

Assembling

1. Toss the fried chicken in orange sauce. Let it simmer and then add 1–2 tbsp water.
2. Finish with 1–2 tsp sesame oil and check seasoning.
3. Serve hot with sticky rice or as a starter.

PO BUNS – BBQ CHICKEN BAO (Makes 8–9 buns)

When Panda graduated from watching Doraemon to Kung Fu Panda, he wanted to eat exactly like Po. That was the beginning of the dumpling era, though we sold him the momo as a dumpling! At some point, he got to taste the bao at a popular restaurant in the city as well and enjoyed it.

The Taiwanese-style open bao – which is like a taco – is a favourite. Traditionally called gua bao or lotus leaf bun, it is stuffed with pork belly and is a popular street food. But one can fill it with whatever one likes – from pulled pork, to spam, tofu and of course, chicken, it all tastes great. As Panda grows, so does his tolerance for spice so sriracha sauce is used in abundance.

The pillowy form of the bao is delightful, the shape looks like a mouth ready to swallow the filling. A failed attempt only adds to the excitement in getting it right the next time round. As Master Shifu said, 'If you only do what you can do, you will never be more than who you are.' We do take Kung Fu Panda seriously around here!

Bao Buns

- All-purpose flour: 200 gm
- Milk powder: 1 tbsp
- Salt: ¼ tsp
- Baking powder: 2 gm
- Active dry yeast: 4 gm
- Sugar: 30 gm
- Lukewarm water: 120 ml + 20 ml if
- required while kneading
- Refined oil: 2 tbsp

1. Sieve together flour, baking powder and salt. Add milk powder.
2. In a bowl, bloom yeast in lukewarm water with sugar for 8 minutes.
3. Add the yeast mixture into the flour and make a soft dough. If required, use the additional 20 ml lukewarm water.
4. Shape into a ball, smear oil and place in a bowl wrapped in a moist cloth. Let it rest in a warm place for 90 minutes.
5. Line the top compartment of the steamer with greased parchment.
6. Remove the dough, stretch and fold.
7. Dust the kitchen counter with flour and roll the dough into a ½ cm thick rectangle.
8. Take a 3½ inch diameter cookie cutter and cut as many discs as possible.
9. Carefully remove excess dough, make into a ball and roll as earlier.

10. Cut discs again. Rub each disc with oil and fold in half.
11. With a rolling pin press down along the edges of the folded disc gently.
12. Place in the lined compartment of the steamer carefully and let it rest in a warm place for 30 minutes wrapped in a moist cloth.
13. Boil water in the bottom compartment of the steamer and place the bao-filled compartment of the steamer on top.
14. Cover and steam for 8 minutes.
15. Remove and fill, or cool and refrigerate.
16. If refrigerated, steam again for 2 minutes and then fill.

BBQ Chicken

- Boneless chicken thighs: 600 gm

1. Cut chicken thighs into strips.

Marinade

- Tongatsu sauce: 5 tbsp
- Garlic: 4 tsp minced
- Ginger: 4 tsp minced
- Dark soy sauce: 3 tsp
- Sesame oil: 4 tsp
- Honey: 1½ tsp
- Sriracha sauce: 2 tbsp
- Salt: 1¼ tsp
- Refined oil: 3 tbsp

1. Mix all the marinade ingredients except the oil together. Taste and check seasoning.
2. Marinate chicken strips for 6 hours in the mixture.
3. Heat oil in a non-stick pan on a medium flame and cook the chicken until it caramelizes.
4. Cover and cook for 5–7 minutes tossing occasionally.
5. Remove the cover and cook the chicken strips until dry and sticky.
6. Divide into 8–9 portions.

Assembling a Bao

- Layer 1: Apply sriracha mayonnaise (2 tbsp mayonnaise mixed with 3½ tbsp sriracha sauce) on the inside of the bao.

- Layer 2: Lettuce leaf – placed inside the bao.
- Layer 3: BBQ chicken strips.
- Layer 4: Peel and trim a carrot. Cut into thin juliennes and marinate in 1½ tbsp red wine vinegar/balsamic vinegar.
- Layer 5: 2 Spring onions green portion, thinly sliced.
- Layer 6: Drizzle sriracha mayonnaise on top.

BHAI'S FRIED INSTANT NOODLES (Serves 1)

Instant noodles for us is the 2-minute revolution that began when I was probably 7 or 8 years old. I don't know of a single person who doesn't enjoy eating what comes out of that trademark bright sunny yellow packet. Mothers add vegetables to make it healthy, some like it soupy – there are endless versions of this popular dish. My brother-in-law has a unique way of making it, fried in lots of butter to make a crunchy mess! Panda's midnight meals are like this!

- Instant noodles: 1 packet (break into 8 pieces)
- Butter: 20 gm
- Refined oil: 2 tsp
- Onion: 1 medium chopped
- Water: 125 ml

1. Heat butter and oil in a non-stick pan.
2. Melt butter for 30 seconds and then add onions and stir fry for a minute.
3. Add the crushed noodles, lightly toss for 5–7 minutes until they crisp up.
4. Add the readymade masala which comes with the packet and mix well.
5. Add water, a little at a time so that the noodles are well coated with the masala. Keep stirring continuously.
6. Serve hot, garnished with chopped onions and coriander leaves.

Photo on p. 468: Bhai's fried instant noodles.

'GIMBAP' ROLLS IN A BOWL (Serves 2)

(Measuring cup size: 150 ml)

The introduction to gimbap and the process of rolling it began with Panda's introduction to the animation series called *Doraemon*. That's where his love for all things Asian, from rice balls to sushi, really began. What Doraemon and Nobita ate, Panda devoured. Lucky for him Salina, who has been a part of his life and ours since he was a year old, knew how to roll gimbap, having learned how to do it from her previous Korean employer. Since we couldn't roll sushi, we began rolling gimbap, which is, interestingly, also eaten as a snack with one's fingers. This deconstructed gimbap simplifies it even further.

- Sushi rice: 1 cup
- Rice vinegar: a few drops

1. Boil rice, strain and keep warm. Add a few drops of rice vinegar to the warm rice.

Sesame Spinach

- Spinach leaves: 2 cups
- Roasted sesame oil: 1 tsp
- Light soy sauce: ½ tsp
- Roasted sesame seeds: ½ tsp
- Powdered sugar: ½ tsp
- Rice vinegar: ½ tsp
- Garlic: ¼ tsp minced
- Black pepper powder: ¼ tsp
- Mayonnaise: 1 tsp

1. Wash spinach leaves and drop into salted boiling water for 10 seconds, and then into an ice bath for a few minutes.
2. Strain in a colander. Press spinach leaves between your palms to remove excess water.
3. Mix roasted sesame oil, light soy sauce, roasted sesame seeds, powdered sugar, rice vinegar, garlic, black pepper powder and mayonnaise together.
4. Combine with spinach leaves and refrigerate for 1½ hours.

Photo on p. 471: Gimbap rolls in a bowl; Photo on p. 474: Oyakodon; Photo on p. 477: 'Chindese' chopsuey.

Chicken and Mushroom Bbq (can be made with either or both)

- Boneless chicken thighs: 1–2
- Mushrooms: 6 split in half
- Onion: 1 medium chopped fine
- Garlic: 4 cloves chopped
- Ginger: 1 tsp minced
- Refined oil: 2 tbsp
- Soy sauce: 1 tbsp
- Brown sugar: 1 tsp
- Rice vinegar: 1 tsp
- Sriracha sauce: 1 tsp
- Roasted sesame oil: 1 tsp
- Salt: ¼ tsp
- Cornflour: 1 tsp mixed in 1 tbsp water
- Water: ½ cup

1. Cut chicken into 1½ inch cubes.
2. Heat oil in a non-stick pan over a high flame.
3. Stir fry garlic and onion until light brown.
4. Add ginger and sauté.
5. Add chicken and mushrooms and cook for 2 minutes.
6. Season with salt.
7. Add all the other ingredients, except cornflour.
8. Cook for 7–8 minutes until the chicken is cooked.
9. Add the cornflour mixture and stir in ½ cup water for additional moisture.
10. Cover for a minute to ensure there is a sticky coating on the chicken. This will add flavour to your bowl. Serve warm.

Accompaniments

- Luncheon meat: cut into slices, pan fried and cut into strips.
- Carrot: 1 cut into thin batons and lightly cooked with a few drops of oil.
- Cucumber: deseeded, cut into batons and soaked in vinegar.
- Eggs: 2 whisked with salt and black pepper powder and made into a thin pancake, then cut into strips.
- Nori sheets: cut into thin strips.
- Sesame seeds: 1½ tbsp roasted.

Sauce

- Gochujang paste: 1½ tbsp/home-made Chinese chilli paste: ½ tbsp
- Sesame oil: 2 tsp
- Rice vinegar: 1½ tbsp
- Honey: 1 tbsp
- Soy sauce: 1 tbsp

1. Mix all the above ingredients.

Assembling the Bowl

1. Place warm rice at the base.
2. Top with sesame spinach and chicken and mushroom barbeque
3. Add all accompaniments.
4. Add sauce as desired and serve.

OYAKODON (Chicken and Egg Fried Rice) (Serves 2)

'Oyako' literally means 'parent and child'. This dish can be a beautiful interpretation of this special relationship. My child continues to eat rice in a bowl, topped with his favourites. That, for him, is bliss. Creating a vegetarian version – sorry, an egg and vegetable version – for myself ensured that I could bond at the table too!

- Sushi rice: 200 gm boiled

Chicken Version

- Boneless Chicken thighs: 200 gm
- Leek: 2 inches cut into thin rounds
- Celery: 5–6 leaves chopped
- Eggs: 2 large (each whisked separately with a pinch of salt and pepper)
- Olive oil: 1 tsp

1. Divide ingredients into 2 portions.

Vegetarian Version with Eggs

- Olive oil - 1 tsp
- Abura-age: 6–8 cubes small (dehydrated and fermented tofu)
- Carrot: ¾ grated

- Mushroom: 2 large halved and sliced
- Leek: 2 inches cut into thin rounds
- Celery: 5–6 leaves chopped
- Eggs: 2 (each whisked separately with a pinch of salt and pepper)

1. Divide ingredients into 2 portions.

Sauce (Makes 2 portions)

- Dashi powder: ¾ tsp
- Boiling water: 125 ml
- Mirin: 1 tbsp
- Kikkoman soy sauce: 1 tbsp

Assembling Oyakodon

1. Mix and boil all the sauce ingredients for about 5 minutes and then divide into 2 equal portions and keep aside.
2. Take a non-stick pan, approximately the size of the bowl in which you want to serve the rice. Add oil and heat over a low flame.
3. Add all the ingredients for one portion, be it vegetarian or chicken except egg and celery, and cook until half done.
4. Add one portion of the sauce and let the ingredients cook covered.
5. Remove the cover, and let the sauce thicken a little.
6. Add one portion of whisked egg and spread in the pan like an open face omelette.
7. When the egg is half done, add celery and turn off the flame.
8. Cover for 1–2 minutes and then flip the egg in the pan.
9. Fill serving bowl with cooked rice until three-fourths full. Transfer the egg on to the bed of warm rice, celery side up. Repeat all the steps for the second portions

'CHINDESE' CHOPSUEY (Serves 4)
(Measuring cup size: 250 ml)

As a nation, we have adapted many Chinese dishes and made them ours. The Hindi–Chini Bhai-Bhai slogan holds true, at least for this aspect of relations between the two countries!

Spending a few years in Kolkata only ensured that Indo-Chinese cuisine like 'chowmein' and 'Gobi Manchurian' became a part of my plate! Entering the lanes of China Town for breakfast in the morning or even New China Town in Tangra for a meal was always delightful. So what if one had to tolerate the stench of the tanneries nearby – it was all part of the experience! I am a great fan of tossing things in a pan, flipping them and enjoying the sound of food sizzling. Fried noodles and a topping of sweet tangy sauce with a fried egg on top gives you chopsuey or, rather, the 'Chindese Chopsuey'. When I was growing up, every club we visited had this on its menu. The joy of eating this gooey mess is unparalleled – and is sacrosanct for Panda. 'You haven't eaten Chinese till you've eaten this!'

Noodles

- Hakka noodles: 160 gm
- Refined oil: for deep frying

1. Boil noodles in hot water until al dente and strain in a colander. Reserve ½ cup boiled noodles. Divide remaining noodles into 4 portions and shape into flat discs.
2. Heat oil in a wok. Deep fry and keep aside.

Gravy

- Cabbage: ¼ piece shredded
- Carrots: 2 peeled and cut into juliennes
- Capsicum: ½ peeled and cut into juliennes
- Onion: 1 sliced
- Beans: 6 sliced diagonally
- Garlic: 8–10 thick cloves
- Tomato ketchup: 2 tbsp
- Light soy sauce: 2 tbsp
- Sugar: 1 tbsp
- Tomatoes: 4 boiled and peeled
- Vinegar: 4 tsp
- Salt: 1½ tsp
- Kashmiri red chillies: 4 soaked in water for an hour and then partially deseeded
- Home-made Chinese chilli paste: 1½–2 tbsp (can be substituted with bottled Sichuan chilli paste, but check spice levels accordingly)
- Black pepper powder: ½ tsp
- Stock cube: 1 dissolved in water
- Water: 2½ cups
- Spring onions: 4 tbsp chopped
- Refined oil: 2 tbsp
- Eggs: 4
- Cornflour: 1 tsp

1. Heat 1 tbsp oil in a wok and sauté onions until translucent. Add a little salt and black pepper powder.

2. Add beans and cook for 2 minutes. Add carrots and cook for 2 minutes.
3. Add cabbage and cook for 2 minutes. Add capsicum and cook for 2 minutes.
4. Remove from flame. Add reserved ½ cup boiled noodles and keep aside.
5. Blend tomatoes, Kashmiri chillies and garlic in a mixer together to make a paste.
6. Heat 1 tbsp oil in a pan and cook the tomato paste until the oil separates.
7. Add home-made Chinese chilli paste, tomato ketchup, light soy sauce, sugar, salt and black pepper powder. Add stock cube, water and boil.
8. To make a thicker gravy, add 1 tsp cornflour dissolved in 1 tbsp water and boil.
9. Check seasoning and add chilli paste to make it spicier if desired.
10. Add the sauce to the already cooked vegetables.

To Assemble

1. Make 4 double fried eggs, season and keep aside.
2. Heat the chopsuey gravy with 4 tsp vinegar and and divide into 4 portions.
3. Place 1 fried noodle disc on a plate.
4. Pour a portion of the chopsuey gravy on it.
5. Top with a portion of double fried egg and 1 tbsp chopped spring onions.
6. Serve hot. Adding stir fried chicken strips in soy garlic is optional.

BURGERS – UNITE THE WORLD
(Measuring cup size: 250 ml)

Who doesn't love a burger and Panda is no exception! The first country to put a ground beef steak between two pieces of bread was America. However, the addition of trimmings like lettuce, onions and pickles happened along the way. Another story goes that the hamburger, as it's called today, is named after the city of Hamburg in Germany.

The hamburger has moved across continents, sinking its teeth into every home. There are numerous versions of it, with globalization and chains like McDonald's making it even more popular. Of course, it helps that a hamburger is always a 'Happy Meal'!

The Japanese were introduced to the hamburger or 'Hambaga' when the US military arrived in Sasebo City of Nagasaki after World War II. The Marines would step out of their base into the city and that led to many restaurants serving the burger to hungry soldiers. The 'Sasebo Burger' was a trendsetter long before American chains reached Japanese shores, with the first restaurant being 'Hikari' which started selling burgers in 1951.

The Japanese Milk Burger Bun is a versatile bun with a pillowy texture. This is something I learnt from someone who worked in a Japanese home in the city. The difference here is the starter dough, which is traditionally called tangzhong. The texture of the bread is its biggest asset. The patty can vary, depending on which part of the world you want to derive flavours from… like we have our very own McAloo Burgers!

Japanese Milk Burger Buns (Makes 9)
Starter Dough (Tangzhong)

- All-purpose flour: 2 tbsp
- Milk: 3 tbsp
- Water: 3 tbsp

1. Cook all the ingredients in a non-stick pan on a low flame to make a paste.
2. Remove from flame and keep aside.

Dough

- Active dry yeast: 1 tbsp
- Sugar: ¼ cup
- Milk: ½ cup
- Milk powder: 2 tbsp
- All-purpose flour: 2½ cups
- Buter: ¼ cup
- Egg: 1 large

1. Bloom yeast in lukewarm milk mixed with sugar for 8 minutes.
2. Mix all the dry ingredients together.
3. Add the starter dough, bloomed yeast and egg.

4. Knead for 15–20 minutes and add butter. The dough will be elastic.
5. Transfer to a greased bowl, wrap the bowl with a moist cloth and proof in a warm place, for 90 minutes.
6. Transfer the dough from the bowl on to a counter dusted with a little flour. Knock back the dough and stretch it lightly.
7. Divide into 9 portions of approximately 83 gm each.
8. Shape into balls. Place a ball on the counter, cup your palms and gently apply pressure from above to get the shape of a burger bun.
9. Place on a parchment-lined tray with gaps between each ball as they will double in size.
10. Proof for 50 minutes.
11. Preheat oven to 170 °C for 10 minutes.
12. Brush the tops of the buns with milk.
13. Bake for 15–20 minutes. Remove from the oven, let the buns cool.
14. Transfer to a wire rack.

Mushroom Burger Patties (Makes 4)

- Mushrooms: 1¼ cup
- Baked beans: ½ cup strained and mashed
- Tofu: ½ cup
- Breadcrumbs: ¼ cup
- Onions: 2 chopped fine
- Worcestershire sauce: ½ tbsp
- Garlic: 1 tbsp minced
- Parsley leaves: 2 tbsp chopped fine
- Chicken masala powder: ½ tsp
- Parmesan cheese: ¼ cup grated
- Chilli flakes: 1 tsp
- Olive oil: 1 tbsp + 2 tbsp for pan frying
- Salt: ½ tsp

1. Heat 1 tbsp olive oil. Stir fry half the quantity of chopped onions with garlic and salt.
2. Add the mushrooms, chicken masala powder and sauté till done. Cool and mash.
3. Mix mashed mushrooms, baked beans and tofu together.
4. Add parsley leaves, chilli flakes, breadcrumbs, Parmesan cheese, remaining chopped onions, and Worcestershire sauce.
5. Mix together and divide into 4 portions.
6. Moisten palm and shape the mixture into a patty.
7. Heat 2 tbsp olive oil in a flat non-stick pan.

8. Place the patties in the pan and cook for 5 minutes on one side. Then flip and cook for 5 minutes on the other side over a low flame. Do not keep flipping as the patty may crumble.
9. To freeze the extras, place patties on an open plate lined with parchment, for an hour. and then transfer to an airtight container. To use, defrost and then place on a greased non-stick pan and cook.

Chicken Burger Patties (Makes 6)

- Chicken mince: 500 gm
- Breadcrumbs: ¼ cup
- Jalapeños: 6
- Onion: 1 large
- Chicken masala powder: ½ tsp
- Parsley leaves: 2 tbsp chopped
- Chilli flakes: 1 tsp
- Garlic: 1 tbsp minced
- Worcestershire sauce: ½ tbsp
- Parmesan cheese: ¼ cup grated
- Salt: ½ tsp
- Olive oil: 1 tbsp + 2 tbsp

1. Grate half the onion and finely chop the other half.
2. Heat 1 tbsp of olive oil in a non-stick pan.
3. Add the grated onion and half the quantity of chopped onions. Add salt and sauté.
4. Add garlic, chicken masala powder and cook.
5. Cool and place on a plate.
6. Add the remaining chopped onions, chicken mince, jalapeños, chilli flakes, breadcrumbs, Parmesan cheese, parsley leaves and Worcestershire sauce. Mix well.
7. Divide into 6 portions and shape into patties.
8. Heat 2 tbsp olive oil in a flat non-stick pan on a low flame.
9. Cook the patties for 7–8 minutes on each side.
10. To freeze the extras, place patties on an open plate lined with parchment, for an hour. and then transfer to an airtight container.
11. To use, defrost and then place on a greased non-stick pan and cook.

Paprika Mayonnaise

- Mayonnaise: 4 tbsp
- Dijon mustard: 2 tsp
- Paprika powder: 1 tsp

1. Mix all the above ingredients together.

Caramelized Onion Rings

1. Cut an onion into thick roundels.
2. Heat a pan and add 1 tsp olive oil.
3. Add onions and ½ tsp sugar.
4. Let the onions caramelize and soften.

Assembling the Burger

1. Cut burger buns in half horizontally.
2. Heat the buns on the pan. Remove and keep warm.
3. Place the burger patty on the pan and let it warm up.
4. Place a slice of Cheddar cheese on it and let it melt.
5. Apply paprika mayonnaise on the inside of the burger buns.
6. On the lower layer of the bun place caramelized onions.
7. Top with lettuce and tomato slices.
8. Then place the patty and the top layer of the bun. Serve immediately.

MIDDLE EASTERN PLATE (Serves 4)
(Measuring cup size: 250 ml)

Getting Panda to eat vegetables is a task, but give him warm pita with hummus and all the brightest vegetables chopped up and it all gets devoured.

SERVINGS

Pita is a round flat wheat flour bread that has a pocket. Baking it is delightful. The bread dates back 4000 years and is probably the simplest flatbread to make. It is also incredibly versatile. Apple hummus ensures a portion of fruit is consumed!

Pita Bread (Makes 6)

- All-purpose flour: ¾ cup
- Whole wheat flour: ¾ cup
- Yeast: 2¼ tsp
- Sugar: 1 tsp
- Salt: ½ tsp
- Water: 3 tbsp + 125 ml

1. Bloom yeast in 3 tbsp lukewarm water with sugar for 8 minutes.
2. Sieve both the flours, add salt and the frothy yeast.
3. Knead into a soft dough, gradually adding water.
4. Transfer dough to a greased bowl and proof for 90 minutes in a warm place, wrapped in a moist cloth.
5. Knock back the dough and divide into 6 portions of 65 gm each.
6. Place the dough balls on a large tray and let them proof again in a warm place for 10 minutes.
7. Preheat oven to 200 °C for 5 minutes.
8. Roll dough balls into discs of 5 inches each and place on a parchment-lined baking tray.
9. Bake for 8–10 minutes until they puff up and are light golden.
10. Serve warm.

Apple Hummus

- Chickpeas: ⅔ cup soaked in water overnight
- Tahini paste: 2½ tbsp
- Garlic: 4 cloves minced
- Apple: 1 peeled and chopped
- Pink salt: 1 tsp
- Lemon juice: 3 tbsp
- Chilli flakes: 1 tsp
- Olive oil: 1 tbsp + extra to top
- Olives: 8–10
- Salt: ½ tsp

Photo on p. 480: Burgers; Photo on p. 485: Middle Eastern plate.

1. Boil 1 cup water add ½ tsp salt and chickpeas and cook until done.
2. Once cool, strain the chickpeas and save the water.
3. Place the chickpeas in a blender with apples, tahini paste, minced garlic, pink salt and lemon juice. Add reserved chickpea water as required. Blend until smooth.
4. Transfer to a serving dish and top with olive oil, chilli flakes and olives.

> Serve with raw or steamed vegetables of choice or cut the pita in half, slather with hummus and fill with chopped vegetables and slices of cooked chicken or salami.

MILK AND COOKIES CAN BE MILK CHOCOLATE COOKIES! (Makes 15)

Chocolate cookies dunked in milk are Panda's go-to evening treat. We have Ruth Grave Wakefield to thank for the concept of these drop cookies that became popular as Toll House Chocolate Crunch Cookies, named after the inn she owned in Massachusetts. She later sold her recipe to Nestlé for a lifetime supply of chocolate!

The popularity of these cookies spread all over America and today most homes would have a chocolate cookie jar. Double and triple chocolate, vegan, flourless – there are so many versions of this simple cookie. Here is my version in the classic drop style, made with milk chocolate. The dough is pretty yummy too!

- All-purpose flour: 150 gm
- Baking powder: ¾ tsp
- Unsweetened cocoa powder: 1 tbsp
- Castor sugar: 60 gm
- Brown sugar: 60 gm
- Butter: 65 gm
- Egg: 1
- Vanilla essence: ¾ tsp
- Milk chocolate covertures/chips: 90 gm

1. Butter and eggs should be at room temperature.
2. Preheat oven to 180 °C for 10 minutes.
3. Line a baking tray with parchment.
4. Sieve flour with baking powder and cocoa powder.

5. Cream butter with brown sugar and castor sugar.
6. Add the egg and vanilla essence and whisk till fluffy.
7. Add flour gradually and whisk further.
8. Fold in chocolate chips. Using an ice cream scoop drop equal portions of the cookie dough onto a parchment-lined tray.
9. Keep at least 1½ inch gap between each ball.
10. Bake cookies for 12–14 minutes ensuring that they don't burn.
11. Remove from the oven. Cool and store in an airtight jar.

ALWAYS COLA! (Serves 6)

Panda loves Cola! He wasn't allowed a sip from this trademark 'red can' of fizzy goodness until he was seven years old. As with everything forbidden, the craving for it only increases.

This cake recipe from a chocolatier is a treat for him and a tribute to the drink we all love —even the diet version, despite the not-so-positive attributes that people so often warn me about reminds me of the yin and yang philosophy!

Mansi's 'Coco' Cake

- All-purpose flour: 150 gm
- Unsweetened cocoa powder: 30 gm
- Brown sugar: 150 gm
- Sour cream: 60 gm
- Cola: 70 ml
- Milk: 2 tbsp
- Baking powder: ½ tsp
- Baking soda: ½ tsp
- Vanilla essence: 1 tsp
- Butter: 100 gm
- Eggs: 2 medium
- Chocolate chips: 1 tbsp

1. Ensure that the butter, eggs, sour cream and cola are all at room temperature.
2. Sift flour, cocoa powder, baking powder and baking soda together.

3. Preheat oven to 170°C for 5 minutes.
4. Grease a 10 inch bundt pan or a 9 inch round pan.
5. Whisk butter and brown sugar until creamy.
6. Add sour cream and whisk further.
7. Add eggs and whisk along with vanilla essence. Add milk.
8. Gradually fold in the sifted flour mixture, alternating with cola. Mix well.
9. Fold in chocolate chips. Pour the batter into the cake pan.
10. Tap the pan on the counter to remove air pockets.
11. Bake for 35–40 minutes. Insert a toothpick in the centre, it should come out clean.
12. Remove from the oven and cool.
13. Take the cake out of the pan. Serve drizzled with cola frosting.

Cola Frosting

- Butter: 50 gm
- Castor sugar: 1½ tbsp
- Chocolate chips: 3 tbsp (mix of milk and dark chocolate)
- Cola: 8 tbsp

1. Melt butter in a thick-bottomed saucepan over a low flame.
2. Add castor sugar, chocolate chips and mix.
3. Add cola and mix.
4. Let it simmer to thicken.
5. Allow the frosting to cool down.
6. Drizzle frosting over the cake.

Photo on p. 487: Milk chocolate cookies; **Photo on p. 490:** Mansi's 'coco' cake.

Acknowledgements

It takes more than a galley to write a cookbook. There are many people who have been a part of this incredible journey, without whom I would not have been able to dish up this sumptuous feast.

Nandini Varma, who designed the book and had the patience to go through the numerous edits, gently nudging, constantly encouraging and working with me diligently.

Taranbir Singh, for working on all my amateurish photographs and infusing life into them.

Niti Kumar, a dear friend and an industry pro who believed this cookbook was a possibility and helped me tread the path.

Kanishka Gupta, my literary agent who helped me foray into the publishing world.

Dibakar Ghosh from Rupa Publications, who believed in me, a home cook and a newbie in the cookbook writing space.

Shyama Warner, for the editing and for setting us on track and ensuring we crossed the finish line.

And last but not least a big shout out once again to my dear family and friends, your love and encouragement has been my greatest strength.

SERVINGS

Notes

SERVINGS

Notes

SERVINGS

Notes

SERVINGS

Notes

SERVINGS

Notes

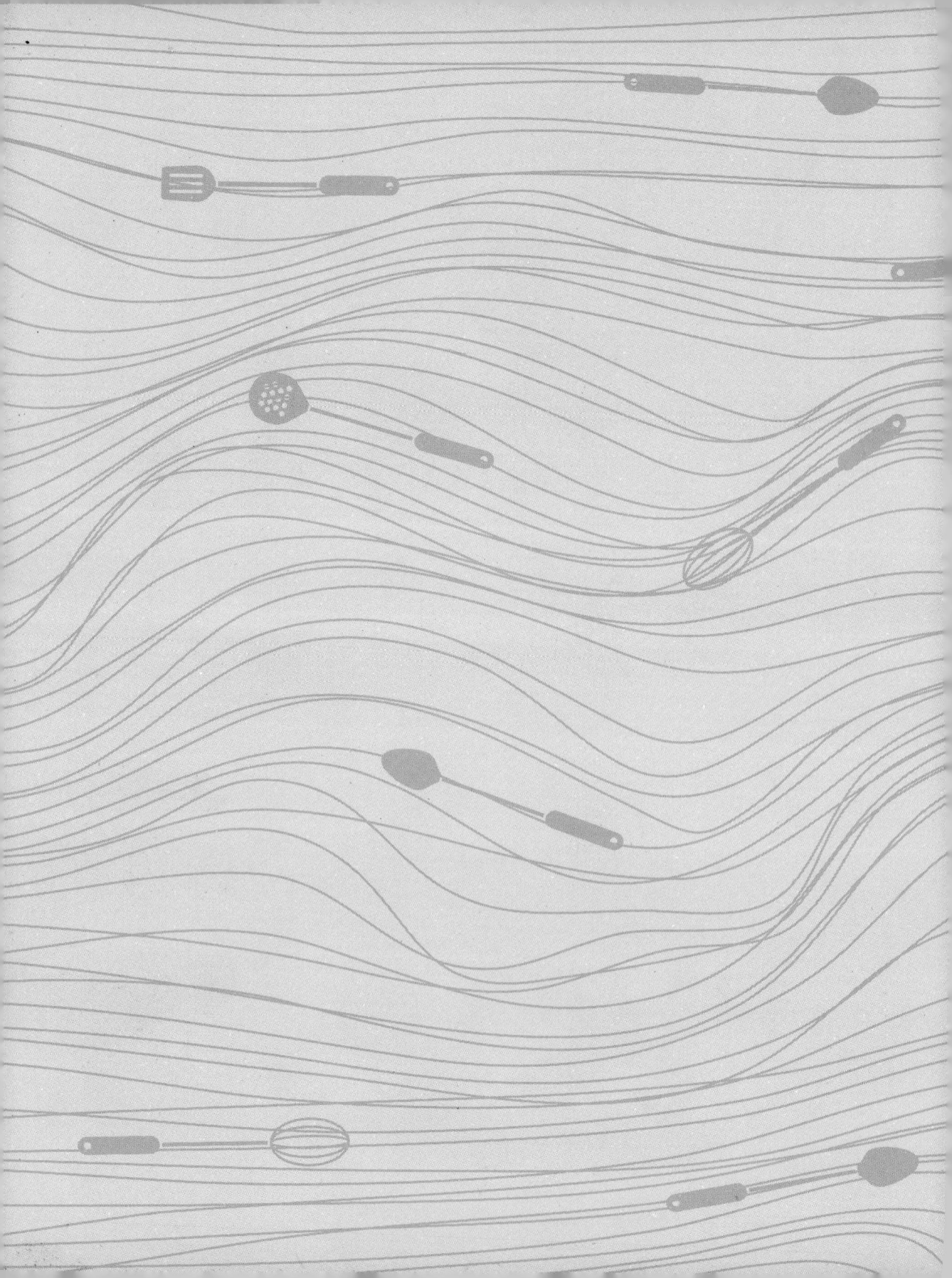